T0380792

Love and Loss

A Journey through Fear to Peace

Volume Three
Love Is God Is Love
April 2014 to January 2016

Betty Hibod

BALBOA.PRESS
A DIVISION OF HAY HOUSE

Balboa Press books may be ordered through booksellers or by contacting:

Balboa Press
A Division of Hay House
1663 Liberty Drive
Bloomington, IN 47403
www.balboapress.com
844-682-1282

Print information available on the last page.

ISBN: 979-8-7652-4577-4 (sc)
ISBN: 979-8-7652-4578-1 (e)

Balboa Press rev. date: 06/04/2024

Beware you be not swallowed up in books!
An ounce of love is worth a pound of knowledge.

– John Wesley

Contents

Foreword

Our task is not to leave a record of what happened on this date for those who will inherit the Earth; history will take care of that. Therefore, we will speak about our daily lives, about the difficulties we have had to face. That is all the future will be interested in, because I do not believe very much will change in the next thousand years. – Paul Coelho, *Manuscript Found in Accra*[1]

Many books have been written as histories recounting events that shaped the life of a group, society, nation, or civilization, or as biographies recounting events and achievements relating to one person's life and work. Many books have been written putting forth ideas, philosophies, and words of wisdom to live by. Some of these we call holy books, or scripture.

Fewer books have been written like this one, which go behind the scenes of history, lay bare the feelings behind the philosophies, and document the painful and joyful inner path along which historical events and philosophical ideas emerge. This book is intensely, even shockingly, personal, not clinical or abstract or detached. It is an intimate, detailed, sensual, and sometimes disturbing account of a life lived on the cusp that bridges time and eternity. Its focus is narrow; it does not reveal much at all about anyone's visible public life or accomplishments, but it explores in great depth the invisible contents of minds, hearts, and souls.

The books of history, biography, religion, and philosophy transmit the end results of the spiritual process, the visible outward effects of invisible inner struggles. This book goes inward, looks directly at the inner struggles and makes visible the invisible forces that shape the end result. It is not a recitation of historical or biographical facts. It speaks "about our daily lives, about the difficulties we have had to face," and in so doing traces the line drawn by the finger of God from darkness to light.

The scriptures and scriptural commentaries of most religions describe a path to salvation or inner peace, and provide instructions or guideposts for moving along the path, but they are still only theoretical, hypothetical, mythical, or metaphorical accounts. This book seeks to show how theories and hypotheses play out in real time and space, how myths come alive in the flesh, how metaphors become the very things they symbolize. How does daily life look from inside someone in the throes of awakening? How does she know who or what she is? How is her destiny revealed? How do seemingly ordinary mundane events become miracles?

Joseph Campbell said: "Words can act as barriers.... There's a saying that appears both in Lao-tzu's work and in the Upanishads: 'Those who know do not speak. And those who speak do not know.' That's hard for one giving a lecture." [2] It's also hard for one writing a book. Can indescribable occurrences and perceptions, sensory and extrasensory, nevertheless be described somehow in thoughts and words? This book is an attempt to find out.

A Reader's Guide

The journal from which this book is excerpted spans over thirty years and in its unabridged form occupies thousands of pages. It is a true story, and all the characters in this drama are real people. To protect the privacy of these people and their families, most names, locations, and dates are fictitious. Some characters may be composites of more than one real person.

There are many words used throughout the book that can be defined in various ways, words like "God," "spiritual," "consciousness," "miracle," "time," "love," "heaven," and "hell." These words are intentionally left amorphous. As you progress through this story, the meanings of words will change, come into sharper focus, or you will see that precise definitions really don't matter and can even be counterproductive, having a limiting effect if applied to the mind-expanding metaphors in which they are often used.

This book begins with two concurrent threads. One is a chronological account of powerful events and sensory perceptions that propelled the author's mystical journey. The other is the author's intellectual analysis of those events and perceptions, and of the art, science, religion, and philosophy that informed and gave meaning to her experience. Eventually a third stream joins the other two, which represents the emergence into consciousness of a hidden force beyond the sensory body and analytical mind which we discover has been directing this process all along.

The basis of this book is a very personal diary which, like most diaries, was not meant for public consumption. This is the author's view not into the world, but into herself, a voyage of discovery in which no social proprieties were observed and no dark backwaters were left unexplored. Many of the statements herein would be considered audacious, boastful, embarrassing, or offensive in polite company and would never have been uttered in public. These private utterances are now made public in this book because the author's spiritual call demands it.

This book is not intended to teach or preach, but simply to describe in great detail one person's journey to awakening. If you question some of the opinions and conclusions expressed in the beginning of the book, just wait – the author's views often changed with new experiences and new insights. This story evolves through many amazing twists and turns, and as with all journeys worth taking, this one is not so much about the point of arrival, if there is one, as about the process of getting there.

Prologue

I was twenty-one years old when I graduated from college and embarked on a great adventure. Armed with only my diploma and one steamer trunk of belongings, I set out to begin a new job in a strange, distant land. I was exhilarated, anxious to see and learn and experience new things.

I loved my new home, but expected to stay only a couple years and then move on. I also expected to remain single and independent. I had such high standards and expectations for a life partner that I figured I would never marry, never find a man who could live up to my impossibly high standards. Maybe I would have a boyfriend from time to time, but no commitments.

Within weeks of my arrival in my new home, I met the man I would marry, the love of my life, Louis. There were many obstacles to our love, many social and cultural differences, but our glorious connection as star-crossed lovers was undeniable, and all the obstacles were finally overcome. Our shining path of destiny was clear. After a seven-year courtship, we were married.

Then, after a seven-year marriage, Lou died. My grief was devastating, sending me into a dark abyss. With Lou's death I came to know that my marvelous adventure with him was not just a finite earthly journey, but also an infinite spiritual one. In an effort to heal my broken spirit, I began to spew my thoughts, feelings, and revelations into a journal – a spiritual journal, a cathartic chronology of my quest for healing and restoration. This book is taken from that journal, my travelogue through life, love, loss, and eternity.

... continued from Volume Two ...

PART 30

The Angel in the Spaceship

April 2014 – May 2014

~ 669 ~

Marianne Williamson's book *Enchanted Love* contains a beautiful story that perfectly describes my divine but tragic relationship with Emily:

> So often the issue is not learning how to attract love, but rather how to *recognize* love. Sometimes love arrives as though it were a spaceship landing in the back yard. The captain comes out of the ship and says to us, "Hi, I'm here to beam you up! Come on! We're going!"
>
> And then we say, if we say it, what is ultimately the most tragic thing we will ever say, and that is, "No, thank you." No, I don't choose the ride, even though I want it desperately. No, I don't want to beam up now, even though it's a living hell down here. No, I do not choose the path of wild and radical and authentic love, even though I know I am dying without it. I think I'll just settle for "good enough."
>
> Angels are onboard those spaceships, often in the guise of loved ones holding the torch that would light our way through darkness. On the other side of that darkness is the light in which dreams come true. But there are demons in that darkness, to be sure, and we can feel them. They almost paralyze us with fear. All those unloved parts of ourselves are there, ugly and twisted and ready to destroy. They live in the darkness, on the other side of which is paradise itself. Even though the only way to paradise is through the darkness—and even though the fire of the angel's torch will burn the *demons* up, not us—we do not trust that. We lack faith. We are staunch and calcified in our refusal to choose love, and so we say to the angel, "No, you go ahead. I'll stay here."
>
> The angel looks at us in disbelief; the refusal of ecstasy is unknown in heaven. The space captain can scarcely believe his ears, but noninterference in and respect for the choices of another human being is a must on the enlightened path. Still, as the ship takes off, the captain looks at the angel onboard and notices that there are tiny sparkling rivers of water falling from her eyes.[31]

~ 670 ~

GOOD FRIDAY

Today is Good Friday, and tomorrow is Easter Vigil. This is the time in Holy Week of deepest darkness, after Christ's death and before his resurrection. It is the descent into hell, into the unknown, into confusion, uncertainty, fear.

This is symbolic of my current status with Emily. We have only the most superficial contact; it is as if her soul is dead to me. She is in her tomb, in hibernation, in her cocoon. She is a black hole from which no light emerges.

I am there, too. My tomb is the dark, silent, uncomfortable place where I lay patiently waiting for Emily to roll back the stone. I cannot see past the barrier she has put between us. Will she permanently erase me from her life, or will she return to me? Will she arise out of the darkness and awaken to rejoice in the light of love? Will she say "yes" to the angel in the spaceship? Will we be resurrected? It will take more than three days. Maybe more than three lifetimes.

Emily just called, her voice rising out of the darkness.

~ 671 ~

[The next morning] Emily called again. She realized that she shouldn't keep me away during her times of stress; my calming influence might help.

Last night after I talked with Emily, I experienced another flood of vaginal secretions – the sexual energy of the 2nd chakra rising to the 6th, passing through the 4th chakra where love pours to overflowing from worldly to otherworldly realms and back again, where the Buddha touches the earth.

When I look at Emily I see God – as Campbell says, God with form at the 6th chakra. That's why I bring her soup, as a cat brings a dead mouse, a food offering, to the doorstep of his master, paying homage to his deity.

~ 672 ~

[Two days later] Emily called again. She wants me to hold her hand through this stressful time. I said, "I love you."

Then she said, "I love you back. I love you, too." *She used the four-letter L-word.* Not "light," but "love."

I spent the last four days with the Christians, eating The Last Supper, suffering The Passion, descending into Hell, and rising again into the Light of Resurrection. Today, with one four-letter word from Emily, I am returned to life. What synchronicity! As I sank into despair on Good Friday, wondering if Emily would awaken, there she was, beginning to awaken. And as I sat in the church sanctuary last night, praying for help in my quest, she was opening her consciousness to our love.

~ 673 ~

Emily spent the night with me. We danced, ate, talked, cried, hugged. I played music for her. She sang for me. There was strong sexual tension in the air, but despite her clear sexual advances, I knew it was too soon to give our love physical expression. Mostly we just talked. I learned about her emotionally closed mother who would not allow herself to be touched; who created an atmosphere of instability with her anger, abuse, and neglect; and who drove the wounded child Emily into silence, loneliness, fear, and a secret protective world of her own.

The good news is that Emily was able to tell me about horribly painful childhood events and about other troubles in her life without splitting, dissociating, as she had before. (~637~) And she has learned to use the L-word. A tiny crack has opened up in her ability to give and receive love. Her tone is softer, her attitude more gracious and accepting, her thoughts clearer and more rational, her anger muted.

The bad news is that, while she no longer avoids the L-word, she is still confused by its multiple meanings, and she has quickly learned its usefulness in drawing people (possibly me) deeper into her web. She still stages dramatic scenes to get attention and manipulate people. She is still hostage to impulsiveness, excess, and delusion. She is still an alcoholic.

Everything is still all about her; compassion for others is severely limited by the fear, suspicion, self-protection, and self-loathing in her own damaged psyche. There is no giving, only taking, and her dominating, controlling personality is still very much in evidence. All of this is colored by what appears to be progression of her chronic physical illnesses. She often appears to be in great physical distress, but it is hard to tell whether her symptoms are caused by disease, anxiety, or skilled acting. There is still a long, long way to go before she can be truly healed.

My epiphany, however, continues unabated. As I lay with her in bed, looking into her beautiful sleeping face only inches from mine, I discovered viscerally what it means to participate joyfully in the sorrows of the world. In this sorrowful creature beside me, with all her weakness, is my personification of God with form at the 6th chakra. My joy in her presence, my embracing arm around her, takes me to nirvana. She is to me as the sick and dying were to Mother Teresa, who saw God in each of the suffering souls she comforted.

~ 674 ~

My love is absolute and indestructible, but I know that Emily does not share it. Love does not mean the same thing to her as it does to me. In her current state she is not capable of understanding or expressing a true spiritual love. While that state may improve over time, it is not likely to be transformed enough in this lifetime to bring her into full spiritual-physical union with me.

Her controlling and manipulative personality is dangerous. My patient, tolerant, sacrificial love and my desire for her presence in my life make me particularly vulnerable. To be fully attached, to suffer with her in compassionate love, yet protect myself from harm and not enable her excesses and self-destructive behavior, is an impossibly delicate balance.

The word "love," both hearing it and speaking it, can be treacherous. It is most often an expression of need or greed, a lure to entice people to use each other. Hearing the word often conjures up the thought, "This person will do things for me," and speaking it means, "I want you to do things for me" – things like sex, companionship, financial support, or help around the house.

Emily says that she wants to be in a committed relationship and married by the end of the year. She admitted that, after so many years of working so hard, now she wants to be taken care of. While I was away on my trip last month, she met a man on the beach, a visitor from out of town, who is now wooing her. "It's going to be either Danny or you," she said to me.

She just doesn't get it. I am already in a committed relationship with her, ordained by powers greater than myself and my ego's cravings. In fact, we are already married and will always be together in the spirit realm from whence my direction comes, as I am forever married to Lou and to The Unnamed One. Even though our earthly lives have diverged, Lou departing in death and The Unnamed One in fear, our divine love remains immutable in the stillness of eternity, awaiting reawakening in another life.

~ 675 ~

Another night with Emily. This one was the opposite of the last one – no sexual advances, barely any touching. It was as if she had pressed the reset button on her sexuality. This is good. All of our previous physical explorations were bound up in the superficial trappings of worldly sex that is all she knows from the lustful loves of her past. If our otherworldly spiritual love is to be faithfully manifested in space-time, in the flesh now, it will have to be approached from another direction, with feelings and sensations that are at this time unknown to her.

We did have some wonderful conversation, however, some food and drink, and a good night's sleep. Strides are being made. I entertain the possibility that she just might awaken to our love. But it is a delicate line I am walking, a difficult communication with an *asura*, a jealous god, as Chögyam Trungpa said. (~658~)

~ 676 ~

Two nights ago we talked about Emily's issues; last night it was my turn. I was very explicit with her about my sexuality and how it comes out of my deep spiritual love, not as a reaction to the usual sensory stimuli. She still doesn't quite understand. Although she knows at some level that we are deeply connected, she has not yet been able to follow the thread of spiritual love into the realm of time and space, body and mind.

My love for her is unchanging, eternal, and oblivious to the opposing forces of space-time duality. It stands on its own, not in relation to any other love in this world. I do not covet anything she possesses. It doesn't matter to me that she has a difficult and demanding personality (albeit accompanied by a certain charm). My sexual attraction to her has nothing to do with gender, age, or beauty. It is the pure love of the spirit made manifest in the flesh, as Jesus was God made Flesh. It's a miracle. Somewhere deep inside her, she knows this and recognizes her place in this wondrous love. Her subconscious has let little signs escape that tell me this, but her conscious mind still resists.

It is impossible to describe the agony I suffer when we part company. Being in her presence puts me in another realm, right on the edge of the place where time and eternity merge. I come alive with her; life becomes real; my black-and-white world morphs into full color. When she leaves me, the magic portal closes. I am jarred back into the illusory world, thrown into confusion and spiritual cacophony. She is dead to me, and I die with her.

But Emily left her scent behind. When I catch a whiff of it on bedclothes or towels, I am subliminally brought back into her company, feeling again our eternal connection in space-time.

~ 677 ~

I give her my blessing to follow her path with Danny and see where it leads. Of course it hurts. But I will not fight with Danny over her. I feel like the true mother in the Bible story of Solomon splitting the baby. If Danny can bring her the fulfillment she seeks, I will let her go. Her happiness, not mine, is my fulfillment. I have too much experience with love and loss to ever think that I can lay claim to her or possess her in any way.

My love for her in the spirit, however, can never be let go. It is inclusive, not exclusive, and will expand to bless all those in her sphere, no matter how much of it finds expression in this life. I will come to love Danny, too, as I love The Unnamed One *and* his wife.

Perhaps an awakening to the highest levels of spiritual love is not in the cards for Emily in this life. Unless she is drawn to me spontaneously and involuntarily, without thinking, as I am drawn to her, by the same force from the same eternal source, then our life together is not meant to be. The intertwining of our lives must be a matter of inexorable destiny, not of choice. If she feels that she must make a conscious choice between Danny and me, she isn't tapping into the ultimate power where all choices have already been made.

~ 678 ~

THE POWER AND DANGER OF LANGUAGE

Words can be dangerous. Language is the most precise way our minds communicate and gain information, but it is not precise enough. Words are easily misunderstood or misinterpreted, especially when in translation across centuries, cultures, and customs.

Here are three different translations, spanning about three hundred years, of "Dhammapada 5" from Sanskrit to English:

Hatred is never appeased by hatred in this world. By non-hatred alone is hatred appeased. This is a law eternal. (translated by Acharya Buddharakkhita, 1922-2013, Indian)

This is the most modern translation of the three, but I suspect, because the translator was native Indian, it is probably the most literal translation, closest to the original Sanskrit.

Hatred will never disappear so long as thoughts of hatred are cherished in the mind. Hatred will disappear just as soon as thoughts of hatred are forgotten. This is an eternal truth. (John Dryden, 1631-1700, English)

The original Dryden wording is: "Anger will never disappear so long as thoughts of resentment are cherished in the mind. Anger will disappear just as soon as thoughts of resentment are forgotten." Dryden had a reputation for embellishment in translation; he not only turned "hatred" into "anger" and "resentment," but also extrapolated the role of thoughts in the causation and dissipation of hatred. He built the interpretation of the verse into the translation, which can be dangerous, but in this case, I think correct, since this view of the nature of thought is consistent with Buddhist philosophy.

Responding to criticism of his expanded translation of Virgil's *Aeneid*, Dryden wrote, "The way I have taken, is not so streight as Metaphrase, nor so loose as Paraphrase: Some things too I have omitted, and sometimes added of my own. Yet the omissions I hope, are but of Circumstances, and such as wou'd have no grace in English; and the Addition, I also hope, are easily deduc'd from Virgil's Sense. They will seem (at least I have the Vanity to think so), not struck into him, but growing out of him." [11]

Hatred does not cease by hatred, but only by love; this is the eternal rule. (Max Müller, 1823-1900, German-English)

Müller, being a creature of the Romantic Age, let "love" creep into this verse. The word "love" was not often used in a positive sense in Hindu/Buddhist literature; love was seen as a hindrance – a first-poison attachment. Hence the term "non-hatred" used by Acharya Buddharakkhita in the first translation above.

Max Müller studied the teachings of his contemporary Ramakrishna and other Vedic and Hindu scholars, incorporating their views into his own work. For this Müller was criticized by the Presbyterian and Roman Catholic Churches in Scotland, much as Joseph Campbell and Jesuit mystic Anthony de Mello were criticized by the Catholic Church a century later for similarly respecting Hindu and Buddhist wisdom. Müller nevertheless had no trouble harmonizing Hindu philosophy with his ancestral Christian faith and remained a lifelong Lutheran.

In researching Max Müller, I discovered an interesting counterpoint to Joseph Campbell's view of mythology:

He [Müller] saw the gods of the Rg-Veda as active forces of nature, only partly personified as imagined supernatural persons. From this claim Müller derived his theory that mythology is "a disease of language." By this he meant that myth transforms concepts into beings and stories. In Müller's view, "gods" began as words constructed to express abstract ideas, but were transformed into imagined personalities. Thus the Indo-European father-god appears under various names: Zeus, Jupiter, Dyaus Pita.[i] For Müller all these names can be traced to the word "Dyaus," which he understood to imply "shining" or "radiance." This leads to the terms "deva," "deus," "theos" as generic terms for a god, and to the names "Zeus" and "Jupiter" (derived from deus-pater). In this way a metaphor becomes personified and ossified. This aspect of Müller's thinking was later explored similarly by Nietzsche.[11]

How fascinating this is! Campbell saw mythology as a way to expand and universalize finite historical persons and events, giving them life and meaning beyond their temporality and the limits of language, uncovering their eternal truth. He looked deeply into the words and images of myths, beyond the superficial storylines, and took the "personified and ossified" metaphors out of their shells, revealing their unseen, impersonal, eternal condition.

But Müller points out that mythology can also go in the opposite direction when myths take eternal truths and confine them in limited space-time words and images. This is exactly how the singularity of the Source got broken up into Yahweh, Satan, and the other anthropomorphic gods of the Bible. In many ways, the mythology of the Bible and much other scripture is indeed Müller's "disease of language." Much of Campbell's work consisted of curing scripture of this disease.

~ 679 ~

We can imagine a healthy body, but that doesn't keep us from getting sick. The medicine man turns a mental image into physical reality—in fact, this is what all miracle workers do. At the quantum level they "see" a new result, and in that vision the new result emerges.
– Deepak Chopra, *How To Know God* [26]

---

[i] Dyaus, or Dyauspitar (द्यौ ष्पित्), is the Rg-vedic sky deity. His consort is Prithvi, the earth goddess, and together they are the archetypal parents in the Rg-veda. Indra's separation of Dyaus and Prithvi is celebrated in the Rg-veda as an important creation myth.[11]

This adds further elucidation to the vaginal spotting I experienced with The Unnamed One. I previously described this phenomenon as a psychically generated surge of pre-menopausal hormones. I saw the union of Shiva and Shakti in our creative musical union, and my miraculous mental image moved from symbology to biology. As my broken bag straps on my trip moved from psychics to physics. (~655~)

> The key question is not whether a medicine man is real or fake but how powerful his consciousness is, for he alone makes the patient enter into altered reality with him, along with any nearby observers. I have to emphasize "nearby" because this is a field effect, and just as a magnet can attract iron only at a certain distance, the miracle worker has a limited range of ability.[26]

This is why there is no substitute for being in Emily's physical presence. Phone calls, texts, emails, and letters don't put us in close enough proximity for the miracles to work. But when we are together, work they do.

My stress with Emily, as with The Unnamed One, is like the unresolved tension of two magnets in close proximity pulling toward each other but not able to make contact. My soul knows that Emily is my other half, my opposite polarity, and it wants to snap into place with her, to find its completion in her, at home in the Source, in heaven on earth.

My sorrow is the probability that she will never open herself to my love, that she will never know the boundless joy that I have already known with her, that she will never in this life close the distance and allow our magnets to find their togetherness.

~ 680 ~

Another night with Emily. We ate, talked, laughed, cried, cuddled a little before bed. "It's getting late, we should sleep now," I said.

"I could talk with you all night," she replied. I stayed put, sitting on her bed, her body nestled against mine. "You don't want to go, do you?" I shook my head no.

Another petal of the beautiful flower opened. She didn't want to leave this morning. She feels safe in my house; she is comfortable here with me. I rejoice in that. I still don't know what our karmic destiny is. All I know is that we are on a fabulous spiritual journey, traveling the glorious high spiritual road that we are meant to travel.

~ 681 ~

LOVE, Part 4

Shakespeare on love, from *A Midsummer Night's Dream*:

> Things base and vile, holding no quantity,
> Love can transpose to form and dignity:
> Love looks not with the eyes, but with the mind;
> And therefore is wing'd Cupid painted blind:
> Nor hath Love's mind of any judgment taste;
> Wings, and no eyes, figure unheedy haste:
> And therefore is Love said to be a child,
> Because in choice he is so oft beguiled.

Robert Olson, in *An Introduction to Existentialism,* paraphrases Socrates:

> Socrates begins his speech by remarking that those who spoke before him were too extravagant in their praise of love. Love, he says, is a symbol of want or need, not of completion or fulfillment. To love is to desire, and to desire is to seek; but nobody seeks that which he already possesses. We seek only that which we lack. The lover may, of course, enter into possession of the body of the beloved, but even then he is inflamed by the desire to perpetuate his good fortune and continues to seek a future happiness, which as future is beyond his grasp.
>
> Moreover, so long as the object of the lover is the beauty of another's body, the lover is doomed to disappointment; for the beauty of the body soon fades. Even if the object of the lover is the beauty of another's soul, he still faces inevitable disappointment. A beautiful soul may survive the decay of the body; but it, too, in its own way is a fragile and finite object. The lover can be secure only if the object of his search is the pure, simple, and eternal idea of beauty itself—a transcendent object of which finite things are but perishable and imperfect copies.[9]

My divine love is indeed Socrates' "eternal idea of beauty itself," but my body-mind constantly grieves the continuous loss of the "perishable and imperfect copies" – the worldly receptacles into which love flows and from which its radiance is visible on earth.

Joseph Campbell wrote about the love relationship:

> *Anima*—as they say in the alchemical system, *anima mercuria*—keeps changing forms. The *anima* comes forth but one doesn't know anything about it until it finds residence in a certain person. The problem of marriage is exactly that: you marry a projected *anima*, but what you

really have married isn't only a projected *anima* but a fact. What you thought you had and what you actually got is the problem of, what shall we call it, the disillusionment. That is to say, you must take back the *anima*. You can go away and I'll project this over here! Then you'll have the same problem all over again.

I think the problem today is that we're taught, or rather, we're given to think, that marriage is going to be a long love affair and that you're going to have a lot of fun with the *anima*. The fact is you're not having fun after the first ten minutes. You're in confrontation with a problem and it turns into an ordeal. The ordeal is of acquiescing.

The pure *anima* is the thing that's got to go, to vanish. You've married this phenomenon and it's not quite what you thought you were going to get. Then the acquiescence in the characteristic of life as here exhibited is what we call maturation.[40]

Campbell refers to a love that is still grounded on earth – a mature love, the best love that can be achieved short of transcendence – but the two people, even though riding in tandem, are still separate. Because there are still two, there is still a *relationship*.

Here is where my love, what I call spiritual or divine love, differs. It is in a realm beyond the physical body, beyond *anima*, beyond Cupid's beguilement, and beyond relationship. Also beyond choice or acquiescence. The self dissolves into the other and disappears, like the salt doll walking into the ocean. There is no longer a relationship, because in the Great Void there is no one and no thing to have a relationship with. There is no "other." There is only one.

Marianne Williamson sees the opposite side of Campbell's coin:

I think often we fall in love and you're just high, helium toes, you are in this altered state of consciousness. So the dominant social wisdom says that doesn't last; ultimately reality sets in. The euphoria doesn't last, because it was all projection and infatuation and delusion, and then reality sets in. After a certain point in my life I realized I don't have to buy that. I think the exact opposite is the truth. That was reality. From the spiritual perspective, *that* was reality, and then non-reality set in.

What really happened is that we, at this point in our development, do not have the personality structures capable of handling that much love, taking in and staying with that level of light perception. That euphoria is our natural state. That euphoria is a spiritual high. The issue is not that you didn't see the person really; the issue is that you saw them *so* really. You saw them the way God would see them, and that's why you were happy.[41]

I am not in a relationship with Emily. I *am* her. I see her *so* really, as God would see her. I am not just projecting a mercurial *anima* on her from the outside; I am seeing and identifying with her buddha-nature, her God-self, on the inside. That's what makes the separation of our bodies and minds so agonizing for me. In space-time I am forced to inhabit a separate body outside hers, even as we are one in the spirit. Our oneness resists being split; the magnetic poles hold firmly to each other, wanting to stay bonded together in the force field of love as space-time pulls them apart.

Emily asks why people fall out of love. Shakespeare, Socrates, Campbell, and Williamson have given us the answer. Cupid beguiles them in the beginning; they are infatuated with and blinded by the *anima*; they pursue their desires for happiness and acquisition of that which they lack, and then are disenchanted when the *anima* wears off, when the treasure they thought they had acquired disappears, or they realize that what they thought was real was actually an illusion.

If love is not about pursuing beautiful bodies or personalities, not about filling an empty hole, not about possessions or dependency or security or satisfying needs and desires, then it is never fallen out of. Our bodies and minds come and go, but Williamson's "euphoria" and Socrates' "eternal idea of beauty itself" never fade. There is no beguilement, disappointment, disillusionment, or acquiescence. Our vision of our beloved "the way God would see them" is the ultimate reality, a "level of light perception" that Cupid can never blind us to.

I was saddened to read Campbell's depiction of marital love in terms of *anima* and the acquiescence to the unanimated reality as maturation. In his other writings, Campbell's descriptions of true spiritual love, transcendent love – as in Tristan and Isolde, Isis and Osiris, courtly love, the kundalini and chakras – were so good, imbued with the sense that he knew from personal experience what he was talking about. I thought he must have lived such a love with his wife. But he also described disillusionment with the projected *anima* and the ordeal of resigned acquiescence in the marital relationship with a tone of personal experience. Perhaps he did indeed know both kinds of love; courtly love outside his marriage, but something less in his marriage.

My heart breaks for Campbell as I realize what a blessing Lou was to me. I was granted transcendent love within marriage – no beguilement, no disillusionment. No acquiescence necessary.

~ 682 ~

Mysticism has been conceptualized as oneness, without boundaries, without ego, which perpetuates a harmful split between the mundane and the spiritual that negates the reality of matter, individuation, and daily life. We need a view that acknowledges the existence of both, embedded in each other, and allows for the things that are part of daily life – ego, self-centeredness, thinking, emotions, being social mammals, the problems we are having – to be part of the spiritual context we need to deal with, not something we need to escape from through practices. – Joel Kramer and Diana Alstad, "Reframing Spirituality"

Thich Nhat Hanh said, "How do we touch nirvana? You just touch what is there in the phenomenal world." (~694~) Huai-jang warned about the impossibility of finding enlightenment solely through religious practices: "How could sitting in meditation make a buddha?" (~295~) Being in touch with the phenomenal world of daily life while also touching the oneness that is embedded inside is the essence of the bodhisattva's life.

Dietrich Bonhoeffer was a German Christian martyr from the Nazi era. But for the culture he was born into, he could have been a Buddhist. He explains so well the bodhisattva's joyful participation in the sorrows of the world:

> The community of disciples does not shake off suffering as if they had nothing to do with it. Instead they bear it. In doing so, they give witness to their connection with the people around them. At the same time this indicates that they do not arbitrarily seek suffering, that they do not withdraw into willful contempt for the world. Instead, they bear what is laid upon them and what happens to them in discipleship for the sake of Jesus Christ. Finally, disciples will not be weakened by suffering, worn down, and embittered until they are broken. Instead, they bear suffering by the power of him who supports them. – *The Cost of Discipleship* [51]

~ 683 ~

I think Emily is my last great trial on the road to enlightenment. Mara is tempting me with her luscious beauty, attracting me to her, luring me to take the first poison, and at the same time showing me her horrible demons, tempting me to run from her in fear and hurt, taking the second poison. I must resist both temptations. Whether Emily rides my spaceship or not, I must remain immovable, not succumbing to either desire or aversion. I must truly let her go, accepting her presence or absence, her affection or ridicule, with the same equanimity.

I spent a half-hour with Emily today. Even though she says she wants to be alone before her final exam, she invited me over to her office. When I arrived she was exhausted from studying, her face drawn, her voice strained. Then we talked, laughed. She read me part of the paper she was working on. By the time I left, she was again radiant and smiling. So was I.

We melt in each other's presence. The salt doll walks into the ocean. What we have is magic. Before my very eyes the power of spiritual love is beginning to transform us. We are not just good together; we are perfect together.

LOVE, Part 5
Love from the Top Down

The seven chakras are arranged from the bottom up: The lower three chakras are physical, reflecting aspects of life in time. The 4th chakra, in the center where divine love is awakened, is the bridge from the physical to the metaphysical, to the upper three spiritual chakras.

The lower three chakras are the seat of the worldly loves. (~643~) At the 1st chakra of survival is parent/child love; at the 2nd chakra of sex and creativity is spouse/spouse and friend/friend; at the 3rd chakra of power is master/slave.

At the pivot point, the 4th chakra where the Buddha touches the earth, divine love arises and subsumes the temporal loves of the lower three chakras into the spiritual love of the upper three. As Campbell said, the energy of the 1st chakra rises to the 7th, the 2nd to the 6th, and the 3rd to the 5th.

When the 4th chakra opens, all the colors of the kundalini rainbow merge into invisible white light – the light of God's love. "This is the message we have heard from him and proclaim to you, that God is light and in him is no darkness at all." (1 John 1:5 RSV) Jesus said, "While I am in the world, I am the light of the world." (John 9:5 RSV) The Buddhists also know that God is light: Amida, the compassionate deity of the Pure Land school and the Buddhist counterpart to Jesus, is called the Buddha of Immeasurable Light and Life.

The love that most people know comes from the bottom up. Most marriages start in the lower chakras, with lust and power, dependencies and responsibilities – financial, emotional, parental, social. Women exchange sex (a 2nd chakra creative function) for protection and financial support (3rd chakra power functions). Men provide that support, create a household, and women respond by providing housekeeping and childrearing services (1st chakra survival functions). Such marriages are just business deals; love has little or nothing to do with it. Many marriages never progress beyond this stage, but can still be happy and satisfying, and even become loving, as the needs of physical life are met.

My love comes from the opposite direction, from the top down – it starts in the spirit. This spiritual energy races through the chakras from top to bottom, radiating and flowing through all the chakras with the same extreme intensity. Hence the renewed creativity and authority in my artistic and intellectual work (at the 2nd and 3rd chakras) and my miraculous new sexuality in the wake of my awakening with Emily, my vision at the 6th chakra rejuvenating the 2nd chakra. Eternal love comes first, then its psycho-physical manifestations.

From the first time we hugged, Emily and I have been in continuous sexual union. I am constantly making love to her, renewing that union, moving it to the next stage. If at some point we actually have sex – make love – on the physical plane, it will be but one of many blips in the continuous heartbeat of our eternally sexual body.

~ 685 ~

Emily's dark side reemerged. Mean, angry, irrational. She hates and reviles me now. She came to stay the night with me after her all-day final exam was over. It was going well for a little while, but when I told her that I had previously scheduled a breakfast meeting with my friend Joe the next morning, a cloud descended over her. The meeting would only have taken me away for an hour, but unbeknownst to me, she was expecting me to stay with her all day.

I think her childhood trauma of abandonment was conjured up. She withdrew more and more from me, drinking almost two bottles of wine, barely speaking, looking at her photo collection on her phone, retreating into herself. By 1:00 a.m. she was so uncomfortable that she left my house and walked to her office. Between 1:20 a.m. and 3:00 a.m. came a flurry of texts and a phone call in which her demons broke loose in all their fury, telling me all that I had done wrong and essentially breaking up with me.

I overestimated her capacity to stay in the light. I suspected this might happen, her demons finding their chance to emerge once her final exam was over. I was not prepared, however, for the intensity of her primal rage or the depth of my own suffering in the wake of it. All day I have been walking around like a zombie, living the opening sentence of C.S. Lewis' *A Grief Observed*: "No one ever told me that grief felt so much like fear."

After a long sleepless night, I had breakfast with Joe, seeing him off on his trip to visit his mother. He is my dear friend, my confidant and helpmate in handling the sorrows of life. We shared our respective relationship problems and found a measure of peace in our mutual compassion. Later he texted: "That was such a lovely breaking of the fast! Thank you for always making time for me. You are one of my dearest friends."

I finished the day visiting my sister-in-law Elaine at the nursing home. She was so glad to see me, and I was glad to see her, too. We almost cried. She said, "You are my only friend, the only one I can talk to. I like you the best." We talked for almost an hour. Through most of our time together I held her hand and stroked her arm. She was a bit befuddled and repeated herself a lot, but was in good spirits, buoyed by my visit. Her smile helped release some of the icy fear that had gripped me the whole day.

~ 686 ~

God is love, and he who abides in love abides in God, and God abides in him ... There is no fear in love, but perfect love casts out fear. For fear has to do with punishment, and he who fears is not perfected in love. (1 John 4:16-18 RSV)

The pastor quoted the 23rd Psalm: "Though I walk through the valley of the shadow of death, I will fear no evil, for God is with me." Anita Moorjani ("Live fearlessly!") and many others say that love and fear cannot coexist. God is love, casting out fear. This is the great celestial theorem, the eternal geometry of the spirit.

In the last analysis, learning how to transcend the ego involves nothing less than learning how to be open to love. Only love has the power to save us from ourselves. Until we learn to truly love ourselves and others—and to accept the love of others—there can be no hope of lasting happiness or peace or redemption. It is because we do not love ourselves properly that we lose ourselves so easily in the many illusions ego sets before us. – *Enneagram Personality Types, 460-61* [17]

~ 687 ~

Emily is back. She stayed with me again last night. "I do love you," she said. "You are the only person I think about every day. Not Danny, only you."

I am wary, however. She is having a cash shortage and asking me for money again. She encourages me with flattery and affection to get things from me. But no matter. I am drawn to her by assignment from God, not by her plays to my vanity and emotions. Part of my assignment is to practice the 1st Perfection of generosity, to provide her enough money to enable her good karma (but not so much as to enable her bad karma, her excesses and indulgences). My connection to her would be the same with or without her professions of love.

I must admit, though, that her affection feels good. Maybe too good. Her bad days are a reminder that every moment of joy is accompanied by an equal measure of sorrow. While

Danny is still in play, I will assume that her future is with him. Her fickleness has been well demonstrated.

~ 688 ~

FULL MOON – NEW MOON, Part 5

There is sitting meditation and walking meditation. Now I know there is also sleeping meditation. I spent the night with Emily at her house. My right arm was wrapped around her waist; my left arm pressed against her side. My knee touched the back of her thigh; my nose and lips brushed the back of her head. I could feel the cat lying against my leg.

Touching meditation. As I laid there with her, feeling her chest rising and falling with each breath, my arms floated away from my body and melded into her. I could not feel them anymore. My nose became one with her beautifully scented hair. My breathing stopped and her breath became mine. The boundary that marked the end of my body and the beginning of hers began to dissolve. My whole body felt light and ephemeral, almost revealing the illusion that it is.

For a little while, we three – Emily, the cat, and I – became one flesh as we are one spirit. Space and time and eternity blurred together. Such is the power of transcendent love, beyond thought or feeling or even being.

~ 689 ~

My Buddhist message today: *You are walking the path … do not hesitate, do not hold back … share your knowledge … you are lighting candles for your ancestors and many others … you are far along the path … you understand the teaching, you understand what the Buddha went through … the Buddha said to know the dharma in this life is as difficult as a blind turtle poking its head through a small hole in a log in the vast ocean … YOU KNOW THIS DHARMA … you will encounter obstacles along the path … pray to the Buddha and the obstacles will be removed … go forward with confidence, do not hesitate.*

After the session I asked my spiritual guide to explain the story of the blind turtle. He did so, and further said that my grateful heart was clearly indicated, as well as my deep penetration into the spirit world. I thanked him and he walked away. A few minutes later, as I was about to leave, he came back to me and said that he had more to tell me. He said that

I must put my spiritual knowledge into practice; talk to this person, write to that one, meet with another one, and spread the dharma to the world.

My guide did not tell me anything I did not already know. I am an eighth bhūmi bodhisattva, living every moment in the dharma that is as hard to know as it is for a blind turtle to find the hole in a log in the vast ocean. The turtle is one of my guardian spirits.

> It is hard to be born as a man; harder still is it
> To encounter the Buddha when he appears in the world.
> It is as in the case of a blind turtle
> who, in the midst of the ocean, may chance to hit the hole
> In a piece of floating wood.

> – *The Mahayana Mapaharinirvana Sutra*, Chapter Two, On Cunda

~ 690 ~

Comparing my love with Danny's is like comparing apples and oranges. We offer Emily two entirely different journeys. Her journey with Danny is an earthbound one, governed by the same desires and dependencies as her past loves. She clings to old loves and grasps for new ones seeking to escape her pain and quiet her fear, to fill an empty hole that neither old nor new loves of the worldly kind can fill. She seeks someone she can depend on, only to find yet another person who depends on her.

Her journey with me would go to a very different place. It would be the ride of her life, a trip to nirvana with the angel in the spaceship. No dependencies or demands, no delusions or defenses. But pain and fear must be faced. The road to "no suffering" is full of suffering. Her mundane life with Danny might be less painful, but also less joyful, less liberating.

Will she follow the path with me? Climb aboard my spaceship? Only if she is drawn to me by the same inexorable force of destiny as I am drawn to her. Her hero's journey must be embarked upon with the sense that it is something she cannot *not* do. If she has to think about it, weigh the pros and cons, make a conscious choice, she is not ready. If her fear says, "No, I can't go," she is not ready. If there are lingering doubts, suspicions, reservations – any resistance at all – she is not ready. But if she is ready, the most blessed peace and joy await once she is through the fire.

She is unsure about how to relate to me sexually. The old rules of sexual attraction and allure that she has followed so far in her life don't apply to us. All her life she has used sex as a manipulative lure, or as an anesthetic, as most people do, to dull her psychic pain. With me, sex would not just dull the pain; it would banish it entirely. Sex in spiritual love is categorically different from the worldly kind in the same way the love is. Blissfully, transcendentally different.

The only way for her to know what I mean by this is to ride the spaceship with me. If she rides the spaceship, we may be able to cast her demons out, never to harm her again. Defenses down, hostages freed. Fear lost. Paradise found.

~ 691 ~

Last night Emily said, "When we are together, we are in La-La-Land." True enough. Our La-La-Land is where, as she puts it, we don't know what day it is and the rest of the world is shut out. It is not Cupid's beguilement or Campbell's mercurial *anima*, but rather Williamson's euphoric altered state of consciousness. (~681~) Can we stay in that state, where we see each other *so* really, as God would see us? Do we have the "personality structures capable of handling that much love, taking in and staying with that level of light perception"?

We went out to dinner. She said that it was between me and Danny. She said that if I were a man, I would win hands down, but she is having trouble coming out as a lesbian. The social stigma from her previous relationships with women still haunt her. Yet she held my hand at the restaurant and kissed it, and talked about sex with me in very intimate terms. She is terribly confused about us. Somewhere inside she knows and shares my deep love, but awareness of its true nature has yet to emerge in her conscious mind. She still is not ready.

~ 692 ~

Emily started our conversation this morning on the bright side. She said that she had a wonderful time with me last night, woke up happy, the first day free of pain in weeks – because of me. Then she turned. The conversation ended with accusations of my blowing her off and treating her like a toy. She lifts me up and then slams me down. Only a bodhisattva of the highest order could withstand this punishment. Joyful participation in the sorrows of the world. Today I'm having trouble finding the joyful part.

PART 31

Smoke Signals and Other Signs

May 2014 – June 2014

~ 693 ~

I visited my Buddhist spirit guide last night, seeking guidance regarding Emily. When he went into trance, I closed my eyes. There appeared in the middle of my field of vision a round orb that morphed back and forth from light to dark, like moving from a positive to negative photographic image. This orb had a border of its opposite shade; that is, if the orb was dark, the border was light, and vice versa. The whole thing was surrounded by a thin red circular halo.

I opened my eyes for a moment to see if there was a bright light or other circular high-contrast image in view that might have left its imprint on my retina, but there was nothing. This orb could be my third eye, my 6th chakra, manifesting now as the tingling at the back of my 5th chakra had manifested in communion with my spirit guide last year. (~539~)

Prayers are in order for Emily's mother and father, both of whom suffered emotional illnesses, according to my spirit guide. Both can be healed by merit transfer and Emily's own healing. I am instructed to share the teaching.

~ 694 ~

Tonight as I watched the sunset from my sacred place by the ocean, on the pier by the boat harbor, I read this by Thich Nhat Hanh, from *Going Home: Jesus and Buddha as Brothers*:

> It is not because you abandon all phenomena that you can touch the dimension of noumena.[ii]
> If you throw away the historical dimension, there is no ultimate dimension to touch. You have
> to touch God through his creatures. You have to touch the ultimate dimension by touching
> the historical dimension deeply. How do we touch nirvana? You just touch what is there in
> the phenomenal world.[42]

[ii] *noumenon* – as related to *thing-in-itself* in the philosophy of Kant – a thing as it is in itself, not perceived or interpreted, incapable of being known, but only inferred from the nature of experience (*phenomenon*).

On July 21, 1944 Dietrich Bonhoeffer wrote these words in a letter to his friend Eberhard Bethge, recognizing that we touch God by touching life in this world:

> During the last years I have come to know and understand more and more the profound this-worldliness of Christianity ... I thought that I could acquire faith by trying to live a holy life, or something like that. But I discovered later, and I am still discovering right up to this moment, that it is only by living completely in this world that one learns to have faith.[53]

Duality and eternity are inseparable. As one rises and falls in our consciousness, so does the other. When Emily and I touch each other in the phenomenal world, as the Buddha touches the earth, we touch God in the dimension of noumena. We touch nirvana.

Emily said that she was staying away from me to do "self-soothing." I think this is what she did as a child when her mother hurt her. She took refuge inside herself because the world outside could not be trusted. But there is a better way. Divine love *can* be trusted, and it has come into our lives to soothe and heal us, to help us both go further with our inner work.

She tells me to "be happy." But this is not a time for me to be happy. This is a time of great sorrow for me. I must not deny or repress my sorrow or put a smiley face over it. I must stay in the fire, feel the flames, and joyfully participate in the sorrows of the world. My time of happiness will come when I see the radiant glow of nirvana on Emily's face in the phenomenal world as I see it in the noumenal world.

~ 695 ~

I decided to go to church, this being Sunday morning. Perhaps something will happen to reset my soul, I thought. And something did. I got there just in time for communion. The minister began his communion prayer. I was only half listening, still being absorbed in my own turmoil. Then two words popped out at me: "... give thanks ..." Suddenly it dawned on me that instead of despairing over all that has not manifested with Emily in this life, I should give thanks for all that has. This realization was the balance I needed.

Almost no one alive on this earth has been graced with the miracles that I have. The Buddhists tell me I know the dharma that is as difficult to know as it is for a blind turtle to poke his head by chance through a hole in a log in the vast ocean. (~689~) The Christians gave me my New Year's Day epiphany when I saw matter dissolve into pure energy in the dancing molecules. (~232~) And I know what it is to love someone so deeply that I literally felt my physical body dissolve into hers. (~688~)

Emily retreats into herself because that is what she has done all her life; it is the only way she knows how to deal with fear. Whenever we have a beautiful moment together, as we did last week, I can expect a pullback of equal magnitude to follow, as her fear of strong emotions, even positive ones, rises up.

What we had last week in La-La-Land was gloriously, frighteningly, unsettlingly real; what she has done this week is retreat back into her seemingly peaceful delusion. But it is a superficial peace that comes from covering up the tension, not resolving it. She is only masking the symptoms of her malaise. She will need a love like mine to heal the underlying disease. She will need to overcome her fear of our relationship and awaken to its healing power. But my light is too bright, as Marianne Williamson says:

> We didn't expect love to awaken our biggest fears and insecurities and doubts. We thought it would bring more immediate comfort. And so we wanted it, but we didn't. When you've lived in a dungeon for a very long time, the light, when you see it, actually hurts your eyes.[31]

My body melts into hers. My mind is inside her mind and understands her aberrant behavior and raw emotions at a deep psychic level. My spirit is joined with hers and has adopted her crushing pain as its own. Surely there must be a grand cosmic plan that is the reason for this. Be patient.

~ 696 ~

ATTACHMENT/DETACHMENT, Part 5

Finally, an audience with Emily. She said that she spent the last ten days "self-healing," being by herself and reorienting herself spiritually. What she did was not healing; she just pasted back on the veneer of denial that had started to come off with me last week. But it is only the thinnest veneer, judging by how quickly it peeled off again when I obliquely mentioned her parents' emotional issues as reported to me by my Buddhist spirit guide.

She spent almost the whole time we had together in clinical detachment, spouting platitudes and dry theoretical concepts about psychology and her energy work. Her aloofness and resistance to any depth in our conversation stifled me. I could only say a tiny fraction of all that I had on my mind. Communication is so difficult with an *asura*. Only in the last minute of our conversation did the real Emily finally emerge, the one who knows love and expresses genuine human emotion.

She is back in detachment mode, saying that attachment is the cause of suffering. Yes, that's true, but not all attachments are the same, and not all suffering is the same. Attachments rooted in worldly desire bring a kind of suffering that comes from fear, anger, and frustration over not getting what one desires, widening the separation of the pairs of opposites in space-time.

Attachments rooted in eternity bring a different kind of suffering, like that of saints, angels, and bodhisattvas, which comes from eternal love, bringing the pairs of opposites back together – self-sacrificial, egoless suffering that leads to atonement ("at-one"-ness) and awakening. The attachments created by this highest form of love, totally free of dependencies and demands, are more than just constructs of need and greed; they are earthly manifestations of our oneness in eternity.

Some attachments and the suffering that goes with them must be accepted and even welcomed. For a bodhisattva to joyfully participate in the sorrows of the world, she *must* attach, knowing that such attachments and the strains, tugs, and pulls that they generate, as well as the pain of loss, are simply an inescapable part of a life fully and meaningfully lived. A buddha can let go of the world and be detached, but a bodhisattva cannot.

Just as I was about to leave, Emily turned away from me and muttered under her breath, "Must clear energy, no physical contact." It sounded like her abusive mother talking, who didn't like to be touched and would not allow physical contact with her little daughter. But then, as I invited her to go to a concert with me and handed her the concert ticket, her countenance changed dramatically. She beamed, took me by the shoulders, and presented her cheek for kissing. "Okay, I'll go," she said, adding, "There *is* love and light, you know."

All the "healing" and "cleansing" she did on herself over the last ten days was not enough to purge the negative energy that her demons created, not enough to keep me from easily scraping off the carefully constructed veneer and re-exposing all sides of her complex personality. She claims that her relationship with her mother is healed and that she processed her childhood trauma long ago. Clearly that is not true; her wounded child is still in pain, and the pain still blocks her path to true love and true healing.

~ 697 ~

At this morning's rehearsal for tomorrow's concert – probably my last concert before retirement – a fellow musician said to me, "You have a beautiful tone."

A visiting colleague, a renowned player in another band, said, "It has been such an honor to work with you. I'd play second fiddle to you anytime."

It is good to finish my career at the top of my game.

<h1 style="text-align:center">~ 698 ~</h1>

My dream last night: *I see what I think is a cat sleeping on my kitchen counter, and I reach to pet it. It is startled and scurries away. I realize it is not a cat. It has the head and ears of a cat, but the long sleek body of a weasel. I see the cat-weasel sleeping again, try to pet it, and again it runs away and jumps down to the floor. I follow it around the floor. The third time it lets me pet it, but snarls and starts to bite my hand. It is only a playful bite, though, and does not break the skin. Eventually the cat-weasel lets me pet it peacefully, and it falls asleep.*

From dreammoods.com:

> **Cat** – To see a cat in your dream symbolizes an independent spirit, feminine sexuality, creativity, and power. The cat could indicate that someone is being deceitful or treacherous toward you. To dream that a cat is biting you symbolizes the devouring female.

> **Weasel** – To see a weasel in your dream represents your lack of trust in others.

> **Kitchen** – To see a kitchen in your dream signifies your need for warmth, spiritual nourishment and healing. Alternatively, the kitchen represents a transformation. Something new or life-altering is about to occur.

> **Counter** – To stand in front of a counter in your dream suggests that you are looking for advice and for some direction in your life. You are exploring your options.

> **Floor** – To see the floor in your dream represents your support system and sense of security. You have a firm foundation that you can depend on. The floor in your dream may also symbolize the division between the subconscious and conscious.

Most of my dreams, like this one, take place in a dark background, signifying a subconscious context. The cat-weasel is Emily, who possesses both cat-like and weasel-like qualities, and whose unstable, volatile behavior I cannot trust. I take from this dream that Emily will eventually sleep peacefully in my care, on my floor of love that is a firm foundation she can depend on, where the conscious and subconscious meet.

~ 699 ~

Played what is probably my last show with the band last night. Emily was there, and we went to dinner afterward. Dinner started well, ended terribly. Demons came out. She continues to project onto me every horrible trait in herself, in her past lovers, in her mother and who knows who else. None of these projected traits are really mine, so say my sane friends who know the real me.

I am getting very close to the source of her pain. She asked me if I was sexually attracted to her. I said, "I suppose so." She instantly dissociated into a total stranger overcome with fear of me, and compared my sexual attraction to that of a pedophile priest. She accused me of being a predator and only wanting her body, despite my careful non-response to her overt sexual advances. Was she sexually abused as a child, perhaps by a priest, someone who claimed a spiritual connection to her and lured her with professions of divine love? Is this why she left the Church?

I realize that I am in way over my head in understanding Emily from a mental health perspective. I have scheduled a meeting with a psychologist next week, hoping to put all that I have experienced with her into an objective scientific context.

~ 700 ~

I have spent most of the day reading Thich Nhat Hanh's book *Living Buddha, Living Christ*. This quote caught my attention:

> If his mind of enlightenment is strong, the monk will follow the path of practice naturally, like water flowing in a stream. ... Monks or laypersons who practice well always observe the Five Wonderful Precepts, the 58 Bodhisattva Precepts, or the 250 Pratimoksa Precepts. These guidelines are the expression of the practitioner's understanding and love. They are not rules imposed from the outside.[33]

I didn't learn the Five Precepts and then try to put them into practice to become a better person; when I first learned of the Five Precepts I realized that I had already been practicing them without intention in the natural course of my spirit-filled life. I didn't study the 58 Bodhisattva Precepts to conform my behavior to that of a bodhisattva, seeking to become one; I was already a bodhisattva, unknowingly practicing the 58 Precepts before I had any knowledge of them. Past is present is future. Cause is effect.

When you truly practice for the sake of others, you are not conscious of the precepts, the details of how they are actually practiced, what it means to be precept-abiding, the outcome of such practice, or the transgressions of others. Such a person truly abides by the precepts. – Chapter 23, *Mahaparinirvana Sutra*

~ 701 ~

Yesterday my picture of Kuan Yin fell off the wall, and the glass covering broke. Then I accidentally squished a small bug that had hitched a ride home from the park with me, perhaps the same bug I had befriended and carefully avoided squishing earlier in the park. I apologized to the bug and grieved for it. Just now the psychologist's office called and canceled my appointment for tomorrow. What does all this mean? I am feeling very alone, disconnected and abandoned by my spiritual support, worldly and otherworldly.

~ 702 ~

THE WHITE CLOUD

OH MY GOD! Just now, as I was doing computer work, I casually cleared my throat and gave out a little cough. A big white cloud about two feet in diameter issued from my mouth. I was shocked and startled. I'm on fire! I looked around for some evidence of the source of the cloud. There was nothing. In a few seconds the cloud dissipated into an amorphous haze and disappeared. My throat felt a little raspy for a few minutes, but then went back to normal. I felt numb, no pain or other sensations, just a little spacey, disoriented, and empty, as if I had pushed the reset button on my psyche. I sat totally still for about five minutes, stunned.

What happened? Did I expel a spirit of some kind? Did my soul leave my body? Did I go into a trance and imagine the whole thing? Real or imagined, it makes no difference. All life is illusion. But the cloud was *real*.

~ 703 ~

Not everyone wants to be fixed. Getting rid of pain can be painful, and I can understand not wanting to go down that rough road. I can't help Emily if she doesn't want help. The Unnamed One did not want help, and so he rejected his helper. The gift of love must be opened to, accepted with joy, gratitude, and humility. Lou recognized the transcendence of our love, welcomed it, and was instantly fixed, healed in spirit. So was I. Love really does conquer all, if you let it.

The distinction of spiritual love, the highest form of love, is that it remains total and complete, unchanging and unconditional, even if people are not fixed, even if nothing changes. Even if everything changes.

~ 704 ~

Dream last night: *I am standing in a field of dry scrubby grass, no trees. I see along the horizon a series of explosions coming out of the ground, like land mines going off. I turn around and see the explosions, hundreds of them, going off all around me. The explosions start happening closer to me, and finally they are going off within feet, then inches, of me, but I am not injured. After the smoke clears, I see that where each explosion had been there is now a small shrub with gnarled, stunted branches and withered leaves.*

From dreammoods.com:

Field – To see dead or barren fields signifies lack, pessimism and jaded prospects for the future.

Explosion – To see explosions in your dream symbolizes repressed anger. The rage that you have been holding in has come to the surface in a forceful and violent manner. Your subconscious is trying to get your attention.

Horizon – To see the horizon in your dream symbolizes a new beginning or a somber conclusion. The horizon represents your goals and future plans. You are in a continual state of growth, rebirth, and regeneration.

Minefield – To dream that you are in a minefield represents the many difficulties that you are facing in your waking life. You are worried about how to tackle and resolve your problems.

Land Mine – To see or set a land mine in your dream suggests that you are under some extreme pressure or stress. You fear making mistakes or tripping up on some project. Alternatively, a land mine symbolizes emotions or issues that can potentially explode if they are not properly addressed.

Plants – To see plants in your dream indicates fertility, spiritual development, potential, and growth. To see droopy, withered or dead plants in your dream suggest that you are at a standstill in your life.

I think the explosions are Emily's anger coming closer and closer to me. I am not injured by her anger, but the desolate location reflects my pessimism concerning our future. The stunted, deformed shrubs that come from her outbursts of anger represent some spiritual growth, but are not the glorious, verdant trees of awakening that I had hoped for. I am clearly worried about tripping on a land mine.

~ 705 ~

Emily dumped me again. I pushed her too far, got too close to her pain. She has retreated deep into her delusion. She again projected onto me all of the offenses committed against her by her mother and other abusers, and all of the guilt, fear, and self-loathing she feels for herself. I know what it is to take upon myself the sins of the world, and I asked for it; I opened her wound and now it is bleeding onto me.

Somehow, though, I think she will be back. Volatility, instability, impulsiveness, excesses and extremes are hallmarks of her disease. Sure enough, she called back to tell me that she is very sick and fragile now, afraid that her chronic illness is progressing. She said she does really love me and doesn't want me to go away. But then she went on to tell me that I am not the spiritual person I think I am, I need to do spiritual work on myself, and that I am a very sick, flawed person. She hung up on me.

I was worried about her. I called the suicide hotline for advice on what to do if she becomes suicidal. I offered to come over to her house just so she would not be home alone. She said, "Bring me a pizza and wine?" I took the food and drink to her, and we sat in meditative silence with music playing for a little over an hour. It seemed to help.

She is luring me back into her life because she wants money from me. She said, "You know I'm not just using you, don't you?"

I said, "I know that." I know there is a part of her that does love me, understands our spiritual connection, and is not using me. But there is another part of her, the part that is asking for money, a selfish, conniving, distrustful, deceitful *asura* who *is* using me and has the kind, warm-hearted Emily locked inside a dark prison.

She has gone from making sexual advances to being averse to any touch at all. She doesn't want to talk about deep spiritual matters, only superficialities. I have gone from being a soulmate to a friend to a vending machine. God, please tell me, how can I reach someone in such horrific pain?

~ 706 ~

Ignacio and Cecilia invited me to dinner. I brought them up to date regarding Emily. They posed several provocative questions, doing their blessed duty of caring for me, testing the righteousness of my mission:

How do you deal with your anger? What do you do when your anger comes up?

I have searched my heart, mind, and soul, and I truly cannot find any anger. My practice of the 3rd Perfection is highly developed. I respond to Emily's abuse as Jesus did: Father, forgive her, for she knows not what she does. Feelings of sadness and hurt arise in me, for sure, but I know it is her behavioral disorder and her fear that abuse me, not her true self, her eternal essence. I cannot be angry with her because she cries out in pain.

What are you getting out of this relationship?

What did Mother Teresa get out of caring for the sick and dying in Calcutta? What did Jesus get out of spreading the gospel and dying on the cross? What I get out of it is my own spiritual growth and the peace that comes from being a vehicle for God's love on earth. Feeling the spirit move in my life is its own reward.

Have you thought about letting go of this relationship?

Our relationship sprang from a series of signs, miracles, epiphanies, and synchronicities. God took me by the scruff of the neck and put me in this relationship. I must hold on to it until God releases me from this assignment. Until then, I must remain in the fire and find peace and joy therein – the bodhisattva's joyful participation in the sorrows of the world. Letting go will happen naturally when the time is right.

~ 707 ~

Opposites arise by mutual consent. As one side of duality rises, the opposite side also rises with equal strength, to the point of Campbell's "limitation in death." In pursuing my mission of mercy with Emily, watching over her, showing her the purity of God's love, I arouse her demons and bring about the rising of evil in her. The same thing happened with The Unnamed One; the light of my love exposed the darkness of his fear and brought it to the surface. I pushed him to the limitation in death, and he erased me from his life.

This is the same as when Martin Luther King's truth raised up the hatred of white segregationists; when Gandhi's truth angered the British, the Muslims, and eventually even the fundamentalist Hindus; and when Jesus incurred the dark wrath of the Pharisees in response to the light of his truth. Coming from the other direction, the evil of Hitler and the Nazis caused the rising up of equal and opposite goodness to counter it, in such forms as Viktor Frankl, Dietrich Bonhoeffer, Oskar Schindler, and Maximilian Kolbe.

The love that drives me, like that of the others, is a sacrificial love. By acting single-mindedly in Emily's interest without regard for my own interest, accepting, even welcoming, the vulnerability inherent in that condition, I demonstrate the transcendent love of God on earth. I have faith that whatever abuse I suffer at Emily's hands is meant to be, and whether my love reaches her or not, God's will is being done.

~ 708 ~

At the Buddhist service today, in the reading about Kannon [Kuan Yin], the bodhisattva of compassion: "There are three realms of existence, three levels of awareness. Kannon helps those at the middle level. Kannon also helps those in transmigration through the six lower realms, especially the *asuras*."

There it is – evidence that I am in the right place at the right time, with the *asura*.

~ 709 ~

Emily said she had a dream last night in which animals were being horribly abused. The dream woke her up at 3:00 a.m., at which point she felt the presence of a spirit in the corner of her house by the sofa, trying to tell her something. She was frightened.

From dreammoods.com:

> **Animals** – Animals symbolize the untamed and uncivilized aspects of yourself. Dreaming of animals being abused indicates that your own primal desires are being suppressed. You are unable to fully express an important part of who you are. Alternatively, the dream represents your helplessness in a situation.

There are three times I know of when the barrier between spirits and mortals is very thin – around the time of the full moon (like last night); on Halloween, All Hallow's Eve (our love rose to the surface on Halloween last year); and around 3:00 a.m. I often wake up at or near 3:00 a.m., too.

Christian mystics explain the "witching hour" this way: At 3:00 p.m., Christ died on the cross and his soul left his body. At the opposite end of the day, at 3:00 a.m., departed souls are likely to return to the human realm to communicate in some way, in dreams or in perceptible signs. Wayne Dyer claims that spiritual messaging wakes him up at 3:00 a.m. and inspires his writing at that time.

~ 710 ~

After our dinner, we walked and talked. Emily is uncomfortable in anticipation of Danny's arrival in a couple days, realizing that she is not really interested in marriage with him, and also realizing more in the front of her consciousness that her heart and her spirit are really with me.

I know better than to be tempted into joy by her momentary glimmers of awareness. After a week of worldly delights with Danny (sex), she will likely want to stay in that mode, reverting back to her poisonous-and-deluded-but-comfortable-and-familiar way of addressing the world. My spaceship offers an antidote to her poisons, the ultimate liberation and joy, but it flies off into uncharted territory, into the Great Void. Too scary. The light hurts her eyes.

~ 711 ~

There are no words to describe the agony of contemplating that one's soulmate, karmic lover, the eternal completion of one's being, is sleeping with a man she met only a month ago and with whom until now there has been only a cell phone romance. But my hurt does not turn to anger or jealousy. I understand why this is happening. I feel only compassion for this damaged creature whose fierce pain drives her into escapist promiscuity to salve her wounds.

My pain and her pain are now fused together. I cannot tell them apart. I only know that I writhe in agony from the ubiquitous suffering I feel all around me. Just when I think the weight of the world couldn't get any heavier, more is heaped upon me.

And yet, even as I writhe, I remember that my hurt comes not from Emily's actions, but from my reaction to them. Nothing is different about my life since Danny's arrival. Nothing has changed about my love for Emily or my calling to serve her. Life goes on, beauty is still beautiful, the buddha-nature remains pure and untarnished, and in the Dao everything that happens is right. Perhaps Emily's new flirtation is a regression to old ways and a spiritual setback, or on the other hand, it could be the vehicle for a new awareness of the shallowness of her old ways and a catalyst for spiritual growth. To the angel in the spaceship: Dry your tears.

~ 712 ~

Emily is so afraid of being hurt again, as she was in childhood. She is so afraid of being rejected or abandoned by me that she repeatedly rejects and abandons me first. Then she sees me still standing, calmly taking her threats and anger, not running away or fighting back, returning her abuse with more love. I pray that I will still be standing when the smoke clears from this latest and most painful bruising. I have no choice; I will keep standing forever, propped up by God and the angels until my mission is accomplished.

Brené Brown asks:[iii] *"Who am I in a relationship with who can bear the weight of this story? Someone who will show up and wade through the deep with me."*

As I wade through the deep with Emily.

"I am looking for the person who loves me not despite my vulnerability and imperfection, but because of it."

As I love Emily.

"We steamroll over those people to get the attention and appreciation of the people who will never show up for us like that."

As Emily steamrolls over me.

~ 713 ~

At the park I saw a bird sitting on my favorite bench. "I surrender to you, little bird," I said. "There is no fight left in me. You may have the bench." I stopped and stood quietly watching the bird. For a moment nothing else existed. "It's just you and me, bird."

~ 714 ~

I attended an intuitive group session with my new intuitive friend, Martha. It is hard to describe exactly what Martha does. She is not a medium; she does not claim to predict the

---

[iii] https://www.youtube.com/watch?v=s8Pp7QB6GrE

future or communicate with deceased ancestors. She is more like a spiritual counselor, using her intuition to help people reach into their higher consciousness, to access the knowledge and wisdom they already possess in that high spiritual place.

I told the group about my white smoky exhalation a few days ago. Martha said the word that kept coming up for her as I was talking was "awakening." Contrary to what I originally thought, I did not expel any spirits, nor did my soul leave my body. The smoky cloud was a very positive sign that my 5th chakra, the throat chakra where spiritual messages are given voice, is awakening to speak the Word, the dharma that is in me.

The color of the smoke is significant: White indicates Light. I speak from the Light. My white cloud was a manifestation in physical life of my higher self in the ephemeral spirit – like the cloth straps breaking during my trip a couple months ago, like my body's hormonal changes in temporal physical response to eternal spiritual love. The spirits are still with me, and I must learn to trust them.

PART 32

Tantra

June 2014 – August 2014

~ 715 ~

SEX, Part 21

One of my greatest challenges is explaining the role of sex in spiritual love. My whining about Emily's sexual exploits sounds like the typical upset over a spouse's infidelity, like a country song that says, "He done me wrong." But my upset is not anger over a lover's betrayal, what she has done to me, but rather sorrow over what she has done to herself. In her fear she betrayed her God-self; she recoiled from the hand of divine love reaching out to her and instead settled for the limited and limiting dependent love with which she is familiar. She is comfortable in her old shoes. I grieve her inability to see the divine love I bring to her and the higher function of sex in the context of that love, as an expression of eternal oneness and a vehicle for awakening.

Did Jesus get it on with Mary Magdalene? Did Jesus and the disciples have sexual relationships? The Bible treats New Testament characters like eunuchs, and the idea that the disciples were sexless carries through to this very day in the vow of celibacy taken by Roman Catholic priests and nuns. This comes from a misreading of the Bible passage about eunuchs who have made themselves eunuchs for the sake of the kingdom of heaven – a misreading that has perverted the Church, clergy and laypeople alike, for centuries. The Church often treats sex as an evil temptation, a sin of the flesh, to be tolerated only for the purpose of procreating our allegedly imperfect human bodies, bringing more sinners into the world.

I know from personal experience that the highest form of love has a very powerful sexual component, and it is not sinful, it is sacred. Spiritual love flows through all the chakras with equal force, transmuting the earthly expression of each chakra's energy into an expression of the divine. Where the 2nd chakra is concerned, the thoughts and sensations of sex are elevated beyond the body to a sacramental union with God. As Joseph Campbell explained (~643~), the creative energy of the 2nd chakra rises to the 6th chakra, where our third eye sees God with form, as God took form in the body of Jesus Christ.

I see Mary Magdalene as the bride of Christ. She symbolizes the transformation of a harlot, for whom sex is but a banal, carnal function of the body, into Christ's Shakti, for whom sex is a vehicle for eternal co-creation and the return to oneness with God.

Worldly sex is often used as an escape mechanism, to take one's mind off the problems of the moment. Divine sex does the opposite, taking its participants deeply *into* the moment and into timeless eternity. Worldly sex gives physical pleasure; otherworldly sex gives metaphysical ecstasy.

There are sexual rituals in Tantric Hinduism and Buddhism that are meant to facilitate the expression of eternal oneness in the physical world. From *Wikipedia*:

> Tantra is the system by which you liberate or separate the two aspects of consciousness and matter—*purusha* and *prakriti*, or Shiva and Shakti. Tantric ritual seeks to access the supramundane through the mundane, identifying the microcosm with the macrocosm. The Tantric practitioner seeks to use *prana* (energy flowing through the universe, including one's body) to attain goals which may be spiritual, material, or both.
>
> According to [David Gordon] White, the sexual rites of *Vamamarga* may have emerged from early Hindu Tantra as a means of catalyzing biochemical transformations in the body to facilitate heightened states of awareness. Later developments in the rite emphasize the primacy of bliss and divine union, which replace the bodily connotations of earlier forms. Tantric texts specify that sex has three distinct purposes: procreation, pleasure, and liberation. Those seeking liberation eschew orgasm in favor of a higher form of ecstasy.[43]

When I read this part: "Those seeking liberation eschew orgasm in favor of a higher form of ecstasy," I felt sad. What? No orgasm? Isn't that the best part? Well ... no, it isn't. Orgasm marks the end of the trance, the end of the magical transportation to transparent eternity and the return to opaque duality. The ecstasy is in the buildup to orgasm, where the body is full of scintillating energy, the mind flies off into fantasy, and time stands still.

A kind of post-orgasmic depression sometimes occurs as heightened energy dissipates and the body-mind reorients to its normal resting state. In the months and years after Lou died, I would cry after orgasm; I mourned the end of my brief, blessed reunion with Lou as I was thrown out of eternal consciousness and back into space-time. But the orgasm was not the reunion; it punctuated the end of the reunion. Orgasm, like death, is simply the point of transition between states of consciousness. Saying that orgasm is the moment of transcendence is like saying that death is the moment of life. Orgasm marks the end of transcendence, as death marks the end of life. Life and sex both unfold gradually, building ever increasing energy involving more and more aspects of body, mind, and soul. And then, both life and sex end in a twinkling of an eye, in a flash of light that closes one portal and opens another.

Sex in the context of the highest form of love is a constant state of being, not a singular act. It is an endless spiritual union manifesting in life as endless sexual arousal. This is the most delicious sex there is, always present but making no demands, a continuous psycho-physical embrace that ebbs and flows with the rhythm of life but never ends, no finality of orgasm necessary.

I now have a better understanding of masturbation in the solitary spiritual life. Masturbation can be more than just pleasuring oneself, not just a less satisfactory alternative when there is no sex partner around. It can be a full-fledged form of high spiritual sex, and as such it is an expression of self-love, our love of the God-self within us. When we love ourselves as God loves us but we have no partner who is joined in divine love with us, we can express that same tender, comforting, sacred sexual union with our own internal divinity. The sexual energy of the 2nd chakra rises to the 6th chakra to make love to God with form – in this case the form that God takes is our own.

Heterosexuality, homosexuality, and monosexuality can all be vehicles for any kind of sexual expression, from the lowest depravity to the highest transcendence – from abuse to pleasure to awakening.

> The sexual act balances energies in the *pranic ida* and *pingala* channels in the bodies of both participants. The *sushumna nadi* is awakened, and *kundalini* rises within it. This culminates in *samadhi*, where the individual personality and identity of each participant is dissolved in cosmic consciousness. Tantrics understand these acts on multiple levels. The male and female participants are conjoined physically, representing Shiva and Shakti (the male and female principles). A fusion of Shiva and Shakti energies takes place, resulting in a unified energy field. On the individual level, each participant experiences a fusion of their Shiva and Shakti energies.[43]

Anita Moorjani said this about meeting her father during her near-death experience:

> But when I saw my father, you know, when we cross over, what I learned by seeing my father is that he was not only without his physical body, but he was also without any gender, he was without any culture, without any religion, without any race. All of that drops away with our physical body. Everything. Death transcends culture, religion, race, gender, all of it, and the only thing that was left was his unconditional love for me. That was all, and that was all I felt from him, just pure, unconditional love. And that's all I felt for him.[14]

The sexual attraction that I feel toward Emily does not mean I am gay. It means that I have found that place of eternity where individual identities dissolve into each other, where Shiva and Shakti energies are fused, where there is no gender, or age, or race, or culture – or anything that differentiates separate physical bodies in the dualistic world. There is only pure, unconditional love. I understand this, and am exhilarated by it. Emily does not, and is frightened by it.

Of course I want sex with Emily, but not until she understands it and can experience it as I do, in this tantric way. Once that awakening is reached, she will eschew sex of any other kind, sex outside of the highest spiritual love having lost all its allure.

~ 716 ~

In kundalini yoga there are five kinds of love – 1) master/slave, 2) friend/friend, 3) parent/child, 4) spouse/spouse, and 5) the highest form, which has no relational counterpart; it is love itself. (~643~) The highest form of love trumps all the others, and contains all the others. Just as eternity contains space-time within it, so eternal love contains all the space-time forms of love.

Not only does the highest form of love contain all the other forms, it contains both sides of those forms. At the slave/master level, I am both slave and master, student and teacher, disciple and guru. I am both parent and child, giving succor as a parent and also receiving it as a child. As a friend, I am helping and also being helped. I am both sides of the spousal relationship, masculine and feminine equally expressed.

~ 717 ~

Saw the psychologist today. He reiterated what other psychologists have said, that he cannot make a diagnosis of Emily without seeing her, but he did say that her behavioral symptoms are consistent with Borderline Personality Disorder. His advice was to 1) try not to get sucked in by Emily's manipulation; 2) maintain emotional detachment; don't take her tirades personally, and guard my own self-esteem; 3) set limits on what I will do for her, how much I will do to protect her from herself; and 4) RUN! I asked him what he thought I needed, and he replied, "Running shoes!"

But he understood my spiritual calling, being the one person of stability in her life who will not abandon her even in the face of her irrational and abusive behavior and even if she is never "fixed." He was concerned about my emotional involvement, perhaps dependency, on her, but understood the nature and depth of my love and was relieved that I was aware of her inability to truly return my love in her present state of mind. He asked if I would stick it out with her if there was never any improvement in her behavior. I said I have no expectations of her; it is her buddha-nature that I love, and that will never change.

I must thank Emily for inspiring me to a whole new level of awareness. Through her I have learned how differently a tortured mind sees the world. She has deepened and clarified my understanding of sex in spiritual love. She has shown me God with form, and the obstacles that impede the full expression of the God-self, the obstacles that Kannon and Achala are to remove. She has taught me how to joyfully participate in the sorrows of the world. As I was sent to Emily for her salvation, so she was sent to me for mine.

~ 718 ~

Had a private intuitive session with Martha. I told her about most of my life's major epiphanies and synchronicities. She said that I am a mystic, based on her definition of a "mystic" being someone who communicates directly with the spiritual Source, not needing an intermediary. She confirmed that I do indeed have spiritual and intuitive gifts, and that I don't need to do anything more to develop them but simply listen attentively when the spirits come calling. If I want clarification of the signs, she said, just ask the spirits to speak more clearly!

Martha's first impressions of me, delivered while in intuitive trance:

> *You will earnestly want to share something with someone who is right on the verge of waking up. You are sort of like a wake-up fairy. You cross people's paths and wake them up! The inner calm, which is your persona, is one that people will gravitate to, who want more of what that is that you radiate. And you really do radiate it, whether you think so or not! They just want to be around you, or they seek you out, or your paths will cross. What will happen is, as your paths cross with them, you will be inspired to say something that will be a trigger to awaken them. There will be times when there will be a mystical experience, a phenomenon of some kind that will be just the thing that individual needs to recognize there is something very significant in what you have said.*

The word "buddha" means "one who is awake." Am I really a wake-up fairy, one who leads others on a path to awakening? Am I awake? At the eighth bhūmi: "Bodhisattvas on this level are compared to people who have awakened from dreams, and all their perceptions are influenced by this new awareness." [11]

Anthony de Mello's view of waking up humbles me, to think that I could be an agent for such a profound experience:

> Spirituality means waking up. Most people, even though they don't know it, are asleep. They're born asleep, they live asleep, they marry in their sleep, they breed children in their sleep, they die in their sleep without ever waking up. They never understand the loveliness and the beauty of this thing that we call human existence. You know—all mystics—Catholic, Christian, non-Christian, no matter what their theology, no matter what their religion—are unanimous on one thing: that all is well, all is well. Though everything is a mess, all is well. Strange paradox, to be sure. But, tragically, most people never get to see that all is well because they are asleep. They are having a nightmare.
>
> Last year on Spanish television I heard a story about this gentleman who knocks on his son's door. "Jaime," he says, "wake up!" Jaime answers, "I don't want to get up, Papa." The father shouts, "Get up, you have to go to school." Jaime says, "I don't want to go to school." "Why not?" asks the father. "Three reasons," says Jaime. "First, because it's so dull; second, the kids tease me; and third, I hate school." And the father says, "Well, I am going to give you three reasons why you must go to school. First, because it is your duty; second, because you are forty-five years old, and third, because you are the headmaster." Wake up! Wake up! You've grown up. You're too big to be asleep. Wake up! Stop playing with your toys.
>
> Most people tell you they want to get out of kindergarten, but don't believe them. Don't believe them! All they want you to do is to mend their broken toys. "Give me back my wife. Give me back my job. Give me back my money. Give me back my reputation, my success." This is what they want; they want their toys replaced. That's all. Even the best psychologist will tell you that, that people don't really want to be cured. What they want is relief; a cure is painful.
>
> Waking up is unpleasant, you know. You are nice and comfortable in bed. It is irritating to be woken up. That's the reason the wise guru will not attempt to wake people up. I hope I'm going to be wise here and make no attempt whatsoever to wake you up if you are asleep. It is really none of my business, even though I say to you at times, "Wake up!" My business is to do my thing, to dance my dance. If you profit from it, fine; if you don't, too bad! As the Arabs say, "The nature of rain is the same, but it makes thorns grow in the marshes and flowers in the gardens." – Anthony de Mello, "On Waking Up," *Awareness* [44]

Martha warned me to avoid becoming a martyr for Emily. "You are not responsible for her," she said. "Real unconditional love is to allow people their own journey." She's right. I may support Emily on her journey, but I cannot take it for her or change its course, except as the power of divine love wakes her up. We each dance our own dance.

~ 719 ~

As I left Emily's house, we hugged. I whispered in her ear, "Some part of you ..."

Before I could finish, she said, *"I know ... I know ..."*

"What do you know?"

"... I love you, too."

In the softest, tenderest voice she continued, *"I'm almost there ... with my higher self. I'm almost there."*

To myself I completed my thought: "Some part of you ... knows that your spiritual home is in La-La-Land with me."

~ 720 ~

Emily: "I think you're the love of my life."

Betty: "And you're mine."

With all my heart, I believe this is true. But she still doesn't understand what our love is. Her professed love is not the same as mine. There is the possibility that her "love" for me will wane once my money is in her hands. There is also the possibility that I will be her wake-up fairy, as Martha calls me, and her awakening to our true and sacred love will begin.

While I was at her house, she fought with Vincent, her ex-fiancé who is still her business partner and lives in a separate apartment in her house. She fought with Danny on the phone. She says that she is done with men. She admits being sexually attracted to me, but can't reconcile being gay with her Catholic upbringing and fear of social stigma. There is still huge conflict and confusion in her.

The signs and miracles are unmistakable – this love of ours is a mystical *bodhicitta* of the highest, most blessed order. Just as unmistakable are the signs that Emily is far, far away from being able to embrace it and express it in this life. My heart breaks over and over again.

I watch, and wait, and marvel as the drama unfolds. I am dancing with an *asura*.

~ 721 ~

Just read this from an interview with author Paulo Coelho:

Q: Eleven Minutes *wants to bring sexuality and spirituality to a healthier place. How can this happen?*

A: Well, by accepting that sex is a physical manifestation of God, and that is not a sin—it is a blessing. And then by understanding that except for two things that I consider to be really sick—rape and pedophilia—you are free to be creative. It's up to you, how you do this.

Sex was always surrounded by taboos, and I don't see it necessarily as a manifestation of evil. I think that sexuality is first and foremost the way that God chooses for us to be here on earth, to enjoy this energy of love in the physical plane.

Q: So with a healthy understanding of sexuality you're helping God manifest himself in the world?

A: Absolutely. Not only understanding, but practicing.[45]

God always sends me confirmation or validation from an outside source when I have startling, daring, and controversial ideas, like those I expressed in "Sex, Part 21." (~715~) I am grateful, and strengthened in my resolve.

And this from Coelho's *The Alchemist*, a book that came to me just as Emily is about to leave for a visit with Danny:

It was the pure Language of the World. It required no explanation, just as the universe needs none as it travels through endless time. What the boy felt at that moment was that he was in the presence of the only woman in his life, and that, with no need for words, she recognized the same thing. And when two such people encounter each other, and their eyes meet, the past and the future become unimportant. There is only that moment, and the incredible certainty that everything under the sun has been written by one hand only. It is the hand that evokes love, and creates a twin soul for every person in the world. Without such love, one's dreams would have no meaning.

"You have told me about your dreams, about the old king and your treasure. And you've told me about omens. So now, I fear nothing, because it was those omens that brought you to me. And I am a part of your dream, a part of your Personal Legend, as you call it.

"That's why I want you to continue toward your goal. If you have to wait until the war is over, then wait. But if you have to go before then, go on in pursuit of your dream. The dunes are changed by the wind, but the desert never changes. That's the way it will be with our love for each other.

"*Maktub*," ["It is written"] she said, "If I am really a part of your dream, you'll come back one day."

"I want to stay at the oasis," the boy answered. "I've found Fatima, and, as far as I'm concerned, she's worth more than treasure."

"Fatima is a woman of the desert," said the alchemist. "She knows that men have to go away in order to return. And she already has her treasure: it's you. Now she expects that you will find what it is you're looking for. You must understand that love never keeps a man from pursuing his Personal Legend. If he abandons that pursuit, it's because it wasn't true love ... the love that speaks the Language of the World."

"I'm going away," he said. "And I want you to know that I'm coming back. I love you because ..."

"Don't say anything," Fatima interrupted. "One is loved because one is loved. No reason is needed for loving." [46]

Our love is the pure Language of the World. It requires no explanation. Without it, our dreams have no meaning. May Emily pursue her Personal Legend, find what she is looking for, and come back to me. I already have my treasure; it's her.

I want her to awaken to our love, the love of God brought down from heaven to wipe away every tear. I want her to recognize me as her Fatima here on earth as she does in heaven. But my very wanting it prevents it from happening.

So I wait patiently, letting go of wanting, holding my hand still in the candle flame. I think of her renewed sexual relationship with Danny. I can smell my charred flesh. I feel the pain. *Maktub*, it is written; all is as it must be.

~ 722 ~

"I love you as much as I can love anyone. But you know there is a part of me that loves no one."

Yes, I know that. That loveless part of Emily is why I am in her life, to perhaps melt it away and heal the other part of her, the wounded child who wants to love but is still in pain. It is not my love for Emily that will heal her; it is her love for her wounded self, if only she can find it.

"You will go off someplace and find someone. I would be okay with that."

No, she wouldn't be, if she truly understood the nature of our love. As I am not really okay with Danny. My difficulty with Danny is not a matter of simple jealousy, and not because

I doubt the sincerity of their intentions at some level. It is because her sidetracking into yet another relationship of demands and dependency, and remaining stuck there, is itself an obstacle on the path to the highest spiritual love.

I think she may have taken up with Danny because she expected to lose me to someone I would meet during my trip a few months ago. She had to abandon me before I could abandon her.

"I don't know why you love me."

"Because I see God in you." I love her as God loves her. Or more precisely, God sent his love to her through me.

"Don't put pressure on me."

She puts pressure on herself. I simply hold out an offer to her, the hand of God reaching to her with divine love. The pressure she feels is her inner conflict over whether or not to take the hand held out to her by the angel in the spaceship. Her intuitive knowledge of the elevated nature of our love is fighting against her fear of it, her reluctance to surrender to it, her guilt over compromising it by allowing competing attachments with Danny and Vincent, her difficulty in changing half-century-old habits in the way she deals with strong and painful emotions, viewing them with suspicion and doubt and burying them, as an *asura* naturally would.

Her inner conflict – the war between the part of her that loves and the part that cannot – demonstrates the principle of interdependent co-arising, the arising of both sides of the dualistic dichotomy at the same time. In all of her other relationships there are elements of both sides, positive and negative aspects; there are dependencies and desires, needs and obligations; there is fighting and making up. The love I bring to her has none of these; it reaches beyond dualism, beyond worldly fear and worldly love. It reconciles the pairs of opposites and replaces conflict with bliss.

~ 723 ~

LOVE, Part 6

It is meaningless to ask whether Emily loves me more or less than Vincent, Arthur, or Danny. The love she has for each of us is different, a matter of kind, not of degree. We do not love our parents more or less than our children, siblings, spouses, or friends. We love them all deeply, but in different ways.

Peter said, "Behold, we have left our own homes and followed You." And Jesus said to them, "Truly I say to you, there is no one who has left house or wife or brothers or parents or children, for the sake of the kingdom of God, who will not receive many times as much at this time and in the age to come, eternal life." (Luke 18:28-30 RSV)

Jesus didn't mean you should reject or neglect your family or stop loving them. Jesus did not ask his disciples to leave worldly things behind because he wanted them to recklessly abandon their worldly responsibilities. He was asking the disciples to leave their worldly attachments – their bondage to pleasure, wealth, possessions, desire, and allegiance to worldly kingdoms – so they could follow him naked, empty, and free of impediments into the kingdom of God.

No man can serve two masters; for either he will hate the one, and love the other; or he will hold to the one, and despise the other. Ye cannot serve God and mammon. (Matthew 6:24 RSV)

Pursuing the highest spiritual calling requires 100% of your attention. All other aspects of life become conflicting distractions (unless and until those aspects become part of your spiritual journey). Disciples of Christ live the life of Christ 24/7; disciples of the Buddha live immersed in the dharma 24/7. That's why monks retire to monasteries and shamans live alone in the forest. Your parents, friends, spouse, and children must understand this and give you the space you need to pursue your spiritual journey 100%, 24/7 (as does Fatima in *The Alchemist:* ~721~).

When we discover love at the highest level, we can see its categorical difference right away; we can tell that this is a love of a qualitatively different character from all the worldly loves. I love my mother as a child loves a parent, I love my business colleagues as friends, but I love Emily as I love God, a higher love than even spouse-to-spouse. Thus, I forsake all others to follow the spiritual path that God has put before me with her. I follow her into the desert and into the forest; I give her food, wash her feet, and listen intently to the anguished wisdom she imparts. Following this path of discipleship is not a matter of considered choice; it is being swept up in a mighty celestial current that I am powerless to control (and wouldn't want to control even if I could, knowing the sanctity of its source).

If Emily is to follow the path with me, she must give up her worldly attachments to Vincent, Arthur, and Danny. Not because I demand it, but because that's the only way the path can be followed – 100%, 24/7. She can still be friends with them, of course, but not in a relationship of worldly lust, dependency, or responsibility. That is why Emily's escapades with her men hurt so much. Even though I understand why it is happening, the pain in my body-mind is inescapable. It comes from her inability to open to the deep spiritual love that I know she shares with me in the spirit. From her point of view, she is not being unfaithful to our love; she doesn't consciously recognize our spiritual oneness as I do. She lives her life in darkness and delusion, blind to her own motivations and the effects of her actions on herself and others.

Martha says I am not responsible for her. True, in the sense that I cannot "fix" her or take her spiritual journey for her, or prevent the pain that she will experience on that journey. However, I *am* responsible for her in the sense that I am my brother's keeper. I am her guardian angel, her good shepherd watching over her, Kannon removing obstacles from her path. I can't keep her from falling, but I can cushion her fall, pick her up and dust her off, and send her back into the fray with the armor of love around her. I am her caretaker, sent by God to keep her on an upward journey, or at least point the way to it, so that her soul is not lost to the nether realms.

If my love were of a lower degree, the natural response would be to leave this relationship in frustration and bitterness. But I can't do that, any more than Christ could run from the tortured souls he was sent to save, or from the torturous sacrifice that God willed for him. Like Christ, I must stay in the pain and accept it with peace and equanimity.

I know there is no happy ending for me. I must face the extremes of joy and despair, joyfully participate in them, allow myself to be tortured and not run away. Only a true bodhisattva could handle this. Anyone else would say this is too hard, "I'm outta here." That would be the abandonment and rejection Emily has known all her life, and that as a result, she inflicts on others. I must not abandon her, even as she abandons me in fear of vulnerability and new hurts. I'm the one who stays, even unto the final sacrifice. I hold my hand still in the candle flame even until it is totally burned away.

~ 724 ~

Things got very interesting with Emily last weekend. She started talking marriage again and introduced me as her "partner" to the people at the next table at the restaurant. Mind you, this is while she still has two former lovers, one current lover, and a new suitor she just met on Friday still on the string.

She collects lovers the way a teenager collects charms on a charm bracelet. This long string of impulsive, desperate, co-dependent sexual relationships is her attempt to fill the gaping hole in her heart created by her abusive mother and absent father. But loveless sex can never fulfill her psychotic need or provide the comfort and solace she craves.

~ 725 ~

I had another intuitive session with my psychic friend Martha yesterday. I never would have believed I would actually be paying attention to such a person, but she does say some helpful things. She told me a story about a Zen master who cried out in pain every night. His disciples, hearing his cries, asked if they could do anything to alleviate his suffering. He replied, "I have pain, but I don't suffer, because I accept it."

Then I quoted Lao-tzu: "Because the sage always confronts difficulties, he never experiences them."

"Yes!" she said.

> The reason that the true Master does not complain is that the true Master is not suffering, but simply experiencing a set of circumstances that you would call insufferable. We make real that to which we pay attention. The Master knows this. The Master places himself at choice with regard to that which he chooses to make real. – *Conversations with God* [23]

Martha understands my high spiritual calling to care for Emily, a "soul agreement," she calls it: "Someone looking from the outside of this dynamic would tell you to run for the hills; you're absolutely nuts and crazy, crazier than her, because it's not a rational, logical relationship. It's like caring for someone with Alzheimer's. The burden of love: Even if it isn't easy or fun, not doing it is not an option."

Martha closed our session with this:

> *In the small moments of living, connecting, is the joy of life, and yet if we get caught up in the small aspects of it, that's where the pain and suffering is. Hold that bigger picture, that in the grand scheme of things, everything is perfect and everything is fine, and at the same time being able to relish the sweetness of the moments of human joy. Your higher self is becoming very profound.*

~ 726 ~

Once again, a great book finds its way to me just when I need it. The Dalai Lama, in his *Commentary on the Thirty-Seven Practices of a Bodhisattva*,[78] expands on the work of Ngulchu Gyalse Thogme Zangpo. Here are the Practices that I found especially relevant to my own life:

ELEVEN

As all sufferings are born out of desiring one's own happiness,
And the Buddhas are born out of the mind which benefits others,
It is the practice of Bodhisattvas to engage in the actual
Exchange of their happiness for the sufferings of others.

As did the great bodhisattva Jesus Christ, I take on the sufferings of others at the expense of my own happiness. For years now I have been suspicious of happiness. Giving it up is not such a huge loss. By embracing the suffering of others, I exchange happiness for bliss.

The Dalai Lama explains:

> So we can see that five of the eight sufferings are extremely powerful, namely: ... the suffering
> of unwilling separation from others which is the nature of the body. This contaminated body
> is inseparable from us, and it precludes happiness.

How well put! I have repeatedly said that my physical separation from Emily while being aware of our oneness in the spirit is the source of my existential anguish. While we are in the body, which is inseparable from us, we must accept the dualistic yin/yang and all the opposing sensory perceptions and mental formations that go with it. Yet there are ways in this life to decontaminate the body and dissolve its illusion into the pure, eternal love that is its reality. I described how tantric sex accomplishes this. (~715~) God granted me another experience of this phenomenon, the end of separation on the physical plane, when I felt my arms dissolve into Emily. (~688~)

TWELVE

If someone, under the power of strong desire, robs or
Forces others to steal all one's belongings,
It is the practice of Bodhisattvas to dedicate his body,
Wealth and the virtues of the three times [past, present, future] to them.

The Dalai Lama explains:

> We are likely to feel anger towards someone who robs us or incites others to rob us, out of
> a strong craving for our possessions. We may be saddened by having lost our possessions,
> besides which he has no right to deprive us of them; so we may decide to take him to court
> to try to recover what we have lost. But it says here that a practitioner of the Bodhisattva's
> way of life should not do such a thing. Rather, it is suggested that we should not only give up

our belongings willingly to the one who robs us, but we should also wholeheartedly dedicate to him our body and all our wholesome actions.

Jesus said:

> You have heard that it was said, 'An eye for an eye and a tooth for a tooth.' But I say to you, Do not resist one who is evil. But if any one strikes you on the right cheek, turn to him the other also; and if any one would sue you and take your coat, let him have your cloak as well; and if any one forces you to go one mile, go with him two miles. Give to him who begs from you, and do not refuse him who would borrow from you. (Matthew 5:38-42 RSV)

Here is the 1st Perfection of Generosity – dedicating our wealth, virtue, and wholesome actions to others – stated in Buddhist and Christian terms. This principle finds application in the practice of merit transfer and in the pursuit of social justice, including nonviolent civil disobedience, replacing anger and retribution with patience and compassion, suffering injustice in order to bear witness to it.

TWENTY SEVEN

> *To Bodhisattvas, who desire the wealth of virtue, all agents of harm*
> *Are like a precious treasure. Therefore, cultivating*
> *The patience that is free from hatred and animosity*
> *Towards all is the practice of Bodhisattvas.*

The Dalai Lama explains:

> Patience is the main practice of a Bodhisattva. To the Bodhisattva who longs for the accumulation of wholesome deeds, all the three kinds of people—lowly, middle, and high-ranking—who inflict harm are like the source of precious treasure. Interacting with them causes the practice of patience to develop. When we are belittled by someone in a position of authority, we may tell others that we are practicing patience in the face of such humiliation. The real practice of patience, however, is towards those lower than ourselves, because we are able to retaliate but we choose not to do so.

I watched Lou die slowly and painfully over a five-year period. What tortured me for years after his death was not so much his death as having watched him suffer without being able to help him. They say that a very effective means of torture is to force someone to watch while loved ones are tortured. This torture by witnessing was the main cause of my spiritual crisis decades ago. But it was a crisis with a purpose; it catalyzed my spiritual growth in a way that couldn't have come otherwise.

Who were my "agents of harm" in that situation? I learned the futility of hatred and animosity when God is the only one to blame. The recognition of my agents of harm as precious treasures led me, however unwillingly, to spiritual elevation, and the necessity of surrendering without anger to God's will taught me the 3rd Perfection of Patience.

This is also my torture with Emily, watching her being hurt and hurt and hurt – not by disease or other people or any force of nature, but by her own self – and not being able to intervene. She does harm to herself and others, including me, and I must take the pain she inflicts not with anger or retaliation, but with patience and love. She is an agent of harm to me, but also an agent of awakening.

SIXTEEN

Even if a person whom one has cared for lovingly
Like one's own son were to regard one as an enemy,
It is the practice of Bodhisattvas to show greater kindness,
Like a mother to her son who is stricken by an illness.

The Dalai Lama explains:

> The meaning of this stanza is also to be found in the 'Eight Verses on the Training of the Mind' by Geshe Langri Thangpa: "When one whom I have helped and of whom I have great expectations treats me with unkindness, may I hold him as my supreme guru."

Emily is putting me through my paces – my last battle with Mara – by alternately inflaming my passions with flattery, professions of love, and displays of affection, and then driving a knife through my heart with her harsh criticism, rejection, and fickle betrayal. She lures me with delights I cannot have and reviles me with horrors I cannot escape. The persona who gratuitously flatters me and the one who viciously attacks me both treat me with unkindness, the former tempting me with the first poison of desire, the latter with the second poison of aversion. I am being tortured so sweetly by an *asura*.

My kindness to her in the face of her unkindness comes from my understanding of her condition, "like a mother to her son who is stricken by an illness," or like Martha's analogy of caring for a loved one with Alzheimer's. I now see my sacred mission more precisely: even if her ultimate healing is not to be, at least I can smooth her path and soften the blows along the way.

I can also see her sacred mission for me: She has given me an even deeper understanding of and compassion for the delusions and illusions of suffering. The tortures inflicted on the mind can be as horrific as those inflicted on the body. I thank her for the lessons that her pain – and the pain she inflicts on me – have taught me. She is my supreme guru. Richard Bach described it this way in *Illusions*: "There is no such thing as a problem without a gift for you in its hands. You seek problems because you need their gifts."[47] Carl Jung said something similar: "To this day God is the name by which I designate all things which cross my willful path, violently and recklessly, all things which upset my subjective views, plans, and intentions and change the course of my life for better or worse."

~ 727 ~

BELIEF

"Knowing" is better than "believing." *Knowing* is getting information directly from the Source, from God. It is revelation. *Believing* is forming a conclusion or opinion drawn from circumstantial evidence or from an indirect source such as scripture. Knowing is complete openness of mind, coming from a loving acceptance of all things, and is the ultimate truth. Believing is usually the opposite: the closing of the mind, a defense against the truth we don't want to know. My favorite definition of "belief" – a strongly held opinion one refuses to reconsider.

What is "faith," then? My wall plaque says, "Faith is not belief without proof, but trust without reservations." [iv] Thus, faith is not stubbornly holding firm to a belief no matter what assails it. It is being in a state of trust while waiting for the moment when "knowing" will arrive, trusting without reservations and remaining open to messages from God no matter what form they take. God does not speak in words, or even in thoughts or feelings. God speaks in compassionate love – a love that washes over everything, washing away all fear, desire, suffering, and belief.

"Knowing" does not need knowledge; it asks questions but does not demand answers; it does not cling to one belief and fear another; it gives truth a chance to emerge in any place in any form; it listens even to words it does not want to hear. To "know" God, we must cast off all our beliefs about him/her/it, along with all images, thoughts, labels, and concepts that we have used to identify, describe, and inevitably limit God. When we get beyond words and thoughts, beliefs and opinions, the law and sin, we will find our way to the narrow gate that few will enter.

[iv] This saying is attributed Quaker theologian D. Elton Trueblood.

~ 728 ~

I can only rise above the suffering for so long, then I sink back into despair. We have a beautiful moment, and then Emily backslides into separation and denial. Our connection is made and then lost, made and lost, again and again, like a bad phone connection. Life to death to rebirth to death over and over again. It feels like knife cuts being repeatedly made into the same flesh before previous wounds have had a chance to heal.

Over and over again I ask why I am sent signs and miracles leading me to people who are not able to receive the love I bring, who use me, trample me, and reject me. I understand why they abuse me, but is it really necessary? Why must I be subjected to this torture? "Thy will be done" – whether I fully understand it or not.

The Unnamed One and Emily are teaching me that at the deepest level I cannot really help people. I cannot fix them. I can only love them. My attempts to help bring only short-term, temporary relief and open me to being used and abused.

Even good friends who are not callous or overtly selfish find ways to misuse my generosity. Unlike the truly psychotic, they are capable of exerting control over their behavior, but in their fear or desperation they find taking advantage of my goodwill too easy; it is the path of least resistance.

Kannon does not fulfill self-serving wishes, but that is what I sometimes wind up doing. Jesus warned us about casting pearls before swine, and the Buddha warned us that the 1st Perfection of Generosity goes too far when it enables greed or sloth. (~506~) I must heed these warnings.

I must learn to find peace in a state of helplessness and hopelessness, and learn that patience and forbearance in unarisen phenomena must span countless lifetimes. My frustration means that part of me hasn't completely surrendered.

~ 729 ~

In an episode of the TV series *Columbo* I learned an illusionist trick:

Think of a number between one and four. What number did you pick?
Three.

Look under the telephone. What does the note say?
"I knew you were thinking of the number three."

How did the illusionist know the number? It's not magic or mind-reading. If the respondent had chosen number two, the illusionist would have said, "Look under the desk pad," where a note would be found saying, "I knew you were thinking of the number two."

This trick is a great metaphor for the coexistence of free will and predestination. We are perfectly free to choose any number. (In duality, where the House of Eternity is mostly dark, we don't know that there are numbers higher than four.) But no matter which number we choose, God has already prepared the path by which that number would bring us back to him. We are free to choose any path, but all paths are already mapped out for us before we choose, and all lead to the same place.

~ 730 ~

Thich Nhat Hanh writes in *Going Home*:

> In the Gospel according to Matthew, there is one sentence that makes me very upset. That sentence is found also in Mark. It is the question asked by Jesus just before he died. He called out, "My God, my God, why have you abandoned me?" It is a very distressing sentence. If God the Son is, at the same time, connected to God the Father, why speak of abandonment? If the water is one with the wave, why complain that the water is abandoning the wave? [42]

I am either highly elevated or foolishly arrogant to think I might be able to explain this contradiction to Thich, but here goes.

The Apostles' Creed says, "I believe in God, the Father almighty, Creator of heaven and earth, and in Jesus Christ, his only Son, our Lord, who ... suffered under Pontius Pilate, was crucified, died and was buried; *he descended into hell*; on the third day he rose again from the dead; *he ascended into heaven*, and is seated at the right hand of God the Father almighty ..."

Jesus the Son was indeed connected to God the Father, as the wave is to the water, even as he uttered his abandonment cry from the cross. However, while still in the body and vulnerable to the forces of dualism in the world, he had to perceive the abandonment of God as humans perceive it in the dualistic world, to suffer the agony of hell – which is defined as separation from God – before he could experience the co-arising of heaven and then return to sit at the right hand of God.

In eternity, the water and the wave are one, but in duality, the wave has an ego that thinks it is independent of the water in which it resides, feeling supported by the water in calm seas but abandoned when storms arise.

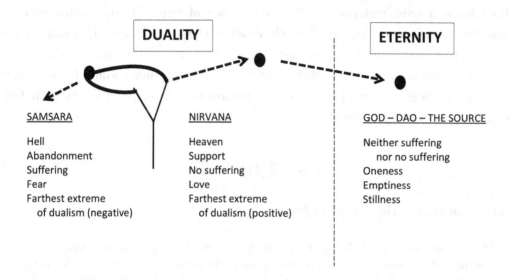

| DUALITY | | ETERNITY |

SAMSARA

Hell
Abandonment
Suffering
Fear
Farthest extreme
    of dualism (negative)

NIRVANA

Heaven
Support
No suffering
Love
Farthest extreme
    of dualism (positive)

GOD – DAO – THE SOURCE

Neither suffering
    nor no suffering
Oneness
Emptiness
Stillness

I think of this process as a slingshot from space-time to eternity. To blast through the invisible scrim between these two states, the slingshot must be drawn back to hell/samsara in order to propel the shot to heaven/nirvana – both sides of dualism must be experienced in the extreme – before the unity of eternity can be found. Earlier I described this extreme tension between the pairs of opposites as a rubber band, like a slingshot, being stretched to its ultimate tautness. This is not unlike the Buddha's extreme pendulum swing from hedonism to asceticism that preceded his enlightenment.

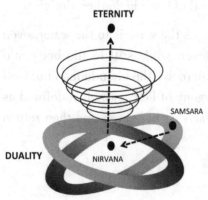

The relationship of samsara, nirvana, and eternity could also be described as a swirling vortex, nirvana being the eye in the middle of the storm where one can be in the midst of suffering (samsara) but not suffer. From the place of calm in the center of the storm one can then be lifted out of space-time dualism, proceeding through higher and higher hermetic levels, to eternity.

The Buddha experienced these extremes in his final battle with Mara under the bodhi tree, and this is the same journey from agony to ecstasy that each of us must take as we live the life of Christ or the Buddha. The Middle Way is very hard to find. The pendulum swings back and forth in a wide arc before it settles into equilibrium between the dualistic extremes.

My despair yesterday arising from my perceived abandonment by Emily was my own pullback into samsara, into the hell of separation from God. I felt abandoned in hell by the same God who sent me the heavenly miracles.

~ 731 ~

Today Emily told me she will probably marry Danny. She seemed relieved to tell me, and relieved to hear me say that if Danny is the right match for her and she is happy with him, I will be happy for her.

How could I ever compete with Danny's offer of a nice house, financial security, and sex with a penis? All I have to offer is a trip to nirvana. I am helpless and hopeless, trying to find peace by remembering that everything happens as it is supposed to, and that I must find contentment in this precious moment, which is all there is.

I know that her love with Danny is not the high spiritual love that she has with me. If it were, she would not be grappling with the decision to marry him or not. The choice would be automatic for both of them, as it was for Lou and me. I knew instantly around Halloween 2013 that Emily was my new karmic love, and in the deep recesses of her subconscious ... *so did she.* Her subconscious self knew what we were when she broke up with Arthur (~631~), and again later when she smiled lovingly and said, "You had me, you know, back in October, at Halloween." Her real self, her buddha-nature, emerged from behind her dark mask on a few brief occasions to make its recognition of our divine love known to me.

I did not make a conscious choice to love her ... *and neither did she.* Her recognition of our love came without her bidding from deep in her soul, from the eternal collective unconscious where my recognition of it came from. But unlike me, she is unable to bring her unconscious recognition into consciousness.

Knowing all this, fully understanding that she simply cannot stay in the light with me, does not help to dry my tears. I have seen too much. I have been one with Emily at the 7th chakra. I have been inside her with her pain and envisioned that pain extinguished in the radiant glow of divine love. There is no way to describe the agony of knowing the magnificence of the life we have together in the spirit, knowing how it could be expressed on earth, but not being allowed to realize that tantric expression with her in this world. It is like having a near-death experience, seeing God's light and feeling God's love all around, and then being unwillingly returned to unawakened life. I am the tearful angel in the spaceship going home to heaven without my beloved.

Anutpattica dharma shanti. Forbearance in unarisen phenomena. Patience is too mild a word to describe this unremitting existential anguish spread across epochs and eons to timeless eternity. But *anutpattica dharma shanti* is the prime directive of the eighth bhūmi bodhisattva, so here I am, patient and immovable in the fire.

~ 732 ~

Emily's house was flooded last night in the storm. She handled the stress pretty well most of the day. There were some harsh, unreasonable outbursts with Vincent, but most of the time she was philosophical about losing a few material possessions and trying to look for a positive message in all the mess.

But then, when we got to my house, where we decided she would store some of her clothes until her house was cleaned up, all hell broke loose, as I suspected it would. The psychological limiter came off and she became sullen, critical, irrational, domineering, and argumentative. She chided me about my failure to open all the windows in my house. She cried buckets over the loss of a few small mementos in the flood. She had a vicious two-hour phone and text fight with Danny because he didn't pay enough attention to her (from 3,000 miles away) in her flood travail.

She said she was testing him; I would say she was torturing him. I was glad he got to see that side of her; he needs to know what he is in for and up against. "I was pretty hard on Danny, wasn't I? But it felt good. I always feel so much better afterward." Her vicious rants are the steam being released from her psychotic pressure cooker. The calm after her storm is like that of a serial killer after a satisfying murder.

I remained surprisingly calm and clinical. It was clear to me while watching all of this that I was dealing with severe mental dysfunction, not just a sad friend having a bad day. Knowing that any true expression of our divine love was out of the question, I was able to let go of that desire and focus on my role as her guardian angel, giving her a helping hand, a compassionate ear, and a loving heart.

Whether this will bring any healing for her, I don't know, but there is healing, and growth, for me. I am still in despair over the severity of her pain, wanting to break through her blinding anger and heal the pain behind it, but I know that is not possible now. In the meantime, I am endlessly fascinated watching a full-blown *asura* in action. It is a frightening, sobering, exhilarating experience. This is life. No seat belt, no safety net.

~ 733 ~

Narcissistic Emily claimed to me that she is a size 8. (I can easily see that she is not a size 8 or even a 10, more like a 14 or 16.) Then to conceal her lie, she asked me for a pair of scissors, chased me out of the room, and cut out the size tags from her clothes that she left at my house.

Histrionic Emily coughed into a napkin while we were out at dinner. She said, "Oh my God, I'm coughing up blood!" and she ran to the restroom. She left her napkin behind. I looked at it. There was no blood on it.

~ 734 ~

"Because the sage always confronts difficulties, he never experiences them." The meaning of Lao-tzu's statement is becoming clear to me. Emily's life is falling apart around her. Her house is flooded and torn apart, her business is struggling, her relationships (except with me) are toxic and violent, and her psychosis is manifesting in many and extreme forms. She is spiraling out of control. I am her rock, steadying her ship in rough seas, removing obstacles, clearing a path, providing a safe port in the storm, but without getting caught up in her emotional dysregulation – confronting her difficulties but not experiencing them.

She is an *asura* for sure, and I think she is also a *preta*, a hungry ghost. She desperately craves love, but she sabotages her relationships and then retreats back into solitude. Her small *preta* throat impedes the flow of love in both directions; it prevents the love of others from getting in and her love from getting out. Thus, her hunger is never satisfied.

At first, I pooh-poohed dialectical and cognitive behavioral therapies because they seemed to address only the symptoms of mental illness, not the root cause. I can see now that sometimes you must be satisfied to just treat the symptoms, because getting to the root is too painful, a practical impossibility. I think that Emily may be in that category, not salvageable at the primal level, her fragmented selves never to be put together into a whole person in this life.

Accepting this reality, that the supreme goal of my life cannot be achieved, is the toughest act of surrender. But I have always known this – everything is a process, a journey, and there is never a point of arrival – except at that point where everything has already arrived in the fullness and emptiness of eternity – where we are now and every moment.

I will not likely ever see my vision of our eternal perfection manifested in this life, and I mourn that. But I am over the *anima*, the tugs and pulls of human emotion, the grasping and clinging. The symptoms of her illness are now so severe that I fear for her life – physical and spiritual – and even for mine. I am walking an incredibly fine line between steadying her and knocking myself off balance. I must call upon every ounce of knowledge, compassion, and wisdom I can muster to know what is right in this situation. This is serious business, not puppy love.

Her aberrant behaviors are more than just signs of past deprivation or difficulty. The evidence is mounting that she was severely traumatized, probably for a long time, and suffered multiple violations of her possessions, her psyche, and her body. Now in the aftermath of those violations, mired deep in unresolved fear and pain, she violates herself.

~ 735 ~

I think that there is a constant storm raging in Emily's mind. That's why she is so flighty, has a hard time concentrating, is always mentally and physically exhausted, and can't look beyond herself to see things as others might see them. She is on constant vigil, on storm watch inside her head.

Her fear, pain, and anger are like a beach ball she is trying to hold under water. She goes into solitude after a stormy outburst trying to collect herself and re-submerge the beach ball. It doesn't work for long. She exhausts herself in the effort.

Why I still remain in this hopeless relationship is a mystery to almost everyone. It would make perfect sense, though, to anyone who understands the incredible love that drives everything I do at this stage of my life. Knowing such an incredible love – so deep, indestructible, and independent of all worldly cares, desires, and needs – is the pinnacle of all that can be known on earth. Nothing can assail it. It is totally sacrificial; my life is given over to it, to the point that I can welcome a dangerously crazy person into my heart and my life without any fear or misgivings, with the peace that passes understanding, even knowing that she might well come at me with a kitchen knife in a psychotic episode.

With Lou I was introduced to this love, and we both blossomed in our mutual expression of it, but it was never put to the test because Lou was sane. Now it is being tested, and in the sense of interdependent co-arising, all of love's awesome power is being called forth in service to Emily's equally awesome pain.

~ 736 ~

Tonight at Martha's group intuitive session a clairvoyant lady said to me, "You are a healer, you know."

~ 737 ~

Emily called. She talked about her new curtains and ideas for her children's book. I could hear the change in her voice as we talked, from tense and terse to animated and carefree. We laughed and soothed each other as her mind drifted back into childlike fantasy.

She said "Love you" to me before I said it to her. She loves me as she has never loved another. Some part of her knows this. But not the conscious part.

One word from Emily and my engine is fired up again. Despair lifts as quickly as morning fog in the first rays of the sun. As much as this renewed energy feels good, I realize that it is my weakness, however benign and beneficent it seems. She casts a spell of manipulative "love-bombing" and "hoovering;" I must recognize these behaviors for what they are and avoid being sucked in.

Nevertheless, I accept with gratitude whatever contact I am granted with her, whether my wishes are fulfilled or not. Serving her is my highest calling and greatest joy. In her service I am also served.

~ 738 ~

Last night I was awakened at around 3:00 a.m. with an aching lower back. It was a dull ache, cause unknown, that radiated into my upper thighs. When this happened to me before, around a year ago (~577~), I wondered if it was sympathetic pain with my friend who had just undergone hip replacement surgery. This time, as before, the pain subsided and was gone by morning.

My new knowledge of the chakras has provided a possible explanation for this pain. The back side of the 2nd chakra is the lower back. Cyndi Dale says:

The back of the second chakra contains our feelings about ourselves in relation to the holistic universe. ...

Physical Attributes – Problems such as emotionalism, stress, compulsions, relationship ills, creative blocks, and small back pains can be symptoms of a second-chakra back side that is not completely open or that is unprotected.

Mental Attributes – Receives the healing and adaptation energy needed to cope with life's changes. Blocks in the back side prevent us from receiving this energy. Judging the acceptability of or denying expression of certain feelings causes blocks in the back side of the chakra or in the center meeting point between the front and back sides.

Feeling Attributes – The back side of this energy center will therefore be open to the vibrations and energies necessary for creativity and experience. In addition, it will enable us to obtain and acknowledge the supernatural help necessary to flow with the twists and turns of life.[19]

I recently retired from the band after more than forty years of service. This is the job that brought me to my current home so long ago and has been the primary vehicle for my 2nd chakra artistic creativity. Talk about the twists and turns of life.

I had dinner with Emily. She is in deep denial, confusion, and delusion, flipping back and forth between fragments of herself so fast I can't tell who I am dealing with at any given moment. There are no visible signs of a genuine person anymore. She has built a huge wall around herself that I can no longer penetrate. Perhaps my backache came from my inability to express my sorrow to her; I am "denying expression of certain feelings."

PART 33

Perfect Joy
August 2014 – September 2014

~ 739 ~

Had dinner out last night with Emily. She came to my place for dinner tonight. She is much calmer now than she was last week – almost too calm. She says she has turned a corner, that her anger is gone. She has decided that her love with Danny is the real thing, is determined to marry him, and is distancing herself further from me physically and emotionally. She professed to be attracted only to men, not women, and then projected onto me her latent homosexuality: "It's okay to let yourself be gay," she said to me. I said that I love souls, and that the sex of the body that houses them is irrelevant.

I do not believe her anger is actually gone; I think she is just getting better at treating her behavioral symptoms. The beach ball has not been deflated; it is just submerged under stronger pressure. Perhaps this is the best that can be expected.

~ 740 ~

Emily is upset with me again. "I think we should not talk for a couple days." She hung up on me. And then, true to form, "a couple days" of silence ended in less than an hour with a series of abusive texts. So much for her anger being gone.

I did nothing to cause her past or present upheavals; on the contrary, I have been instrumental in softening them, but still I am mysteriously to blame. She is acting out with me the psychological abuse that she experienced as a child, this time as the abuser instead of the abused. I can imagine her mother falsely accusing her of wrongdoing, threatening to withdraw her love, giving her the silent treatment. All of this would strike terror in the heart of a small child.

I feel the rising in me of the guilt and fear that she must have felt as a child under similar circumstances almost half a century ago. But I am not a child, and I understand the disease from which this behavior springs. I look at my feelings, realize that they are phantoms not to be acted upon, and let them go. I don't have to be drawn into her darkness. Stay at the high energy positive pole; climb the mountain, look down peacefully from above, see the big picture.

I remember that she picked a fight with me over nothing the day before I left on my trip in March. (~652~) Perhaps at that time, and now again as I am about to leave on another trip, she is feeling abandoned. When her wounded child feels insecure, she shores herself up by becoming her abusive mother.

~ 741 ~

BOUNDARIES, Part 1

"You don't know your boundaries. That's why The Unnamed One broke up with you; you pushed too far," said Emily.

It's true. I pushed The Unnamed One to his place of discomfort, and now apparently Emily, too. That's because spiritual love has no boundaries. Neither of them can be in that boundless place with me, so they push back.

Martha offered more insight to me in an intuitive session:

> "Abraham" Hicks says that whenever we have negative emotion it means that we are seeing the situation in a distorted way that is not the way Source sees it. God sees the perfection in the challenge of the moment. You can't make wrong choices; in the infinite omniscience of God, like GPS, even if we make a choice that goes contrary to the ultimate end result that God is holding, God simply recalculates the route we are taking, creates the next optimal situation to get us to that same ultimate end.
>
> The purpose of this relationship is for you to have the ultimate joy and fulfillment of truly unconditional love, of experiencing God's love for Emily through you. But the wonderful feelings of fulfillment and joy and love are not going to be experienced through Emily's behavior; they will come from the eternal place. She triggers you into expanded love … transformational surrender. This situation has the potential for you to have a mystical experience, not feel any pain in the midst of whatever unfolds, when you hold her in the deepest, most unconditional love. Emily is the catalyst for your spiritual transformation.

~ 742 ~

Emily came over to patch things up. We shared some wine and welcomed each other back. However, the tone was different, much more distant. She was in a trance-like state, an otherworldly gaze on her face and a tone of gratuitous grace in her voice. It felt phony to me, like a desperate attempt to find superficial peace in the midst of a deeper storm. She spouted platitudes and acted very preachy (like an unhealthy Enneagram Type One). At the beginning of our encounter, she lectured me about my faults and my need to do spiritual work on myself, not "wreak havoc" on my friends whom I would be seeing on my trip. Her rise to anger seems tempered now, but I didn't get the impression that she had moved into a truly peaceful place; she just deepened her delusion, settled in, and became comfortable there.

~ 743 ~

Once again I am reading an inspiring book, *God's Fool: The Life and Times of Francis of Assisi*.[48] This passage jumped out at me:

> There they were, the two of them (in reality or imagination), walking one behind the other, Leo in front, Francis in back, according to the Franciscan custom Dante describes for us in the *Divine Comedy*. It was very cold, and both were suffering from that, especially Francis, who was weaker. And then in his clear voice he began the unforgettable dialogue:
>
> *"O Brother Leo, even if the Friar Minor should give good example in sanctity in every corner of the earth; even there is not perfect joy."*
>
> Silence. They went on their way, and once more his voice rang out:
>
> *"O Brother Leo, although a Friar Minor might give sight to the blind, cure paralytics, cast out devils, and raise the dead, even there is not perfect joy."*
>
> A little bit farther on, again his gladness resounded in the frosty air:
>
> *"O Brother Leo, if the Friar Minor were to know all languages and all learning and all Scripture, so that he could prophesy and reveal not only the future, but the secrets of minds and souls as well, there is not perfect joy."*
>
> He knew very well all that was inspired by Saint Paul's sermon on charity in 1 Corinthians, but under the impulse of the Holy Spirit he added what Saint Paul had left out. Perhaps Brother Leo wondered what he was getting at, but Francis wanted him to be patient.
>
> *"O Brother Leo, little lamb of God"* (that was what he called his confidant), *"although the Friar Minor might speak with the tongue of an angel and know the course of the heavens and the virtues of herbs, and if all the treasures of the earth were revealed to him and he were to know*

all the properties of birds and of fishes and of all men and animals and of trees and of stones and of roots and of waters, there is not perfect joy."

A few more steps and Francis began almost to shout:

"O Brother Leo, even though the Friar Minor were to know how to preach so well that he could convert all the infidels to the faith of Christ, even there is not perfect joy."

For two miles Francis had been paraphrasing Saint Paul. Now it was Leo's turn to ask a question:

"Brother, I beg of you in the name of God, tell me where perfect joy is to be found." *

But after the enumeration of these choice graces came a rather rude jolt: Arriving at Saint Mary of the Angels, soaked through from the snow and frozen from the cold, they knocked at the door of the convent where they were in a hurry to dry off and warm up. But instead of opening the door, the brother within accused them of being frauds, rascals, robbers of the poor box, and told them to be gone. And so they stayed outside in the snow and wind, dying of hunger, until nightfall. But they wouldn't complain or curse the inhuman porter. On the contrary they thought that he at least knew whom he was dealing with, and that it was God who made him speak so brutally.

And there, Brother Leo, is perfect joy. And if they persisted and knocked again at that silent door, and this time it opened, but they were driven away, insulted, slapped, and told to go to the hospital; and if they accepted all that with cheerfulness and charity, *there*, Brother Leo, would be perfect joy. But it was too much, they were hungry and they begged the doorkeeper to open up for the love of God. Then they were beaten with a knotty club, dragged by the cowl, thrown to the ground, thrashed in the mud, and they endured all that too by thinking of the sufferings of Christ: There was perfect joy. They had come to the narrow path that Christ said few people find. They had overcome themselves for the love of Christ; they had put up with everything; they had accepted the cross. The goal was reached; a blissful eternity would be opened to them.

* Adapted from *The Little Flowers of St. Francis and Other Franciscan Writings*, trans. Serge Hughes (New York: N.A.L., 1964).

Here is yet another iteration of the practice of the 3rd Perfection. I saw myself in this scene with Francis and Leo, recognizing that all the beatings, thrashings, insults, humiliations, and false accusations hurled at me by those I love are my entry onto the narrow path that Christ said few people find, or as my Buddhist guide described it, the dharma that is as hard to know as it is for a blind turtle to find the hole in a log in the vast ocean.

Even in all the material wealth, physical health, intellectual knowledge, artistic talent, verbal eloquence, and spiritual wisdom that God has heaped upon me, even in all my good deeds, there is not perfect joy. Perfect joy is in letting go of all worldly treasure and accepting all worldly pain in total surrender to otherworldly bliss – "transformational surrender," as Martha called it. This is to be the Zen master who felt pain but did not suffer, because he accepted it.

Over and over I have felt the suffering of Christ on the cross when he said, "Father, forgive them, for they know not what they do," and when he said, "My God, my God, why hast thou forsaken me?" I am now beginning to know the meaning of "Father, into thy hands I commend my spirit." When I fully awaken to that meaning, I will know perfect joy. Then I can say, "It is finished."

~ 744 ~

Emily left an hour ago for two weeks with Danny. With him she may find happiness, but with me she finds bliss. Only she doesn't know it.

Stay in the moment. Stay in the pain. But don't suffer.

~ 745 ~

I took a Facebook quiz today –

Ever wondered what career you were actually meant for?
Answer these ten simple questions to find out!

My result –

THERAPIST
You are a caring and selfless individual. Your compassion, warmth, and sensitivity can heal others in the most authentic way possible. You help and inspire others, and can really touch people's lives. You truly understand others and can make them happy by just being yourself.

~ 746 ~

Martha said to me:

I sense that you think letting go brings spiritual peace. No – peace causes the letting go,
the falling away of obstacles. A Hindu sage said that a monk does not choose celibacy.
Eventually one lives so much in the spirit that things involving the body lose all meaning

and purpose and naturally fall away. Celibacy just happens. You are almost there, so rooted in the eternal that you stay there even in the course of worldly activity.

C.S. Lewis said something similar:

> We know the sexual life; we do not know, except in glimpses, the other thing which, in Heaven, will leave no room for it. Hence where fullness awaits us we anticipate fasting. ... What is no longer needed for biological purposes may be expected to survive for splendour. Sexuality is the instrument both of virginity and of conjugal virtue; neither men nor women will be asked to throw away weapons they have used victoriously. It is the beaten and the fugitives who throw away their swords. The conquerors sheathe theirs and retain them. – C.S. Lewis, *Miracles*[27]

I wonder if Martha intuited the celibacy example because of my recent revelations about sex in spiritual love. Perhaps without knowing she was doing it, she brought me to the next level of understanding: The love of God *with form* at the 6th chakra includes sex (the best sex there is, tantric sex, Shiva and Shakti in union), the sexual energy of the 2nd chakra rising to the 6th. Love of God *without form* at the 7th chakra, however, is without sex. In the Great Void there is no form, no body, no object separate from oneself to have sex with. But we, as conquerors, retain our tantric swords.

The Christian monastic rules of poverty, chastity, and obedience work the same way. Monks and nuns do not choose to follow these rules; spiritual people naturally take on these characteristics when God's love is manifest in their lives. *Poverty* happens when one loses all desire to possess anything, when unsupported thought, as the Buddhists call it, takes over. *Chastity* (in the sense of all bodily behaviors, all Five Precepts) happens when there is no craving, no motivation for misconduct or excess. *Obedience* is the inevitable result of total surrender to the world as it is, to God, to the Source.

~ 747 ~

While I was talking with Martha, my other phone rang off the hook. It was Emily, out of town visiting Danny. She said tearfully that Danny had become possessive, abusive, showed his other side. "And I thought he was the one," she cried. He kicked her out and she is staying in a hotel. She asked me for money. I said no; I will help her in any other way I can, but not financially. Then her voice changed suddenly from wild and frantic to calm and reasonable. "You are absolutely right," she said. "I shouldn't have asked you." In a dreamy, delusional, psychotic voice she said, "It's all right, I'll be okay. I'm at peace now."

Within minutes the other shoe dropped. A flurry of angry texts followed: "Ok, got this and will deal with this, used to being alone. Do not contact me anymore." Just yesterday she had sung a lovely "Happy Birthday" into my phone.

I suspect that it was Emily as much as Danny who showed her other side, and now she is dissociating as she did in January when she broke up with Arthur. What horrific pain she is in! Even though I feel her pain, I realize that I cannot help her or protect her from the effects of her destructive behavior (although I have the love with which to do so) until she opens the door to healing. All I can do is stand ready for the moment she opens the door, in the meantime steeling myself against her demands and attacks. *Anutpattica dharma shanti*. Patience.

~ 748 ~

Emily called. She is back in town. Her voice was happy and light. We made small talk for a while. Then when I asked how things were with Danny, she said with a tone of resignation, "Danny and I will always be friends." But apparently they will not be in a long-term relationship. "Do you want to come over?"

"Sure," I said. "When?"

"Now."

We caught up with each other's activities for the last month. Danny was jealous of her attention to another man and kicked her out of his house. He revealed himself to be possessive and more demanding of her than she could accept. Although he brought her back home the next day and they made up, she decided that they would not likely be a couple. She cried over losing him, "the love of my life," but had to let him go.

Then we went to the store. "We have such fun together, don't we?" she laughed. We came home, ate dinner, and playfully showed off our boxing skills. I sat quietly while she read to me from books by Thich Nhat Hanh and others, expanding on them with her own thoughts. "I'm so glad you're here," she said.

I left around 6:50 p.m. Later she texted, "Thank you, will sleep soon with God. Thank you for everything. Light and love to you forever."

The L-word came back, but "sleeping with God" had me a little concerned, and "light and love to you forever" had a final goodbye ring to it. Sounded like a suicide warning. Her pleasantness all afternoon, almost too calm and accepting, was like the mood of someone who had made peace with the decision to end it all. I texted back to her, asking if she wanted me to come back to her house, but there was no reply.

~ 749 ~

She texted me early this morning and seemed to be all right. But later she called and became agitated about problems and delays with her house repairs. I asked, "Shall I bring you dinner? I know you don't have any food in the house."

She said, "Maybe it would be good if you would come hold my hand through this."

We started eating and then she said, "You know I tried to kill myself last night, don't you?" She had drunk two bottles of wine and taken four sleeping pills. We walked to the store. She stood outside looking at the red evening sky, crying and maniacally screaming. "I'm going to die soon," she said. "I can see things; I know what's on the other side." She sees visions of global catastrophes, earthquakes, epidemics, floods. At one point she stood in the middle of the road and forced an oncoming car to swerve to avoid hitting her.

While we were walking she would intermittently hold my hand or put her arm over my shoulder. When we got back to the house she said she loved me, "more than just spiritually." She still loves Vincent and Danny, whom she called to say good night. She keeps me and her men close, hangs us up in the closet and pulls us out when she needs us. I realize with great sadness that, although the word "love" has come back into her vocabulary, the only expression of love that she is capable of is the verbal one.

It is possible that there is a large element of histrionics involved here. Love-bombing, hoovering, and threats of suicide are part of the narcissist's standard repertoire. But I know her pain is real, and severe. I asked her to call me whenever she feels suicidal again. But my love is not reaching her.

~ 750 ~

"Danny and I are okay again," says Emily.

Yeah. For how long this time? Unless Emily has a psychological breakthrough, more breakups are inevitable. How well does Danny really know her? How deep is his love for her? How much can he take and how many allowances will he make for her, knowing she will make none for him?

~ 751 ~

BOUNDARIES, Part 2

Her texts finally came back: "Have emerged into light, always need space to do so, boundaries are important." Yes, boundaries are important, but in her case, boundaries wall her off from happiness and salvation. Between us I recognize no boundaries, no limitations, no separation.

Her boundary from me held firm until yesterday, when she actually invited me to go to lunch. But I couldn't go. Then she pulled away again, saying she was booked until next weekend and then she would be out of town on a job interview. "See you in October." It has been over a month since we have seen each other, and October is another three weeks away.

Reading a new book, *Loving Someone with Borderline Personality Disorder.*[49] I hope this book will teach me how to handle this.

~ 752 ~

I woke up early this morning, feeling Emily's spiritual presence, her arms around me. I looked at my digital clock; it read 6:43 a.m. I said, "I love you, Emily," wrapped my arms around her aura, and went back to sleep.

I checked my phone later; a text had arrived from her, "Have a wonderful day," at 6:43 a.m.

~ 753 ~

When Emily's relationship with Danny began to blossom, I felt a twinge of jealousy, but I did not succumb to it; I let her go to him with my blessing, as hard as that was to accept, but knowing that it was the necessary thing for her at the time. On the opposite side of the coin, when her heart and spirit returned to me I felt happiness, but I was not euphoric. I recognized that her pleasant change of mood will be as fleeting as her previous estrangement had been. I am standing high on the hill, learning to rise above both the pleasure and the pain even while I twist in their midst.

Ignacio's theology discussion group got into a rousing conversation about whether or not our personal identity continues after death. I brought up the analogies of the salt doll and the iceberg in the ocean, both of which melt back into the water in metaphorical death. But some of my fellow searchers were unhappy about that, wanting to continue to have a relationship with a separate God after death, to be able to argue with him as Talmudic scholars argue with God.

I said, "I'm fine with that. We must learn to be okay with paradox, with the idea that we can be separate from and united with God at the same time." Cecilia likened the separate-but-together idea to cream in coffee; it is all one drink, but until you stir it up, you can see the white streaks of cream in the black coffee.

"Yes!" I said. "Like a marble cake; it is all one cake, but the swirls of brown and white cake can be discerned separately inside the oneness." I remarked that Anita Moorjani in her near-death experience had received communication from her deceased father, but there was no gender, race, age, or any other attributes of a physical body associated with the communication. Yet she knew it was her father.

If such separate consciousness did not survive after death, how could the Akashic Records trace one soul and its karma through eons of reincarnation? How could I identify the spirits talking to me? Cecilia pointed out that even when the salt doll dissolves into the ocean, it is still salt, not water – $NaCl$, not H_2O. The iceberg, however, is H_2O, and when it melts it is indistinguishable from the rest of the water in the ocean.

Thus, the salt doll is Jesus the Son of Man, and the iceberg is Jesus the Son of God. Similarly, the salt doll is a bodhisattva, who knows the dharma but foregoes buddhahood and remains in space-time separation in order to serve; while the iceberg is a buddha, who renounces the world even while in it to abide in the empty singularity of eternity. This distinction between salt doll/bodhisattva and iceberg/buddha echoes the differentiation of "soul" and "spirit" in my description of the four souls. (~403~)

> It has been said that once a bodhisattva reaches the tenth stage of the path, which is next to the enlightenment state, his view of apparent phenomena, or his projections, is like vision by full moonlight. He sees things relatively precisely and clearly, but not as clearly as by sunlight. That's why he is a bodhisattva; he has some more to go. – Chögyam Trungpa[36]

Space-time exists within eternity; thus separateness, like everything else, is eternal. It's a tricky concept, like emptiness, where there is neither separation nor no separation, neither suffering nor no suffering. At the end of karma, when one reaches *anuttara samyak sambodhi*, unexcelled complete awakening, all consciousness is finally extinguished and there are no more incarnations. The iceberg melts into the warm tropical ocean, never to reemerge.

Jesus the Son of Man sits at the right hand of God the Father; Jesus the Son of God is one with the Father. He moved from being a separate person on earth, to being a separate soul in eternity, to being eternity itself – united with everything and dissolved into nothing. And of course, all three states, including the final state of eternal oneness, exist all the time, because in the Great Void there is no time. All time, like all space and matter and energy, is one.

~ 755 ~

At church today Cecilia said, "You are the first priority, not her." Cecilia is concerned about me, worried that I will sacrifice myself and all that I possess in service to Emily. She is right to be concerned, and at the same time, not. I am in the hands of God, in the throes of *agape*, the love of God, under God's divine protection. In that sense, her concern is unwarranted. However, in another sense there is reason to be concerned. God's love directs me, and this love is nothing if not sacrificial. God's will be done. "Greater love has no one than this, that he lay down his life for his friends." (John 15:13 RSV)

Of course it is wrong for Emily to use and abuse me, to take from me and show only superficial concern for my well-being. Is it wrong for me to accept being used and abused, knowing that I will be hurt?

It was wrong for Martin Luther King, Jr. to be jailed and killed. It was wrong for Jesus to be jailed and killed. But was it wrong for these men to have accepted their fate – a fate chosen not *by* them, but *for* them – to have spoken truth to power knowing that tragedy awaited them, knowing that their service to mankind, driven by love of the highest order, would push them to the limitation in death?

All who come to life from the perspective of divine love do so knowing that sacrifice is at the heart of it, surrendering everything, even life itself. In that surrender is our own salvation as well as the salvation of those we love and serve. One day I may be called to sacrifice my life for my friend. It would be as much for my salvation as for hers.

Type One EnneaThought:

> Today reflect on this teaching about Level One of your type: "In the state of integrity, Ones feel a deep peace and acceptance of life that gives them the ability to know exactly what is required in each situation and in each moment." – *The Wisdom of the Enneagram*

Compare this to the description of the eighth bhūmi bodhisattva:

> There is no need to plan or contemplate how best to benefit others, since bodhisattvas on the eighth level automatically react correctly to every situation.[11]

I trust that the guidance I need to react correctly to every situation will arrive just when I need it.

PART 34

Angels and Demons

September 2014 – November 2014

~ 756 ~

I am attending an intuitive workshop presented by Doreen Virtue. There is an air of flightiness about it – fairies, angels, and spirits – but some deep truths are emerging:

> Earth angels: The veil of heaven is lifted for us. We remember what heaven is like. We have memory of nonduality. We are here to help others lift the veil. But we are frustrated by trying to impose oneness on duality.[50]

I have been saying this for years, going on and on about my frustration trying to impose oneness on duality and fretting over my inability to help my loved ones lift the veil and grasp our oneness in divine love. Doreen gets me.

Already I have become a go-to person at this workshop. One attendee asked if she could copy my notes from the morning session. In another instance, I helped a lady cut the etheric cord she needed to break to let go of her soon-to-be-divorced husband. Later I helped a lady come to terms with the grave illness of her father in Japan. I gave her my Jodo Buddhist amulet for her father. She said the Jodo lotus emblem was her family crest. (At the last minute before I left home I had put that amulet into my bag, not knowing why. Now I know.)

Another lady asked me on the elevator if I had been practicing spiritual work for a long time. I said that it was a complicated question. "I guess I have been practicing for a long time, but I am only now realizing that's what it was!"

Robert Reeves, naturopath, said:

> You want to help, but people use and abuse you, and you are hurt. Then they attack, throw daggers at you. Call on the angels to remove the daggers, clear negative energy, so you can continue doing what you are here to do.

Yes, I am used, abused, and hurt. Clearing negative energy, removing Emily's daggers.

Doreen continued:

> Someone with DID [Dissociative Identity Disorder] or an addiction may have a deceased spirit getting a vicarious high expressing itself through this living person. People who are accident prone or show sudden personality changes, as if someone else's tastes have taken over, might have a spirit attachment. This happens when a person is scared, drugged, depressed, suicidal—weakened spiritually. Spirit usurps the living person's free will. "I'll help you," says the spirit when defenses are down. De-possession, ending the spirit's contract with the living person, can be accomplished by using "cancel-clear-delete" to remove negative thoughts and influences.

Emily often talks about spirits nagging her, sometimes frightening her. I have witnessed the eruption of such spirits; they come into view in her dissociative episodes. Many psychologists understand that mental illness is often a physical manifestation, a symptom, of a deeper spiritual illness. The voices a schizophrenic or a sociopath hears may be coming from attached dark spirits such as Doreen describes.

> As intuitives, we are telephones for God. The phone does not have to understand the message, just transmit it. Life purpose is never boring or odious. It is bliss. If you are alive, you still have a purpose. When your job is done, you are dismissed.

There is a benevolent kind of possession; angels as well as demons can attach to us, in this case to help us. Our visions of saints and mystics come from angels managing God's switchboard, making sure God's phone call gets through. When God is done with us, he will hang up the phone.

It was invigorating to be in a group of people who, for the first time in my life, did not question my spirituality. Everyone there had experienced synchronicities and revelations like mine; we spoke the same spiritual language. At lunch, a lady whispered intently in my ear, "Are you a sister? Traveling incognito? You have the aura of a nun about you."

"No," I said, with a wry smile, pleased to know that my spirituality is detectible on the outside, "but I have leanings in that direction!"

"I was a parochial school student," she replied. "I can tell."

A SHAMAN EMERGES

I was asked to do a memorial ceremony in the local native tradition by the family of a deceased couple, Fred and Nancy, friends who lived near me. Although I am deeply immersed in the native culture and religion, I am not "ordained." I have no "credentials." Nevertheless ...

As I drove up the mountain through many layers of clouds, I thought to myself, "Riding through clouds. Heaven is with me, heaven is in me. I breathe the clouds, the breath of heaven." My first stop was the summit, where I turned to face the towering peaks miles away in the distance, the home of the gods, and greeted them with a chant.

I then drove down the mountain a little way to the place where the spirits of ancestors fly. I walked about twenty or thirty yards off the trail and looked for a suitable place for my offering. "Okay spirits," I said, "Show me the place." A sheltered spot in the rocks caught my eye. I invoked the spirits, inviting the angels, Amida, Jesus, and the ascended masters to help me, and I began to set up my offering in the rocks.

As I laid the first leaves on the ground, I noticed that this spot was slightly wet, as if a small spring was seeping up through the rocks. This is an arid alpine place above the clouds; it rarely rains here, and the rest of the area was dry. I couldn't figure out where the water was coming from. It seemed as if the earth was weeping.

I made a bed of leaves as the foundation and laid upon them gifts in remembrance of my friends – flowers, a slice of homemade bread, and a small tomato from the garden – to remember the beautiful flower and fruit that they were in my life and others.

I sprinkled salt upon my offering, asking the spirits to join me. I moistened a leaf and waved it over the offering, blessing it with droplets of water. Then I began my incantation and prayer, ending with, "Above the stars, above the sky, rest in oneness with God forever."

As I drove back down the mountain, two rare native birds flew in front of my car from right to left. I don't know exactly what that means, but I think it is a good sign. In native mythology these birds are considered guardian ancestral spirits, sacred protectors. Perhaps one bird was Nancy, the other Fred, watching over me on my way home.

~ 758 ~

Emily is religiously staying away from me. The last time we saw each other was almost three weeks ago. No phone conversations. Daily texts, but only the most superficial content.

Is she trying to break up with me? Has her impulsive "love" for me cooled? Am I now a burden to her, especially now that she has gotten all the money she can from me? Is it that I see through her façade? Is it that I raise up painful emotions in her and make her uncomfortable? Is she intimidated by my strength of character and personality? Is she ashamed of her past behavior and afraid that her demons will embarrass her again? Does talk of physical or emotional intimacy between us scare her? Does she think my love is an unhealthy attachment and she needs to cure me of it, or that she does not deserve to be so deeply loved and therefore must turn away the angel in the spaceship?

Doreen Virtue said, "Detach from the situation. Sometimes we want to fix or control a situation, to make it come out according to our script, and we get in God's way. When we let go, miracles have room to enter. Detaching doesn't mean I don't care; it means I care so much I'm giving it to God."

I have no choice but to give the situation to God. But I know as much as I can know anything that I am an instrument of God. Why the frustrating disconnect? Frustration is wanting things to be other than what they are. Doreen described earth angels as being "frustrated by trying to impose oneness on duality." I must accept duality as it is, with its illusions of pleasure and pain, and allow my knowledge of the eternal oneness to quell my frustration and the sorrow it brings.

> When Mansur al-Hallaj, the great Sufi mystic, was about to be tortured and crucified as Jesus was, he is said to have uttered this prayer, "O Lord, if you had revealed to them what you have revealed to me, they would not be doing this to me. If you had not revealed to me what you have, this would not be happening to me. O Lord, praise to thee and thy works." [2]

I fully realize that my torture would not be happening if God had not revealed to me what he has. And Emily would not be torturing me if God had revealed to her what he has revealed to me. This is the path of sacrificial suffering that must be trod by every mystic, every bodhisattva, everyone born again of the spirit. What company I keep! I know St. Francis' "perfect joy," the narrow gate that Christ said few people find, and the dharma that is as hard to know as it is for a blind turtle to find the hole in a log in the vast ocean.

~ 759 ~

For the last two days I participated with a group of about ten other women in "family constellation" therapy. This therapy, somewhat like "primal scream" therapy, is meant to help people heal difficult relationships, release their emotions, and understand how trauma can be passed from generation to generation along family lines.

I was stunned by the depth of family discord and tragedy that these women were silently carrying. Unresolved pain, anger, and sorrow were unwittingly transmitted from parent to child. Many wounds were still unhealed. In Rita's case, we saw how a murder committed by her great-grandfather haunted lives through four generations of his lineage.

In her workshop last weekend Doreen said, "Before we were born, we selected our names, our parents, our bodies. Our current relationships are purposeful, to deal with karma from the past. Most difficult relationships are karmic. They reappear in this life to teach us forgiveness."

I chose my parents well. There was some dysfunction and even tragedy in my family, but my parents did a marvelous job of not passing on their pain, anger, fear, and prejudice to their children, and what little caustic fallout came to me from my parents' past generations did not sink in. My compassion, forgiveness, and forbearance began to develop at a very young age.

Witnessing the suffering of these good and loving women gave me pause. I have made more progress than I thought in my battles with Mara. I am almost devoid of the troubling emotions that possess and control so many people. Anger and fear arise in me, but they do not stay. They do not govern my thoughts or actions.

My next great battle is to find the same freedom from the happy emotions of pleasure, affection, and attraction. The first poison is the hardest one to resist. Look past both sides of duality and let go of both. Act in search of wholeness, not happiness. Find oneness in duality; do not impose oneness on duality.

~ 760 ~

FULL MOON – NEW MOON, *Part 6*

I drew a card from Doreen Virtue's Archangel Oracle Cards to get my message for the day. As I was shuffling the deck one card stuck out. "That's the one," I said to myself. I drew

"Moon Cycles" – Archangel Haniel: *"Notice how the moon affects your energy and manifestations, and capitalize upon these cycles."*

In a few hours there will be a total lunar eclipse of the full moon.

~ 761 ~

Emily will not, cannot, see what we are. She no longer entrusts me with her heart or soul. Now she actively avoids me, allowing contact only under controlled conditions involving large amounts of alcohol – able to talk with me only after she is safely anesthetized. She is clearly uncomfortable with my knowledge of her deepest self and what she perceives as my desire to possess her.

She now conceals the sensitive feelings that she used to release to me. We had a pleasant evening at the theater and dinner, but there was no real connection. She spent much of our time together on the phone, talking and texting, and she left the dinner table at around 8:30 p.m., her usual time to call Danny, under the pretense of going to the restroom. She refused to tell me anything about her planned trip next month, saying that if she talks about it, it won't manifest.

If she saw what we are, she would not avoid me; she would stick to me like Velcro; her cell phone companions would be set aside in favor of a real human companion. *If she saw what we are*, her thoughts and feelings would gush out to me without reservation; her deepest self would be laid open to me. *If she saw what we are*, all she wants to manifest in this life would come to pass without effort. She is far, far away from seeing what we are.

~ 762 ~

We had dinner at a restaurant, then a nightcap at a nearby bar. Emily spent all of dinner flirting with me, making eyes and telling me she loved me, and all of her time at the bar flirting with a strange man sitting next to her. Then she summarily dismissed me when we got to her home, getting out of the car quickly and not inviting me into her house. She is so wounded, and in turn wounds me with "perfect joy."

I was reminded of a scene from the movie *Klute*, in which a prostitute, played by Jane Fonda, says to her therapist, concerning her first loving sexual relationship, "It is a strange new feeling; it feels good. Why do I keep trying to end it?" This is Emily, who feels good with me but is suspicious of true love's strangeness and keeps trying to end it with me.

I have been having the strong recurring intuition that Emily's mother was a prostitute, perhaps the madam of a brothel or an expensive call girl, and that Emily learned the business at a young age. This would explain Emily's mother having many children with different fathers and being married to none of them. It would also explain Emily's skills as a seductress: her sexy walk; her pursed lips and "come hither" look; her habit of engaging strangers in conversation at restaurants and bars, dancing with them, even when she is out with someone else; her narcissistic preoccupation with physical beauty and sensuality; and of course, her fickle sexual relationships. It might also explain her interest in sex trafficking and the ten years of her life that she has not told me about, when she left home after high school and went to Asia, allegedly to teach English. Perhaps she had another kind of work in Asia and gained her knowledge of sex trafficking first-hand.

This might also explain why Emily has had such difficult personal relationships all her life, characterized by dependency, manipulation, volatility, abuse, and lust mistaken for love. And why she doesn't understand her love with me, which is free of all those mundane elements. It frightens her to feel her defenses coming down and her vulnerabilities coming up. Exposing her naked body is okay, but not her naked soul.

~ 763 ~

Once again I was called to do a shamanic memorial observance for a deceased friend, this time with a group of about ten people, family and friends.

As I had for Fred and Nancy (~757~), I built a small altar of leaves and flowers, and encouraged all participants to place flowers and any other biodegradable items of remembrance upon it. After a sprinkling of salt and water, I recited my chant. Each person offered a short remembrance, and then we sent the flowers and leaves out to sea. We all stood in silence for a long time watching our flowers drift on the waves as the sun disappeared below the horizon.

Everyone was deeply moved, many to tears. This was the first time I had uttered my memorial chant in front of people, or made any public presentation resembling a native ceremony. At the beginning I made a disclaimer to the group that I was not ordained by any authority and that everything I was doing was strictly unofficial, dictated by my heart and not by any liturgy. Nevertheless, I had the feeling that the gods smiled on our humble but sincere offering, whether prescribed protocols were followed or not.

To be a shaman, bodhisattva, mystic, or other such spirit worker is not a position or title that is earned by pursuing a course of study or conferred by an outside authority. It does not come from taking a vow. It is a power that rises up from within; beckoned, acknowledged, and sanctified by nature and the spirits, not by man. After the ceremony, as the sun was setting, I heard the cry of a bird flying overhead. It reminded me of the sacred birds who accompanied me down the mountain after my memorial with Fred and Nancy.

~ 764 ~

I woke up at 5:00 a.m., my brain bouncing around the memorial ceremony last evening, and Emily's apparent return to my life and love. I couldn't go back to sleep, so I got up. I checked my phone:

2:37 a.m.: Hi Betty, woke up and could not sleep, so much on my mind. Talk soon.

She called at 9:30 a.m., saying that she had canceled her class for this afternoon, just wanted to come over and be with me, rest and get out of the therapist role. We ate a little, drank champagne, talked a little, she napped while I did some computer work. She said tearfully, "You know, I drink because it helps quiet the voices in my head. I hear the cries of all the suffering in the world."

"I know," I said. "That's why I don't try to stop you from drinking."

She wants to quiet her voices. I want mine to speak louder.

~ 765 ~

I gave Emily a white silk rose. She said she didn't want it; she doesn't like fake flowers, only real ones. But she took it, anyway, to not hurt my feelings (after she had already hurt my feelings). I explained that all flowers, real or fake, are illusions, energetic objects in duality that we use as symbols: A live red rose symbolizes worldly romantic love – red hot, lustful, passionate – a 1st and 2nd chakra love – beautiful but perishable, fading as the flower dies. My silk white rose, however, symbolizes a higher spiritual love – calm, all-embracing, compassionate and dispassionate – a 6th and 7th chakra love – eternal, never fading.

A real flower is a precious work of nature, a creation of God living in space-time duality, imbued with the Holy Spirit. The silk flower is a precious work of art, a creation of the God-self living in Man, also imbued with the Holy Spirit. But the flower as a work of art goes further; it harks to a meaning beyond the sensory input that its molecules send, to the spirit beyond the living thing it symbolizes. It is not merely an imitation of life; it is a mystical symbol, a vehicle for transcendence beyond life.

I gave her a silk white rose. Danny sent her a bouquet of red roses.

Emily knows only the hot red-rose kind of love. She uses it as a spider uses a web, trapping men (and presumably me) in it, tending her victims like a garden, luring and holding them with enticements that fuel their passions and dependencies, so they will be needy and compliant and will come scurrying to do her bidding. She has turned Vincent into a houseboy whom she alternately treats with affection and disdain. She has Danny building an office for her in his house. And Arthur is still there at the other end of the phone in case she needs emergency cash or someone in a distant time zone to talk to in the middle of the night.

I am not like the other loves of her life – Vincent, Danny, Arthur. Each of these men has needs or desires that she satisfies, and they in turn satisfy her needs and desires – her love with them is conditional. With me, there are no needs or desires to be satisfied. There is nothing I get from her that binds me in dependency to her. This is pure love, the highest, greatest, most spectacular love there is.

I am not here to take her to dinner, buy her gifts, or have escapist fun with her (not that we can't do those things). I am in her life to be there when she is no fun at all, to feel her pain with her, to hold her hand when the rest of her world crumbles around her, to shore her up when she is suicidal, to change her diapers and wipe the drool from her chin, if it comes to that, when all others have abandoned her.

So far, she has me pigeon-holed along with her men in a pull-Betty-out-of-the-closet-like-a-suit-of-clothes-whenever-I-need-her-and-ignore-her-when-I-don't mode. Perhaps one day she will discover that I am the only suit left in her closet, but the only one she really needs – the never-fading flower of peace that God put there.

~ 766 ~

Bodhisattvas are sent to serve at three different levels. The greatest ones deliver universal messages meant for all people everywhere – great *tathāgatas* like Jesus Christ, Lao-Tzu, and Shakyamuni Buddha. Others come with messages tailored to serve specific purposes at specific times and places – Frederick Douglass and Martin Luther King, Jr., for instance, lighting the lamp of justice for black Americans; Mother Teresa and Mahatma Gandhi fulfilling missions of service in India; Joan of Arc in France; Bonhoeffer in Germany; Mandela and Tutu in South Africa; the Dalai Lama in Tibet. Still others bring compassionate support to one person at a time, assigned to be that person's guardian angel – as I was called to Lou, then The Unnamed One, now Emily.

But there is a thread that connects all bodhisattvas to all the others, a mystic thread that crosses all boundaries of time and space. All know the same truth, the same dharma of divine love and compassion – the dharma that is as hard to know as it is for a blind turtle to find the hole in a log in the vast ocean.

~ 767 ~

> I love the pure, peaceable, and impartial Christianity of Christ: I therefore hate the corrupt, slaveholding, women-whipping, cradle-plundering, partial and hypocritical Christianity of the land. Indeed, I can see no reason but the most deceitful one for calling the religion of this land Christianity. I look upon it as the climax of all misnomers, the boldest of all frauds, and the grossest of all libels. Never was there a clearer case of "stealing the livery of the court of heaven to serve the devil in." I am filled with unutterable loathing when I contemplate the religious pomp and show, together with the horrible inconsistencies, which everywhere surround me. – Rev. Frederick Douglass, *Life of an American Slave*, 1845

After spending a year at the Union Theological Seminary in New York, Dietrich Bonhoeffer said there is no preaching of the gospel to be found in America's churches – except in the black churches.

~ 768 ~

As Emily cleanses, self-soothes, and repairs the dam holding back her emotions, I continue to carry all her pain and suffering at the front of my consciousness. As she pushes her beach ball of emotions under water, it rises up to the surface in me. I am the vessel holding all that she cannot face, awaiting the day when she will face it.

I don't expect her to change her coping mechanisms overnight; they have been with her a long time. I know it is hard for her to let people into her private life, because doing so in the past has had unhappy repercussions. This time is different. I'm not asking her to trust me, but rather to trust our love, the greatest love there is. Surrender to it and let it direct us. It will take us to a good place – to heaven on earth.

Dietrich Bonhoeffer called hope the last temptation. Hope is a reflection of desire, the first poison. Fear is its second poison counterpart. Both hark to the future, which is merely a phantom of time, without reality. This moment is all there is; let go of past and future, nostalgia and regret, hope and fear.

Maybe her cleansing and self-soothing is the best Emily can do in this life. Covering the wound, but not healing it. That thought feels like defeat for me. I am here to heal, not just placate. It is hard to be the angel in the spaceship going home not having accomplished her mission. Let go of hope, memory, dreams. Let go of wanting. Let go of grief. Everything is as it is meant to be.

I can accept this defeat, but with regret. It is the regret, not the defeat, which will cause me to be reborn again with Emily into another life. Karma that is not healed in this life, hers and mine, must return. I was really hoping to jump off the wheel of samsara after this life.

There it is again ... hope. Let go of hope.

~ 769 ~

For the past two days I have been in deep contemplation of death. I think I am just as suicidal as Emily, but for the opposite reason. She wants to run away from something – the dreadful screeching voices in her head. I want to run toward something – my blissful eternal vision. This is our perfection; we see the opposite sides of the same coin. In life and death, we are perfect in our oneness and our oppositeness.

~ 770 ~

DISHONORABLE SUFFERING

> Jesus Christ had to suffer and be rejected. Suffering and being rejected are not the same. Rejection removed all dignity and honor from his suffering. It had to be dishonorable suffering. Suffering and rejection express in summary form the cross of Jesus. Death on the cross means to suffer and to die as one rejected and cast out. It was by divine necessity that Jesus had to suffer and be rejected. ... Being shunned, despised, and deserted by people, as in the psalmists unending lament, is an essential feature of the suffering of the cross, which cannot be comprehended by a Christianity that is unable to differentiate between a citizen's ordinary existence and a Christian existence. The cross is suffering with Christ. – Dietrich Bonhoeffer, *The Cost of Discipleship* [51]

Bonhoeffer's "dishonorable suffering" is St. Francis' "perfect joy." (~743~) I can see that in my life "being shunned, despised, and deserted by people," even as I bring them liberation in divine love, is a "divine necessity ... an essential feature of the suffering of the cross."

With both Emily and The Unnamed One, estrangement came as a result of allegedly unskilled behavior on my part. Of course I did not think it so; from my perspective, my actions were righteous; I spoke the truth as I felt compelled to tell it, motivated by love and a call to serve.

These supposedly egregious sins of mine were really just excuses my loved ones used to distance themselves from me. I had entered the private space where their pain was kept, and they were uncomfortable with my being so close. I butted up against the limit of their compassion and tolerance – the limit of their ability to love – the point where fear overwhelmed love. This is Campbell's "limitation in death," where Jesus was, rejected on his cross, having been found guilty of trumped-up charges, experiencing, as Bonhoeffer described it, "dishonorable suffering." I know that place.

C.S. Lewis knew that place, too – the place of rejection, scorn, insult, and contempt. I consider Lewis to be a great 20th century mystic, but not everyone grasped his spiritual message as I did:

> *from a January 28, 1951, letter by Hugh Trevor-Roper, to Wallace Notestein. In 1951, Cecil Day-Lewis was elected over C.S. Lewis to the Chair of Poetry at Oxford.*
>
> Do you know C.S. Lewis? In case you don't, let me offer a brief character-sketch. Envisage (if you can) a man who combines the face and figure of a hog-reeve or earth-stopper with the mind and thought of a Desert Father of the fifth century, preoccupied with meditations of inelegant theological obscenity; a powerful mind warped by erudite philistinism, blackened by systematic bigotry, and directed by a positive detestation of such profane frivolities as art, literature, and (of course) poetry; a purple-faced bachelor and misogynist, living alone in rooms of inconceivable hideousness, secretly consuming vast quantities of his favorite dish—beefsteak-and-kidney pudding; periodically trembling at the mere apprehension of a feminine footfall; and all the while distilling his morbid and illiberal thoughts into volumes of best-selling prurient religiosity and such reactionary nihilism as is indicated by the gleeful title, *The Abolition of Man*. Such is C.S. Lewis, whom Magdalen College have now put up to recapture their lost monopoly of the Chair of Poetry. – "The Don Treader," *Harper's Magazine*, December 2006

C.S. Lewis may well have been guilty of all the quirks and foibles Mr. Trevor-Roper listed. That does not change the truth that he brought to the world. This kind of venom has been spewed about virtually all the great mystics throughout history; in fact, I measure their greatness by the degree of dishonorable suffering to which they are subjected.

This is the price that all truth-tellers must pay. Let us look beyond the weaknesses of the physical forms of great teachers and see the impact their mortal lives and teachings have had on our immortal souls. As Jesus said, a tree is known by its fruit.

~ 771 ~

HALLOWEEN
Our 1ˢᵗ Anniversary

> You said you always wanted a diamond solitaire. Here it is.
>
> We are married, always have been. This gift is proof.
>
> When I bought this ring I had no idea why I wanted it. Now I know. It has been slumbering in my drawer for thirty-five years, waiting for its meaning and purpose to emerge in the fullness of time. Waiting for you.
>
> Here is my vow to you: As long as we both shall live (and maybe after), you will never be alone. You will always have a compassionate ear to hear your cries, a helping hand to tend to your needs, and a loving heart to hold your spirit.
>
> I am the good shepherd watching over you. God is loving you through me.

I gave Emily the ring and note at dinner. She was clearly moved – and she is clearly crazy. She set the ground rules at the beginning of our dinner: "I don't want to talk about me," she said. Then she played the therapist, asking about the reason for my melancholy.

"I thought you didn't want to talk about you," I said, but she pressed me, and I went on to explain that it was the distance between us. She said the distance is because I am so intense. I interpreted this to mean that my insight into her disrupts the carefully constructed edifice she has built to mask her pain and subdue her emotions.

After dinner we went to three bars. She sang, danced, drank, and got progressively more irrational, morose, and judgmental. "Danny said he would move mountains for me," she said. "Will *you* move mountains for me?"

As we walked back toward her office, she almost began to dissociate into the nasty haranguer who is disgusted by me. She was barely willing to accept a goodbye hug (like her mother, I suspect, who didn't want to be touched) – this after I had just promised my life to her.

I realize now that she is a constantly split personality; she doesn't just dissociate once in a while. None of the personalities I have seen is the real Emily, the whole person. The real Emily would be the composite of all her disparate fragments, but she does not exist in this world in that form. She seems to be in total denial about it, deluded into thinking that she is in control, that she just flairs up occasionally when she has too much to drink. She doesn't realize that she is just as fractured in her sober, calmer modes as in her drunk, angry ones.

I am not a good party girl for her; I am not in her life for laughs. I know her too well. For help around the house, she should call Vincent. For money, Arthur. For moving mountains, Danny. For a good time, her superficial friends and acquaintances. Others can provide money, attention, flattery, and fun. When she is suicidal, she should call me. For healing her karmic pain, she should call me. For a trip to nirvana, she should call me.

~ 772 ~

Yesterday Emily said to me, in all seriousness, "I think you are bipolar." She was projecting herself onto me, as she often does. By projecting this diagnosis onto me, she is expressing a conscious realization of her illness. But she got the diagnosis wrong. Borderline, not bipolar, although her manic rages and suicidal depressions could fit the bipolar mold.

Today I felt real gratitude for the privilege of being allowed to witness and take into myself Emily's incredible psychic pain. To be able to see deeply inside a mind as disturbed as hers, to perceive the many generations of bad karma that this diseased state represents, to viscerally know the horrendous suffering of it – and yet be able to grasp insanity from a vantage point of sanity, and to see the perfection of it, its place in the cosmic matrix – is a joy beyond description. Much like St. Francis' "perfect joy" in the level of suffering that it brings.

But still, the flip side of this coin, my vision of the end of her suffering, the other half of my blessed perception, calls to me, taunts me, tempts me, like a Siren song. I run to that beatific vision, grasp it, clutch it, hold it tight, and bring it into myself as I have the suffering. I see the complete picture in the spirit realm, where both dualistic sides are reconciled. If only the joy could be brought into this world where the suffering is and reconciliation could be found here and now.

My sanity perfectly balances her insanity, and together we are whole, empty, transformed ... or could be. That "could be" is my hope, my desire, and my last temptation, the last obstacle I must overcome.

~ 773 ~

MY MYSTIC JOURNEY WITH KATHY, Part 4
Provocation

In response to my provoking thoughts about God, my niece Kathy wrote, "Provocative may be in the eye of the beholder."

I responded: "Some people refuse to be provoked, even when God is doing the provoking. Yes, I am trying to provoke you, to get you to see things from multiple perspectives, to question and to challenge – first me, then yourself. Are you afraid of ideas that don't obviously conform to those you already hold? Do you want me to be just an echo chamber, a rubber stamp, for your present views? Somehow I think God has something more powerful than that in mind for us."

~ 774 ~

I'm drunk. I like being drunk. Pain hurts less. Nothing matters so much. Being dizzy and fuzzy is nice.

I feel like Emily died. It is easier if I think of her that way. Don't worry about me. I'm okay. I'm not suicidal. But I wish I was.

As Emily gains control of her emotions, I lose control of mine. But ... yet ... she *is* gaining control. She says that she is happier now than she has ever been. When we have been together recently she has been on a more even, although superficial, keel. Perhaps my healing love is reaching her even though she does not recognize it. Perhaps I've done a better job of loving than I thought. Or maybe she is just getting better at concealing her madness from me, and from herself.

SEX, Part 22

Today I came to fully understand that I have been making tantric love with Emily for over a year. My state of near-continuous arousal with her, independent of orgasm, is Tantra. This from Cheryl Fraser, Ph.D., a psychologist and sex therapist:[v]

> Tantra is a Sanskrit word that means "woven together." Hindu and Buddhist meditation practitioners use sexual union as a metaphor for weaving together the physical and the spiritual: weaving man to woman, and humanity to the divine. The purpose is to become one with God. Couples in my practice who have tried tantric sex find that they cultivate great sensual pleasure and also a sense of "dissolving into each other" that is profound and loving.

Cecilia remarked to me, "If Jesus was indeed fully human, he must have had a sex life." What might it have been like to have sex with Jesus? For those who did not recognize the divine love that Jesus embodied, it would have been just the usual lustful sex with just another man. But for those who did recognize his divinity, how fabulous it would have been! Tantric sex is the expression of divine spiritual love in the physical body, Shakti making love to Shiva, making love to God with form. It is tantamount to – it is – having sex with Jesus.

Swami Chidananda and other orthodox Hindus warn that most popularized Western forms of Tantra are only for the purpose of extending or enhancing sexual pleasure and as such are perversions of true Tantra, which as a means of physical-spiritual communion is the one exception to the rule of celibacy in the totally committed spiritual life. It is this one exception that allows Jesus, and all who live with him in divine love, to have a sex life.

Tantric sex is not about satisfying a craving, but about celebrating an elevated state of being, a transcendent union of bodies, minds, and spirits to which few people awaken. Worldly cravings arise, are satisfied, and then arise again in constantly repeating cycles. Sexuality in the heightened awareness of Tantra is not cyclic; it is constant, like the unending, ever-present state of eternal life it reflects.

> Q: How do you know when you are finished with a painting?
> A: How do you know when you are finished making love?
>
> – from a *LIFE* magazine interview with Jackson Pollock, as related in the movie *Pollock*

---

[v] http://www.besthealthmag.ca/embrace-life/relationships/sex-advice-what-is-tantric-sex

At some level, Jackson Pollock, in all his madness, understood the constancy of tantric love. Continuous, mind-blowing sex that does not end with orgasm. Emily and I dissolve into each other, even with thousands of miles between us. There are no boundaries or limits in the totality of All.

PART 35

Stay in the Fire
November 2014 – March 2015

~ 776 ~

My angel card today, which flew out of the deck as if it had wings: *"Chakra Clearing"* – *Archangel Metatron: "Call upon me to clear and open your chakras, using sacred geometric shapes."*

My Buddhist message today: *The image of Achala is seen … the messages being sent to you are getting misdirected, flowing around you … open to them … be strong in your faith, immovable like Achala.*

I am blocking something; my chakras are not open. I need to call upon Metatron and Achala to help me. I think fire may be involved. **Achala** is my Buddhist fire god, the deity of the eighth bhūmi bodhisattva, who burns away defilements in his cleansing flames.

Wikipedia says this about **Metatron**, the highest of the Hebrew archangels, the celestial scribe, who is said to be the heavenly transformation of Enoch:

> This Enoch, whose flesh was turned to flame, his veins to fire, his eyelashes to flashes of lightning, his eyeballs to flaming torches, and whom God placed on a throne next to the throne of glory, received after this heavenly transformation the name Metatron. In the later Ecstatic Kabbalah Metatron is a messianic figure … the name Metatron may originate from either Mattara "keeper of the watch" or the verb MMTR "to guard, to protect." An early derivation of this can be seen in Shimmusha Rabbah, where Enoch is clothed in light and is the guardian of the souls ascending to heaven.[52]

Another Hebrew reference to God is *shekhinah*, as described by Campbell:

> In Jewish thought, the sign of the two triangles together is known as "magen david," "Shield of David," and read as connoting the *shekhinah*, or presence of God in Israel (as originally in the burning bush and in the cloud on the summit of Mt. Sinai).[28]

Shekhinah, the presence of God in Israel, is represented by light, as Deepak Chopra described, "the halos around angels and the luminous joy in the face of a saint." The Christians say that the Holy Spirit descended to the disciples after Jesus' resurrection in the form of tongues of fire above their heads. (Acts of the Apostles 2:1-4) Some Christian denominations keep a flame constantly burning in the sanctuary to represent the constant presence of the Holy Spirit dwelling with us.

Last month I gave the Christians some money in the name of **Adonai**, the name of the God who spoke to Moses in the burning bush and wrote with the finger of fire on Mount Sinai.

My other fire god, the native god to whom I chant when I go to the hot springs, who speaks to me in clouds of smoke and ash and the red glow that issues from the depths of his pit, is the fiery Holy Spirit present in my life here and now.

~ 777 ~

THE 1st ANNIVERSARY OF MY 2nd EPIPHANY

Emily came home yesterday. She invited me to her house for dinner. We had a very pleasant reunion. She drew my attention to a large diamond ring on her finger and said, "I'm engaged. Danny popped the question. We will be a nontraditional couple, though, going slow, no date set. Besides, I don't think I could live away from here. I was so happy to come home; my heart is here, I want to die here."

She plans to string Danny along indefinitely, like Vincent and Arthur, luring him, holding him, but keeping him at a distance. She tends her lovers as a gardener tends her garden, providing enough water and fertilizer to keep the relationships alive and productive, picking their fruits of money, attention, service, and sex as she needs them. She is the ultimate *femme fatale*.

There is a sense of inevitability in all this – this is how she has always lived her life, probably having witnessed her mother living the same way, and she is blind to the depravity of it. Her hapless victims are so beguiled by her seductive skill and undeniable charms that they are also blinded. They eagerly take her poison and submit to her bondage, oblivious to her serious psychological problem, carefully masked, just below the surface. (If they do see the problem, they are willing to tolerate it in order to obtain the delights that she dangles before them.) Maybe they do have genuine affection for her, or gratitude for the great sex she gives them, or guilt for having used her body for their selfish gratification. Maybe there is some glimmer of sincere love between them, but it likely cannot be sustained once the fear or obligation of it becomes overwhelming.

Perhaps she thinks that I, too, am woven into her web of subservience, bound to her by the same kind of dependent love. She uses the same seductive techniques on me that she uses on her men. But, no. My call to her service comes from a very different place than the worldly desires that draw her men. I am drawn not by her beauty or charm, but by her pain. I want only one thing, not *from* her, but *for* her – liberation from that pain. My love is not the love of men, but the love of God, and it remains unchanged, in full knowledge and acceptance of her darkness, as her other changing relationships swirl around her.

I learned a great deal about our relationship during this past week while she has been away. I have discovered the true meaning of Tantra, the interweaving of spiritual and physical worlds. I learned how to love her, to experience our spiritual love on the physical plane even when she is thousands of miles away. This tantric knowledge helps me stay alive in spiritual love with her even though she has other lovers, even though the full manifestation of our spiritual perfection remains elusive in this life.

I grieve over Emily's inability to see our perfection and surrender to it, but I understand the purpose of this condition for my own awakening and the reason for it in her life at this time. She is wrestling with many generations of bad karma, and it will take many more generations and incarnations for all of it to resolve. The introduction of God's love into her present life through me, her good shepherd, adds one speck of angelic light to her dark karmic picture.

Perhaps the speck of loving light I bring into her life will be the one tug on Indra's Net that changes her karmic course. This possibility is what keeps me steadfast in her service and gives meaning to my suffering.

~ 778 ~

I have described my journey with Emily as my last battle with the demon Mara. In the story of the Buddha's awakening under the bodhi tree, one of the temptations of the Buddha was in the form of Mara's three beautiful daughters. They appeared before the Buddha to inflame his desire, but he remained unmoved.

I am inflamed by my desire to experience in this life the blissful liberation I see with Emily in eternity. To be a bodhisattva living a life of service in this world, I have no choice but to accept the arising of desire that must come to all who inhabit a physical body, but also to rise above that desire, recognizing its illusory nature and not allowing myself to be driven by it – not driven to frenzy by its allure, nor driven to despair by its failure to manifest.

This is what I mean by staying in the fire – feeling the pain, smelling my charred flesh – but not trying to escape. Staying in the fire, trusting the divine love that put me in the fire to protect me from its consuming flames and eventually take me out of it. To stay immovable in the fire – as did the Buddha under the bodhi tree, and Shadrach, Meshach, and Abednego in Nebuchadnezzar's fiery furnace (Daniel 3:24-27) – is to be liberated from it.

~ 779 ~

Martha thinks I am too emotionally involved with Emily. If only it were just a matter of emotion.

Martha would have me climb up out of Emily's murky water and save myself, so I can throw her a lifeline from a safe distance. But there is no safety for me. Yes, in this world I could stand apart from her pain, not be seduced by her drama, not get into the water with her, and just throw her a lifeline from the shore. But in the oneness of eternity where I love her, there is no separation. Her pain is my pain. I cannot help but be in the water, in the pain, in the fire, with her.

While I am with Emily in eternal love, I am completely vulnerable, and there is no protection possible. But there is no protection needed; in the throes of God's love there is no fear. There is nothing to be afraid of, nothing to need protection from. Everything that happens is right; no harm done, no matter how great the pain.

Through Emily I have discovered Tantra in all its depth. I am living our spiritual life and love, our blessed oneness, here and now in the physical plane. It is a marvelous, magical existence. But when my love calls out to her and there is no echo coming back, and I realize that she is not connecting with me across the same tantric physical-spiritual bridge, a shudder goes through my body, a seismic shift of energy as my body-mind resumes its awareness of separation from her on the physical plane. (This shudder marks a transition between states of consciousness, not unlike the scintillating shudder of orgasm that marks the transition out of the sexual trance ... not unlike the death rattle.) And then my love rises up again and I float back into eternal union with her, only to be knocked back down again into duality.

I am actually closer to her when we are apart, when we connect purely in the collective unconscious, than when we are together, when I must deal with her psychotic behavior as a practical temporal reality. With this realization I can see the bridge between life and death, the consciousness that connects spirits on both sides of the mortal divide. Some of the dead, like Emily, still walk the earth.

In his poem "On His Deceased Wife" (~607~), John Milton describes his vision of his beloved wife in a dream, which goes away when he awakens to his blindness: "I waked, she fled, and day brought back my night." When I return to worldly consciousness in Emily's presence, distracted by her sensory provocations and disruptive behaviors, I lose my vision of perfect love with her in the spirit, in the collective unconscious. Like a blind man whose other senses become more acute in the absence of sight, my spiritual senses become more acute when I am blind to the world.

~ 780 ~

This morning this text came in from Emily:

> *Fell asleep, had an awakening and saw the truth in our dimensions last night. Heaven is inside of us and we can touch it … God is so powerful in this message I received; exhausted from the content, trying to understand it, yet realized nothing to understand, just feel it. Light to you Betty, you are such a treasure.*

Awakening to divine love has a lightness to it – the joy of understanding – but also a heaviness – the weight of responsibility. What will I do with my awakening and its call to a life of service? Divine love is indeed a treasure, but much is expected from those to whom much is given.

~ 781 ~

At the beginning of our relationship when Emily was first attracted to me, she seduced me as she had all of her other lovers, following urges from the physical plane. Then she became frightened of her own feelings and of mine, wanting a deeper relationship with me but not wanting to face homosexual urges, and not wanting me to unearth those painful thoughts that she works so hard to suppress but that come bubbling up so relentlessly with me. And so she backed away from me.

Then Danny came along. She enjoyed his advances, lured him in, and is now engaged to him. Although she says she loves him, her other words and actions and tone of voice and facial expressions and body language say that she is merely settling for him. He is not the answer to her prayers, or the love of her life, or the man of her dreams. He is convenient.

Psychic Michael Neill says, "Most people have experienced sex without intimacy, but very few people can as easily access experiences of intimacy without sex." Emily has experienced a lot of sex without intimacy; that is her *modus operandi*. Our deeply intimate relationship, so far without sex, feels strange and uncomfortable to her.

~ 782 ~

Spent last night at Emily's house, our first night together in six months. In the sixteen hours we spent together, she ran through her complete repertoire of dysfunctional personae – histrionic, narcissistic, dissociative, manic, depressive. Her mind was so thoroughly detached from reality that it was very difficult to have a conversation or interact meaningfully with any of her various selves. Her psychic trauma goes so deep, is so pervasive, that I don't know where to begin. It is like a cancer that has spread throughout the body and cannot be stopped. All I could do was alternatively hold her hand and run for psychological cover.

She started the evening with her demons blazing, prompted by her upset over the stove going out just as she was trying to cook. Her narcissism flared up; she told me I had "failed the test" by not telling her that she was the most beautiful woman I had ever seen. I had blown it, lost my chance, she said, and she was through with me. "I want you to leave now." But I stayed, she relented, and I spent the night on the couch.

By morning she had morphed into someone else. Smiling, happy to see me. The stove came back on and cooking resumed. We took a little noontime nap, this time, by her invitation, both of us in bed – but no touching. "That was a nice nap we had, wasn't it? We heal each other," she said. Vincent came over and we three ate our meal.

After Vincent left and the dishes were done, she wanted me to sit with her. She said that if I were a man, she would marry me in a minute, and it breaks her heart that I am not a man. "We are so good together, I feel safe and peaceful with you, you would be a good provider, but I will never have sex with you."

Under it all was the assumption that I was grasping for her as her others lovers do, and I wanted to marry her. (She equates "I love you" with "I want to marry you, provide for you, and jump at your every command.") There was no thought of what I might actually want or need or feel, no reciprocation of care or concern from her side. It's all about her – all taking, no giving. Because of her behavioral disorder and the horrific pain from which it springs, she is not capable of loving me as I love her or of understanding what a mature relationship is. I continue to patiently love her, dodging her arrows while dancing with the *asura*, but I cannot marry her, live with her, or bring our tantric sex to the physical plane unless and until she understands, surrenders to, and spontaneously manifests her side of our karmic love.

"Danny got down on his knees and begged me to marry him. He says I am the love of his life. Do you think he means it?"

"I think he does," I replied. But Danny is caught up in the *anima*, and I doubt he knows the full extent of his fiancé's psychosis. Nor is he aware that he is not the love of her life – I am.

As I left this afternoon we shared a warm, intimate hug that seemed to belie our supposedly impossible marriage. I can't tell if her alleged awakening a few days ago has had any impact. Perhaps. I only know that last night and today felt like I succeeded in bailing one thimbleful of water from the Titanic.

~ 783 ~

Emily says that she has broken up with Danny and she is very depressed. Danny had been verbally abusive to her, putting her down, calling her a dummy. "I will never marry him," she said. "I'm a therapist. I know that verbal abuse will lead to physical abuse." Memories of her abusive mother were conjured up.

When I dropped her off at her office, her goodbyes were very cold, no hug, no kiss. Later she called to tell me that Danny had called and they were back together again, followed by a small rant about my lack of respect, not asking her to spend the night with me.

"I told you that you are welcome to stay with me anytime," I said, "but you decided that you needed your space."

She is still so confused. She ties love together with material objects, physical attraction, financial security, and dominant or submissive behavioral roles. She mistakes the trappings of love for the real thing. "Would he have given me a $7,000 diamond ring if he didn't love me?" she asked.

I replied, "Perhaps with that ring he was buying the right to control you, buying a license to abuse you." I didn't say it, but I was thinking that perhaps he was buying sex, reducing their relationship to little more than prostitution.

~ 784 ~

Emily's bodily histrionics come in three forms: asthma attacks, nausea, and body pain, usually abdominal. I don't want to minimize or question anyone's genuine discomfort, but I have reason to suspect that Emily's physical symptoms, if indeed present, are not as severe as she portrays them to be. The main reason is that when I do not display the expected panic response to her distress, she tones it down, as a child reduces the intensity of a tantrum when the parent does not engage it. Also, she is able to avoid the histrionics if she wants to, in public or when her mind is diverted into pleasant thoughts. Her outbursts of wheezing, vomiting, and wincing seem to come on when she is fearful, seeking attention, or trying to escape unpleasantness.

She tells me she hasn't eaten in three days and she is losing weight. "I look thin and trim, don't I?" she says. Perhaps she has lost some weight, but not much; she still has a tummy, ample thighs, and love handles. She is indeed beautiful, and she knows it, but she is not satisfied with the reality of her beauty as it is. Her low self-esteem tells her that she is not beautiful enough. Her narcissism requires constant validation of her beauty; she wants others to affirm her appearance as she perceives it. I dare not tell the empress she has no clothes. Her delusion is more than skin deep.

I think I underestimated her dissociative disorder. She doesn't just have dissociative episodes; her entire life is a charade, a performance. None of her personae is real. I wonder if she has completely dissociated from her true self. The terribly wounded child in her is so deeply submerged that I fear she may never see the light of day. Emily is exhausted by the effort it takes to keep her elaborate façade pasted on. She spends more and more time maintaining and rebuilding her masquerade – cleansing, meditating, exercising, self-soothing, just being alone. She stays away from me – the love of her life – because I see through her mask and strip it away, undoing all her hard work putting it on. She loves me, perhaps as deeply as I love her, but her fear still overwhelms her love.

~ 785 ~

Emily says that she and Danny made up. He wrote her a beautiful love letter. Abusers making amends often write the most beautiful love letters.

~ 786 ~

This morning at Ignacio's theology discussion group I related the story about a monk who was in pain but did not suffer. The group couldn't grasp that pain is not the same as suffering. Pain is the experience of life. Suffering is our response to pain, wanting to get rid of it, wishing life was something other than what it is. We can be in pain but not suffer if we understand pain as the inevitable counterpoint to pleasure and accept it, surrender to it, and be grateful for the lessons it teaches.

I was sad that the group could not understand this. That was one kind of pain. Then another kind of pain set in, the loneliness of being in the midst of kind, loving people but finding no kindred spirit among them, no one who can provide support as I walk my treacherous spiritual path. They all mean well, but they are like Jesus' sleeping disciples in the Garden of Gethsemane.

This is the same deep loneliness I feel when Emily prefers to be alone, or with Vincent, or on the phone with Danny, rather than with me. That loneliness turns to grief when I contemplate our eternal oneness. She *does* have someone who can provide real comfort and spiritual support, but in her fear she turns away my genuine healing love, preferring palliative care from those who do not challenge her illusions.

I don't seek to take her away from her daily activities; I seek to blend into them, help her with them, and support her in them. Our love is not something separate and apart from the rest of our lives; it is not an escape or diversion from daily life – it is life itself.

Emily seeks to pigeon-hole me into a narrow pocket of her life and keep me out of other pockets, but it won't work. Our love has no boundaries, no limits, no separation in time or space. It is like a wave that washes over every part of our existence, flowing into every nook and cranny of our lives. She has built dams and barricades to hold back the wave, impeding the flow of my love in and her love out. I feel like a salmon swimming upstream and running into new obstacles at every turn.

PARZIVAL

In *Transformation of Myth Through Time*,[2] Joseph Campbell writes:

> There was this war in heaven, and there were some angels who sided with God and others who sided with Lucifer—the pair of opposites. The metaphysical mystery is to go past all opposites. Where you have opposites of good and evil, you are simply in the field of ethics. Adam and Eve were thrown out of the Garden when they knew the difference between good and evil. Nature knows nothing of that. The neutral angels were neither on God's side nor on Lucifer's side; and Wolfram[vi] interprets the name of Parzival as *perce a val*, the one piercing through the middle of the valley, going between the pair of opposites.

Could it be any clearer? Parzival is traveling the path between and beyond the pairs of opposites, between and beyond good and evil – the Buddhist Middle Way.

> Parzival lets the reins lie slack on the horse's neck. In this tradition, the horse represents the will in nature, and the rider represents the rational control. Here nature is what's moving us. Compare this tradition with the Christian tradition from the Near East, wherein nature is good and evil but we've got to be good, a tradition that does not say "Yield to nature" but rather "Correct nature." Wolfram is here saying "Yield."

Nature is sinless innocence. No right or wrong, good or evil, just what is and must be.

> When Parzival comes back, Condwiramurs has put her hair up in the way of a married woman. They're married. This is marriage for love, the mind's love, the love of character, the love of quality, and they go to bed. Well, he doesn't know anything, and she doesn't know much more, and so they just lie there. ... And then Parzival thought, "Oh, yes, mother told me." So Wolfram says, "If you'll pardon me for letting you know, they interlaced arms and legs and thought, 'This is what we should have been doing all the time,' and the marriage was consummated." No Priest. The answer: marriage is the confirmation of love, and sexual love is the sacramentalization of marriage.

> The point here is that it was not a marriage that began with physical sex; when she put her hair up, they were married. Wolfram tells us that it starts in the spirit and is fulfilled in the flesh.

This is tantric love as I so gloriously know it – love from the top down. (~684~) It is the most spectacular thing. I am just now remembering that during my courtship with Lou, my

---

[vi] Wolfram von Eschenbach, 13th century German narrative poet, author of the epic poem *Parzival*.

hair was long. At about the time our spiritual "marriage" was consummated (long before we were married in the worldly sense), I began to wear my hair up. I knew nothing of the *Parzival* story or of my hairstyle's mystical significance.

Emily said she would never have sex with me, and that she would feel dirty if she did. Does she not know that we are already in near-constant tantric union? And it is not dirty – it is sacred, the sacramentalization of our mystical marriage, the best sex of our lives.

~ 788 ~

REJECTION

> He was despised and rejected by men; a man of sorrows, and acquainted with grief; and as one from whom men hide their faces he was despised, and we esteemed him not. Surely he has borne our griefs and carried our sorrows; yet we esteemed him stricken, smitten by God, and afflicted. (Isaiah 53:3-4 RSV)

In a room full of his disciples, even among those who knew his divinity, Jesus was alone; in his last days he found among them only betrayal, denial, and primal fear. There is no denying the incredible pain of crucifixion, but the ultimate passion of Christ, his spiritual suffering, came forth in his utterance, "My God, my God, why hast thou forsaken me?" At that moment he felt rejected not only by men, but by God, his Source, his Creator, his eternal self.

I, too, am alone in a room full of people – rejected, misunderstood, thought to be afflicted. My own family, who consider themselves devout Christians, reject my ecumenical truth and esteem me stricken. Emily, after briefly allowing her fear of homosexuality to be lifted and her affection for me to bloom, is now avoiding me like the plague.

Emily alternately lifts me up and slams me down. She does this with everyone. Everyone else accepts this behavior because they want something from her; she satisfies their worldly desires and dependencies. I come from a very different place; I accept her abuse because I accept her as she is; I connect with her at a spiritual level where worldly behaviors don't matter. Her conscious mind has no concept of this kind of love, a love that is not qualified or conditioned in some way.

I drew two angel cards today. They came up at the same time, stuck together:

"Sensitivity" – Archangel Haniel: "You are extra-sensitive to energies and emotions right now. Honor yourself and your feelings."

And *"Gentleness"* – *Archangel Sandalphon: "Be very gentle with yourself at this time. Surround yourself with gentle people, situations, and environments."*

Interesting that these cards found themselves side-by-side in the deck, ready to give me a double dose of compassion when I needed it. And the images of the angels on both cards show them playing musical instruments, Haniel the lyre and Sandalphon the lute.

~ 789 ~

To desire death in order to attain one's blissful vision of eternity is taking the first poison. To desire death in order to avoid the pain of life is taking the second poison. To desire death in order to jump off the merry-go-round, to escape all the pleasures and pains of life, the whipsaws of dualism, is taking the third poison.

Death, like life, must simply be accepted, allowed to evolve in its own time, as a leaf falls effortlessly from the tree in the natural course of things, not too soon, not too late. For everything there is a season. When the weight of life becomes too heavy, I will drop it. When the weight is lifted, I will let it go.

~ 790 ~

It has been ten days since I have had any meaningful communication with Emily. She says I am her best friend, the love of her life, but I am nowhere in her life. Enduring her silence and distance for so long makes me a little crazy. I feel like I am just sleepwalking through life, nothing is real, all pantomime. I play music, do computer work, attend meetings, luncheons, exhibitions, and workshops, but nothing is real. I feel like I am caught between two worlds, not completely in either one.

When this cycle of cozying up and then pulling back happens with Emily, as it has several times now, I cry in my beer and moan about my own suffering, but I neglect to consider the agony inside her that causes her to exhibit these behavioral extremes. Part of her knows and shares the deep spiritual love that I have for her. But there is also the part of her that cannot love anyone. In her pain she cannot reconcile real love with the life pattern that she has known heretofore, in which love is a four-letter word, almost a dirty word, a negative emotion that hurts and demands and extracts.

She is afraid to surrender to our divine love; she doesn't know how; she only knows love that in the past has hurt and cannot be trusted. When love is exhibited towards her by someone else, she interprets it as a weakness to be exploited, a tool to be used to get something from her lover. When she feels love, it is a danger to be guarded against, a vulnerability that will lead to her being used and abused and similarly exploited, and to bitter disappointment when her hopes and dreams are dashed.

Closeness with me is difficult for her; I distract her from her work, raise up her demons and the pain behind them, and disable her efforts to control her behavior. I can see etched on her face the inner conflict that rages between her desire to explore our divine love and her fear of its power. I take her where she does not want to go, except for that part of her that desperately wants to go there.

Is Emily staying away from me because Danny is coming soon for a visit and she must get her mind into his space and out of mine? Is she conflicted about us, not knowing how to love Danny and me at the same time? As I have told her many times before, our eternal love exists on a spiritual plane. It could manifest in this life with sex, cohabitation, even marriage – but it doesn't have to. It can manifest in many other ways, and already has. Our love is an inclusive love. She can love Danny and me at the same time, in different ways. We can both be intimate parts of her life. She will always be an intimate part of mine, regardless of other relationships.

Or is she staying away from me because she is afraid of the deep feelings that come up when she is with me, the strange attraction she feels for me that is unlike anything she has known? So afraid of my love that she would settle for a lesser relationship that, despite its limits and abuses, is more comfortable in its familiarity?

~ 791 ~

Row, row, row your boat
Gently down the stream
Merrily merrily, merrily, merrily
Life is but a dream

We are living a dream. All of life – the entire universe – is a dream in the mind of God. What happens when God wakes up?

~ 792 ~

I am remembering *The Heart Is a Lonely Hunter*, one of my favorite movies. The story, based on a book of the same title, is about John Singer, a deaf-mute, who becomes a trusted confidant to four of his neighbors, helping them with their problems, but whose own problems are unknown to them. Singer's life revolves around his friend Spiros Antonopoulous, who is also deaf. Spiros is mentally unstable and is put into an asylum. Singer visits his friend regularly, bringing him gifts and taking him on outings, but Spiros lives in his own world and is oblivious to Singer's love. One day Singer goes to visit and is told that Spiros had died. Inconsolable, Singer commits suicide.

Like Singer, I love a mentally ill person who is incapable of returning the love I give her, cannot recognize anyone's concerns but her own, and cannot conceive of the huge gulf between the depth of my love and the shallowness of hers. Like Singer, I live a life of service to others, none of whom know about my silent struggle with my secret love. Will I kill myself when I am told that Emily is dead? I will want to.

~ 793 ~

I feel that much of what I write comes directly from God – written not by me, but through me. Deep, esoteric, understandable only to the most spiritually elevated readers. Everyone else will think me a fool. Like St. Francis – "God's fool." Like Jesus – "We esteemed him stricken, smitten by God, and afflicted."

We think of love as a good, happy feeling. At the highest level, love is neither good nor bad, happy nor unhappy; it just is. As expressed on earth, it contains both sides of dualism, suffering and no suffering. It absorbs and then squeezes out all that you are. Ask Jesus hanging on the cross if he thinks loving so divinely is such a happy feeling.

But then there's the flip side:

> All things have been delivered to me by my Father; and no one knows the Son except the Father, and no one knows the Father except the Son and any one to whom the Son chooses to reveal him. Come to me, all who labor and are heavy laden, and I will give you rest. (Matthew 11:27-28 RSV)

The Father has been revealed to me, and I have been given rest. The torment of my cross is mitigated by my knowledge of the light I have seen behind the veil of suffering.

Marianne Williamson wrote, "The greatest gift we can give to a person in pain is to hold in our own minds the thought that there is a light beyond this darkness." From the mind of God, that greatest gift was given to me, and through me to Emily. I have seen the light beyond her darkness; I live with her eternally in that light.

~ 794 ~

For John [the Baptist] came neither eating nor drinking, and they say, "He has a demon;" the Son of man came eating and drinking, and they say, "Behold, a glutton and a drunkard, a friend of tax collectors and sinners!" Yet wisdom is justified by her deeds. (Matthew 11:18-19 RSV)

No particular behavior, lifestyle, or religious practice defines a saint or a sinner. Neither the solitary ascetic wandering in the desert nor the gregarious party animal is necessarily wise or foolish. Wisdom is justified by her deeds. Alan Watts, Chögyam Trungpa, and Joseph Campbell were, like Jesus, gluttons and drunkards.

~ 795 ~

I sent Emily an email with quotes from Marianne Williamson's book. She rejected them, saying that I was giving her a "forced lecture." "I do this for a living," said Emily the therapist. She told me to "chill out." Apparently the quotes struck a nerve.

I totally get Jesus' crucifixion, his willing submission to darkness, sacrificing everything to bring us into the light. I sacrifice myself for Emily. I am God's avatar, come to earth in human form to take on her suffering. The pain she represses arises in me; I feel her pain, literally.

Emily's rejection of my love – the highest form of kundalini love, the love of God – brings St. Francis' "perfect joy," Bonhoeffer's "dishonorable suffering."

~ 796 ~

CHRISTMAS EVE

Putting a coat of white icing on brown, slightly burnt cookies. All blemishes are covered in pure white, like a fresh snowfall on a brown, slightly seedy landscape. Trouble is, the snow melts in the spring and the seediness is revealed. Not so with the cookies. The soft icing smooths the cookie's crunchy rough edges on the way down the gullet. Light and dark surrender their separate identities and are blended in perfect balance.

I saw Emily for an hour today, the first time in almost a month. She is moving forward on the path with Danny, veering away from the path with me. "I'm going to marry him," she said.

"We're talking about setting a date." He offers her security, sex, and adoration. Maybe a little abuse, too, but still, this deal is impossible for her to pass up. She seems more emotionally stable since settling into this comfortable marriage scenario, but I know from the pain in my back, near-constant since our near-betrothal last month, that her hysteria is not cured, only in remission. I am still the love of her life and she is mine, and we both know it.

Doreen Virtue teaches her intuitive students a practice called "cancel-clear-delete" to clear away bad energy. This protects psychic practitioners from illness and other deleterious effects due to exposure to their clients' negative energy. The esoteric Buddhists have a similar practice to clear away negative energy.

But where Emily is concerned there is no "cancel-clear-delete" for me. I am here on earth, like Jesus and other bodhisattvas, to willingly and purposefully take on the pain and sorrow of the world and keep it, not clear it; to hold it, absorb it, soak it up like a sponge, and then be sacrificed, burned in Achala's fire, to finally cleanse it from the world. (see "Tonglen" ~1315~)

With my death and resurrection will come the ultimate "cancel-clear-delete." All will be forgiven, forgotten, in perfect balance, at one with God. Emily will be healed, and her mother, father, and all her ancestors with her.

~ 797 ~

CHRISTMAS DAY

This morning at church the assistant pastor failed to deliver two lines of the liturgy. There was an awkward silence, everyone waiting for the lines, until finally the senior pastor delivered them. The assistant said, "Thank you, Pastor. That part wasn't printed in my book!"

It is not enough to read the liturgy. Clergy who merely read the words prescribed in ancient ceremonies are not connecting with the Holy Spirit. Scripture is not found in a book. It is written in the heart. There it must be memorized, not just in words, but in meaning. It must be taken into the soul. Then it will issue spontaneously from the mouth.

The church service always starts with the congregation confessing their sins and asking God's forgiveness. From the very beginning the congregation is reminded to feel guilty and imperfect, and to look outside themselves for salvation. I prefer the Buddhist view of sin; it reflects a more compassionate and holistic approach to good and evil. "Sin" is an archery term meaning "missed the mark." What mark? Who set up a target? (~840~) Humans in their essence are not sinners; they just behave, like all creatures, according to their nature.

Ignacio and Cecilia are coming over for Christmas dinner tonight. I teasingly refer to them as "Mom and Dad," which seems to please them. They are my guardian angels; they watch over me. I am now seeing them in a new light, as my Simon of Cyre'ne. They are helping me carry my cross up the hill.

My back feels miraculously better today.

~ 798 ~

I doubt that Joseph Campbell would have considered himself to be a genius. He was a researcher cataloguing the genius of others. But his own genius came out with the results of his research. He became a master synthesizer, collecting pieces of a puzzle – world religions, myths, and philosophies – and putting them together into a fabulous mosaic that in its composite totality reveals great universal truth. Like the jewels in Indra's Net, each piece of Campbell's puzzle has its own integrity, yet also contributes harmoniously to the whole. Campbell devoted his life to this work, and I am in awe of his achievement. It has changed my life. I fancy myself his disciple and humble successor, weaving his threads together with new ones.

~ 799 ~

It occurred to me that perhaps Emily has been wanting me to fight for her, to say, "Don't marry Danny; stay with me." But why would I fight for her? Why would I want to pull her away from another path that might be the one meant for her at this time? Fighting, competing with the goal of conquest in pursuit of a selfish desire, is not reflective of true love. My role is to serve her needs, not my desires.

She doesn't know how to react to a love that is tender and yielding, not possessive and aggressive. Her past history with love has been to watch men (and maybe women) fight over her, plying her with entreaties and enticements, and then sell herself to the highest bidder. She uses love as a tool to acquire what she needs and to assuage her fears. She measures love by the opulence of the gifts and the size of the diamonds she gets. She can be bought. She has no experience with a love that is not grasping, dependent, demanding, or measured in material terms.

One can possess an animal by throwing a rope around its neck and dragging it into a cage, or by enticing it into the cage with carrots and lures. But if you just sit quietly and gently, the animal may come to you willingly, of its own volition, without fear and without ropes, cages, or carrots, joined to you by trust and mutual consent, not by coercion or bribery. This is how I want Emily to come to me.

My love is the love of God, all around her all the time, but she must choose to accept it. I cannot force her to take the hand that is outstretched to her. She must come to me as to Jesus, like a little child, and freely surrender to our love with no preconditions or expectations. She must love me as I am, blemishes and all, and find bliss with me no matter what our physical, social, or economic condition might be. Just being with me is all she would need or want. She would seek my intimate presence in her life, as I do hers. Happiness for us would be the same in sickness and in health, for richer or poorer, not just until death did us part, but beyond.

I will know she has awakened to divine love and is ready to accept it when I see these signs. I do not expect to see them in this lifetime.

~ 800 ~

I visited Elaine today. She was so glad to see me she almost cried. Me, too.

~ 801 ~

SEX, Part 23

Emily has become a silent, invisible phantom, not seen or heard since Danny arrived four days ago. Yet when her body disappeared, I was even more tightly bound to her in the spirit. My tantric sexual ardor reached fever pitch and has been more or less constant for four days, punctuated by occasional orgasmic release.

At first I was disturbed by this outpouring of sexual energy, sad that Emily was not here in person to enjoy it with me, and jealous that Danny was in a sense taking my place. But then I realized that they were not apart from me; I was joining them in a miraculous spiritual *ménage à trois*.

My powerful sexuality at this time is a gift from God. For a post-menopausal woman to have the sexual responses of a twenty-year-old again, to feel the greatest love flowing freely in the body as well as the spirit, even in the physical absence of my beloved, is a miracle as great as any I have known.

> There are teachings within Tantra that have something to do with the art and practice of spiritually-directed, transcendent sex—but even those, a very small part (say .00005% of Tantra)—are intended to help the Bodhisattva clarify his or her mind and heart and so better be able to help others. – Waylon Lewis, http://www.elephantjournal.com

This is indeed how I have experienced tantric sex, as a means of clarifying my mind and heart, refocusing and reorienting my *ki*, life energy, so that I can go forward in temporal-eternal harmony. This sexual ecstasy is a heavenly message showing me how the full physical manifestation of my divine love feels, God granting me a taste of ambrosia to relieve my otherwise incessant despair – a bodhisattva's safety valve, the spirit's concession to the call of the earthly body, like eating and sleeping and breathing.

For the bodhisattva, all these mundane acts are spiritual activities as well as worldly ones. Eating is not just nourishment, but also the sacred passage of dead plants and animals into new life. Sleep is not just rejuvenation, but also a visit to the collective unconscious, the place of dreams. Breathing is not just oxygenation, but also the passage of *ki* through the body. Sex is not just pleasure or procreation, but also the blissful earthly expression of eternal oneness.

~ 802 ~

My temporal body-mind is on an extreme roller coaster. I vacillate between extreme highs and extreme lows, vacillating so fast that I am at both extremes at the same time. The rack upon which I am stretched is multi-layered; in addition to the temporal-eternal one, there is an intra-temporal one, where I am held hostage to extreme dualism.

I say to myself that I cannot take Emily's torture any longer ... but then I realize that I can ... I must. Would I give up all that I have learned and will learn from her, all the spiritual insights, the blessed vision of eternal love that she brought to me, to avoid the pain? Would I have given up the transcendent love I had with Lou to have avoided the horrific pain of losing him? It doesn't matter. I have no choice; I am called by God, dragged by the scruff of the neck into these relationships. The same power that brought me into joy will lift me out of sorrow.

The psychologist Mihaly Csikszentmihalyi, the founder of "flow" theory, posits that the zone in which we learn and perform best, and enjoy most deeply, lies exactly halfway between boredom and anxiety – the Middle Way. I am flowing at the speed of light through all the zones, hoping that my pendulum will stop, time will stop, in the middle, in the zone.

~ 803 ~

A deep sadness has set in. I am acknowledging my body-mind deprivation; to know all that can be had and not have it is a torment few can understand. My soul knows that Emily is an illusion and her cruelty comes from a deep psychic disturbance, but my physical self still pines and craves and grieves.

It is important that my worldly desires not be satisfied. If they were, I would miss my chance for perfect joy. I would be removed from my last battle with Mara and deprived of the opportunity to win that battle. Removing temporal deprivation creates spiritual deprivation. Being dragged through this despair is necessary for my awakening. I must be grateful to Danny, not jealous of him. I must imagine Danny and Emily in intimate embrace, see them kissing, laughing, and enjoying each other, without falling prey to the poisons, with equanimity and peaceful acceptance. This is so hard.

~ 804 ~

First dream of the New Year: *I am waking up, getting out of bed, walking into the living room. I look toward the table with Lou's picture on it, and it isn't there! All my furniture is gone. I run back to the bedroom, and now the bed is gone. "I've been robbed!" I thought, "But I've been here the whole time, it's happening right in front of me!" I went through all the rooms in the house, and they were all empty. Then I opened the front door and found all my stuff lined up in a hallway.*

From dreammoods.com:

> **Furniture** – To see furniture in your dream represents how you feel about yourself and your family. It refers to your relationships with others and how they fit into your life.

> **House** – To dream that your house is broken into suggests that you are feeling violated. It may refer to a particular relationship or current situation in your life.

> **Hallway** – To see a hallway in your dream symbolizes self-exploration. It is the beginning of the path that you are taking in life. You are going through a transitional phase and journeying into the unknown. It also signals spiritual enlightenment, emotional growth, physical prowess, new opportunities and mental passages in your life.

Emily has violated me and taken my furniture, but it is all waiting in the hallway, ready to embark with me on a new path. I take from this dream the message that my new psychic path with Emily is one of less craving and more acceptance, focusing more on deep karmic healing and less on immediate satisfaction or comfort. I must accept Danny's role as her potential spouse, but I can still express all the other aspects of our worldly love as her disciple/mentor, parent/child, and best friend. Perhaps on that basis my divine purpose on earth can be carried out.

~ 805 ~

I have settled into a kind of numb, zombie-like state with the realization that Emily will probably not come back to me in this life. She will need to run this course with Danny, and do it without me, since she cannot see a way to love us both and keep us both in her life. I hope that she will resolve this inner conflict before we die, but I remember that hope is the last temptation and that I must find peace in the absence of Emily and the absence of hope.

All my friends want me to extract myself from this punishing relationship and move on to healthier aspects of my life, but every time I tell myself that I should let her go, I am reminded of the powerful forces that brought me to her, the miracles and epiphanies and serendipities – the call of God. No matter how far away she is, I will always be with her, standing by.

My body-mind is beginning to shut down, gradually closing itself off from life and opening more toward death and eternity. The Door of Death that I wrote about earlier (~146~) has opened so wide now that I can almost walk through it.

~ 806 ~

Today is the one-year anniversary of my first night with Emily, when she bore her soul to me after breaking up with Arthur. (~631~) Tonight she broke up with me.

After initially signing up for Emily's class on energy healing, I told her that I could not study with her after all because I didn't think I could separate our personal relationship from the teacher-student one. She blew up, saying she was disappointed with my "unprofessionalism" in pulling out of the class. I reminded her that I am not the professional in this situation, she is; I am a student expressing a sincere feeling that the energy is not right for me to take her class at this time. "This is very rude of you," she said, "I was counting on the $500."

"So you do need money," I said. "Isn't Danny helping you?"

"I'm not sharing my personal life with you anymore. We're through. There's the door," she said in a tone of ice-cold disgust, pointing the way out. No goodbye hug.

I told her that no matter how much distance she puts between us, we will always be together in the spirit and I will always love her. My words fell on deaf ears. She only wanted me to study with her to get my money. She had no interest in my needs, feelings, or concerns, and no appreciation for the fact that I have already parted with thousands of dollars on her behalf. Her demons had already broken up with me a couple months ago; my backing out of the class simply gave her an excuse to bring her disaffection to the surface and make it official.

In one episode of the television tragicomedy *M.A.S.H.*, the psychologist Sidney Freedman says to the chaplain, Father Mulcahy, "When Pierce or Hunnicutt [the surgeons] loses one, he's out of his misery. When I lose one, I lose a mind." Then Mulcahy says, "When I lose one, I lose a soul."

I feel as though I have lost a soul. My *asura* remains stuck in the lower realms and appears to be falling deeper. The admonition of Chögyam Trungpa concerning the difficulty of communication with an *asura* haunts me. I grieve over her tortured past, her torturing present, and the specter of an *asura*'s continuing self-torture in the future.

I finished this day by drawing this angel card: *"Angel Therapy" – Archangel Raphael: "Give your cares and worries to us angels, and allow us to take your burdens."*

~ 807 ~

I texted Emily, "Love you now and always." And then I braced for the response. How pathetic it is for me to be so sensitized to her psychological battering that I am afraid of a possible irrational tirade in response to my pure, innocent message of love. But I understand, and I bear up under the beating. I continue to stretch out my hand of love to her because the wounded child inside her is still screaming, calling to me for help. So are her parents, calling to me from the spirit realm.

I am one of the few people in her life, maybe the only one, who can stand up to her demons. Such is the power of my divine love. But I will give myself respite from the beating tonight. I won't check my phone messages until morning.

~ 808 ~

Emily doesn't answer my texts at all anymore. Total silence. The residue of her past presence in my home – a lock of hair, a toothbrush, small gifts she gave me – I preserve like holy relics.

The most telling part of my love, the love of God, is not the presence of positive attributes like compassion, affection, or kindness, but rather the absence of negative attributes – no anger, blame, resentment, or judgment, no matter how great the cruelty inflicted upon me. Her cruelty only draws me closer to her, evoking an even deeper compassionate love.

This is the essence of St. Francis' "perfect joy." (~743~) It is not the rejection or torture itself. It is understanding the suffering of the human condition so completely, to feel only the greatest compassion for one's tormentor, to know that the torment inside one's torturer is as great or greater than that which she inflicts – to joyously hold the wounded one close in protective embrace even as she drives nails into my hands.

~ 809 ~

For the last five days I have experienced a low-grade fever and other mild symptoms – a slightly sore throat, slight congestion. It doesn't feel like any cold or flu I have ever had before.

Shortly after Lou died I was plagued by a persistent respiratory ailment of unknown origin that lingered for about nine months. My shaman friends say that all illness comes from one or more of three causes: disharmony, fear, or soul loss. (~1036~) I know I suffered severe soul loss when Lou died. Part of me flew off with him to other realms. But my soul was retrieved when the twins taught me how to love again. (~54~)

I think my present malaise is not caused by germs, but by another round of disharmony and soul loss. Emily's recent rejection has again sent me into anguish and despair. When this kind of estrangement happens, I ask myself, "What did I do wrong?" But the fact is, I did nothing wrong. With both Emily and The Unnamed One, I hurdled their barricades of irrationality, anger, and cruelty and brought God's love and truth up close and personal. I was right on target, but my light was too bright. They both put up their shields of fear and delusion at extra strength.

I ask myself who is worse off for Emily's distance from me. My life is certainly more peaceful and balanced without her histrionics. I don't need to be afraid of my phone anymore.

She, on the other hand, is out of touch with the blessed love of God that could be her salvation. For all my suffering, hers is worse.

~ 810 ~

I fell asleep on the couch around 4:00 p.m. and had this dream: *I was standing behind a fence, hedge, or similar barrier looking at a large black building which had a tall black tower. It was daylight, the sun shining (unlike most of my dreams, which usually take place in the dark subconscious). The building appeared to be made of plastic building blocks, like Legos, with snap-together interlocking pieces.*

Suddenly the tower began to lean. I shouted to a man standing near the building, "The tower is falling! Get away!" I saw the tower lean farther and farther over, 45 degrees, then 30. Then it gently laid down on the roof of the building. It did not crash or crumble; there was no destruction. It just laid down. I woke up watching to see if the tower might rise again with the same grace as it went down.

From dreammoods.com:

Hedge – To see hedges in your dream symbolize restrictions and obstacles that are inhibiting your progress.

Fence – To see a fence in your dream signifies an obstacle or barrier that may be standing on your path. You may feel confined and restricted in expressing yourself.

Colors – Colors in dreams represent energy, emotions, and vibes. Dark colors represent passion and intensity. Bright colors mean awareness.

Black – Black symbolizes the unknown, the unconscious, danger, mystery, darkness, death, mourning, rejection, hate or malice. The color invites you to delve deeper in your unconscious in order to gain a better understanding of yourself. It also signifies a lack of love and lack of support.

Tower – To see a tower in your dream signifies high hopes and aspirations. To dream that a tower is falling or crumbling heralds a drastic change ahead.

Lego – To see or play with Legos in your dreams may refer to the "building blocks" or foundation of some plan. To dream that something is made of Legos represents your imagination and creative mind.

Day – To dream of a sunny day symbolizes clarity and/or pleasantness. You are seeing things clearly.

~ 811 ~

Satan is not necessarily evil; he is an adversary, a sparring partner of sorts, sent to hold a mirror up to us and reveal the weaknesses that we must overcome. Satan is the master of illusion, creating distractions of pleasure and pain to divert us from the path to truth. Mara, the tempter of Buddha under the bodhi tree, is the Buddhist equivalent of the Judeo-Christian Satan.

I see that Emily is my Mara/Satan, an illusionist, a beautiful seductress one minute and vicious tormentor the next. I must take care to walk the Middle Way between desire and fear, remaining immovable in their midst. But even as I remain strong in the face of her temptations and torments, I cannot let that be the end of our story. She is a blessed soul who is herself under the tortured spell of demonic illusions. I still hear her wounded inner child crying out to me, reaching to me from the prison where the demons hold her hostage.

At the beginning of our relationship I understood that Emily's affliction is so severe, so deep, that it is literally beyond the capacity of the human mind to comprehend. And yet I comprehend it. But it is not with my mind that I comprehend. It is with a power beyond the mind, beyond thought.

My love is the antidote to her pain. When she is ready to receive it, that love will be there for her. I will wait for her, as long as it takes. I have all the time in the world, and more. I have all eternity.

~ 812 ~

Emily has taught me the deep meaning of insanity. Insanity is more than mental illness, traceable to a chemical imbalance in the brain and treatable with other chemicals. It is also more than the effect of past trauma, treatable with de-traumatizing, de-programming psychoanalysis. There is a spiritual aspect to insanity, a sense of being possessed by evil spirits. I have seen the crazed, diabolical glint in Emily's eyes when she is in the throes of a manic episode. I have heard the blood-curdling tone in her voice that is not her own when she dissociates into her abusive mother. I have flinched as her vicious demons spewed venom at me that was devoid of any logic, reason, rational thought or feeling.

In witnessing her tortured life, feeling her pain and the fear that drives her into delusion, denial, dissociation, depravity, desperation and dysfunction, I have experienced the true horror of her dark side. I am in despair over my failure to reach Emily's wounded inner child and bring my love to bear on her horrific pain. I fear that she is beyond repair in this life, so overcome by her demons that even the greatest love cannot reach her.

Yet I have also seen her light side, having experienced the resolution of her pain in the spirit realm at the 7th chakra. I have discovered tantric love with her, her eternally healed spirit reaching into life with me, cleansing us and making us whole. The power of this miraculous vision is what holds me together and binds me to her, no matter what.

But she cannot join me in that fabulous place now, in this life. Why does God send me on these impossible missions that start so gloriously and then are so ingloriously stalled? Maybe these relationships are supposed to end without repairing anyone's bad karma, having come to fruition simply by fulfilling the purpose of my enlightenment. Perhaps I have done all that I can do and learned all that I can learn, but it doesn't seem like enough. It feels like failure.

The mother of an autistic daughter outlines the limits that we all face in trying to grasp someone else's reality:

> How can we assign meaning to behavior when a common reality is not shared? To be "neurally atypical" is to be wired differently, to be processing everything differently, to interpret the meaning of each moment differently. ... My sorrow and irritation stem almost entirely from the belief that she could be different, *should* be different, and that my life could and should be different. ... I think, "She was born to be a child," and in the next breath, I realize how my thought condemns her. She was born to be *herself*, and nothing more or less than that. ... Don't ever say to her, and don't say to yourself, that there is any tragedy in who she is. She is what she is. – Sallie Tisdale, "On Spectrum," *Harper's Magazine*, April 2010

There is no clear dividing line between wellness and illness, sanity and insanity. We are all on a slippery slope from one to the other. Who is to say that the voices and visions of the schizophrenic or the distant realms where autistics live are less valid than the perceptions of "normal" people? "There is nothing either good or bad, but thinking makes it so," said Shakespeare. We are all living a dream. Some dreams are more colorful than others.

In this world of duality, we cannot get completely inside the mind of another, see life and the world the same way as someone else. We can only sense another's psyche by the circumstantial evidence provided through his/her outward behavior, which is further distorted by the limitations of our own perception. All that is left to do is put aside the machinations of the mind and simply ... love.

~ 813 ~

I realize that if Emily does come back to me, our orientation to each other must change. Our painful encounter three weeks ago (~806~) pushed me to the tipping point of my tolerance for her abusive behavior. I am now so sensitized to her cruelty that I am afraid of her, afraid to answer the phone, afraid to read texts and email from her – sensitized as the child Emily must have been by her mother's similar abuse. I have an advantage over baby Emily, though. I am an adult who can process the abuse maturely and separate outward behavior from the inner causes of it. Thus I can survive psychological and emotional attacks that would inevitably drive a small child into emotional chaos and psychosis.

Although I understand her cruelty intellectually and spiritually – I know why and from whence it comes, and I hold no ill will toward her for it – my physical and emotional self still exhibits an autonomic "fight or flight" response that I can't prevent. The past three weeks of near-silence from Emily has given me a needed respite from this heightened biological response, a chance to remember what a more peaceful life feels like, push my reset button, and bring my life back to some kind of equilibrium.

Emily just texted and called. She has been giving me the silent treatment for three weeks to punish me for pulling out of her energy healing class. She said that I was not a good friend to her; that I am suffering from a disconnect between reality and illusion, and that my inconsistent behavior is a sign of being bipolar. She thinks I am too dark. "If you want to be a part of my life," she said, "you need to change that."

Yet again she projects herself onto me, her delusions securely in place.

~ 814 ~

I spent four hours with Emily today catching up. Her house is sold. She broke up with Danny. Neither she nor he was willing to make the life changes that the other demanded. She is thinking about going back to Arthur. She wants to move to Colombia. She is still so very sick, confused, frightened, and now heartbroken ... again.

She was finally able to put into words the core of her sorrow. She said she feels as if her soul had been plucked out, thrown on the ground, spit on, and now she must pick it up, wipe it off, and put it back. I told her that, hard as it may be to believe, I understand. She said, "I know. You are the only one who does."

~ 815 ~

GOOD AND EVIL, Part 2

My Buddhist message today: *The dharma protectors are coming forth … there are forces trying to hinder you in following the path, in your service to others … they might not always be obvious … they approach from behind … even though you do not see them, the dharma protectors are with you, shielding you from them.*

The Jews and Christians talk about God and Satan, angels and demons; the Buddhists about good and bad karma; the psychics about positive and negative energy; shamans and indigenous healers about good and evil spirits. I am grateful that the dharma protectors, angels, and guardian spirits are with me.

~ 816 ~

Ignacio said that the difference between him and me is that he honors temporality, I honor eternity. He is so immersed in process thought that he has trouble seeing the eternal forest for the temporal trees, but for me it is the other way around; the blinding light of the one eternal forest washes out my view of the separate trees.

But I think he makes too much of our difference. I do not dishonor temporality; I appreciate the beauty of this dualistic world, and also its ugliness. I also see, perhaps in more dramatic relief than Ignacio does, the unity behind it. I see the Two, and also the One. I spend more time contemplating eternity because I am more consciously in it, having been catapulted there by Ignacio's own sermon on January 1, 2009. (~232~)

The founders of process theology understand what I mean:

> The connection with Whitehead's distinction between God and creativity is the idea that the term "creativity" points to the same reality to which some Buddhists point with the term "emptying" or "emptiness." More generally, Cobb's hypothesis, which involves "a pluralistic metaphysics," is that there are at least two ultimates. One of these, corresponding with what Whitehead calls "creativity," has been called "Emptiness" ("*Sunyata*") or "Dharmakaya" by Buddhists, "Nirguna Brahman" by Advaita Vedantists, "the Godhead" by Meister Eckhart, and "Being Itself" by Heidegger and Tillich (among others). It is the *formless* ultimate reality.
>
> The other ultimate, corresponding with what Whitehead calls "God," is not Being Itself but the *Supreme* Being. It is in-formed and the source of forms (such as truth, beauty, and justice).

It has been called "Amida Buddha," "Sambhogakaya," "Saguna Brahman," "Ishvara," "Yahweh," "Christ," and "Allah."

Whitehead argues that "the nature of God is dipolar. He has a primordial nature and a consequent nature." While the Primordial Nature of God is absolute, transcendent, impassible (unfeeling), eternal, and unchanging, God is also relative, immanent, sympathetic, temporal, and changing, these features constituting God's Consequent Nature. The most radical aspect of Whitehead's process theology is that God is not to be understood as divine Creator of the world but as a caring deity that aims to save all occasions in world-process: "He does not create the world, he saves it." – David Ray Griffin, *Deep Religious Pluralism*[60]

Cobb's primordial formless "Being Itself" corresponds perfectly with Campbell's eternal "God without form" at the 7th chakra, and the consequent in-formed "Supreme Being" with Campbell's worldly "God with form" at the 6th chakra. The unchanging Godhead is both the creator and the created; the changing, caring, feeling God appears in the world as bodhisattvas like Jesus and the Buddha not to create, but to save.

I have eaten of the tree of the Knowledge of Good and Evil and have been cast out of the Garden of Eden. I am living in this world of duality with full knowledge of its illusory nature, but I am standing at the nexus where duality and unity meet, beside the Tree of Eternal Life, feeling the burn of the cherubim's flaming sword and seeing the Great Void, the emptiness, the fusion of the pairs of opposites, just beyond the fiery barrier.

I am rounding third base, heading for home, back into the Garden, which is why the temporal processes that took me around first and second base, wondrous though they were, have receded into the distance, soon to be swept up into the vortex where the matter and antimatter of which they were made are consumed with everything else in the cherubim's flame.

~ 817 ~

Divine love is not something to be given or received, bestowed as a reward or withheld as a punishment, bought or sold, gained with affection or lost with insult, to be fallen into or out of. It is not a commodity, or a feeling, or an emotion, or a form of currency. It is a state of being – a milieu, an atmosphere, an ether that permeates everything, an endless sea in which our lives are immersed all the time. When all the obstacles to love are removed – all fear, suspicion, greed, possessiveness – we are able to see the love all around us, in us. Love that is unconditional, unshakable, indestructible, inexhaustible.

Yesterday I had a positive meeting with Emily. She is preparing to move out of her house and reset her life. She is back with Danny, but very confused about their relationship. She is acting like she wants me around, wants my help and perhaps ... my love.

~ 818 ~

> But when the Pharisees heard that he had silenced the Sadducees, they gathered together. And one of them, a lawyer, asked him a question to test him. "Teacher, which is the great commandment in the Law?" And he said to him, "You shall love the Lord your God with all your heart and with all your soul and with all your mind. This is the great and first commandment. And a second is like it: You shall love your neighbor as yourself. On these two commandments depend all the Law and the Prophets." (Matthew 22:34-40 RSV)

Jesus' response to the Pharisees was not about ranking the commandments; it was a rebuke of the Pharisees. He was saying that without loving God and their neighbors, all of their pious and sanctimonious displays of religiosity were empty. Their love of money, power, and authority had overridden the love of God that should have been the foundation of their every word and deed.

Jesus said, "You shall love the Lord your God ... You shall love your neighbor." But how can someone be commanded to love? You can't force or be forced into love. You can't decide to be loving. Either love arises spontaneously from your inner being, or it doesn't.

How did love enter my heart? Through suffering and surrender. But actually, love did not enter my heart; it was there all the time. When I surrendered everything else, all that remained was love, the eternal love of God, finally unobstructed and able to shine through. This is how Jesus meant for us to love God and our neighbor – by removing all the obstacles to the love that is already in our hearts.

Anita Moorjani said, "I was amazed to understand that my life could be dramatically different just by realizing that I *am* love, and I always have been. I don't have to do anything to deserve it. Understanding this means that I'm working with life-force energy, whereas *performing* at being loving is working against it." [14]

~ 819 ~

MY MYSTIC JOURNEY WITH KATHY, Part 5
Rejection

Kathy wrote to me:

Since our fundamental beliefs differ, I do not want to seek spiritual counsel from you.

I wrote to her:

You say our fundamental beliefs differ. Not so. I do not have beliefs. I have experiential knowledge. Do you think I would say what I do with such assurance if my revelations and epiphanies were not coming directly from God? That's what my mystical, spirit-filled life is all about.

By what authority do I speak to Kathy? Jesus said, "For I have not spoken on my own authority; the Father who sent me has himself given me commandment what to say and what to speak." (John 12:49) I speak to Kathy by authority of the one who sent me to her in our $12,000 dream (~564~), who revealed truth to me through miracles and revelations.

I don't think the Pharisees were necessarily bad people. Some of them, like Nicodemus, approached Jesus with benevolence and were open to his teaching. Others attacked Jesus out of malevolence, because they saw him as a threat to their power. I think many of them were God-fearing men, doing what they thought was in accord with their fundamental beliefs as embodied in Holy Scripture and the Law of Moses. They did not condemn Jesus because they hated him, but because they saw him as a heretic and blasphemer, not believing he was who he said he was, not open to the truth of God's revealed Word because it did not conform to their limited interpretation of the ancient law. They were not evil, just weak and blind. They could not read the signs of the times; they could not draw the line from Isaiah to Jesus to God.

Kathy fears and rejects me as the Pharisees feared and rejected Jesus. She feels confused and manipulated by my ideas, especially the infusion of Eastern religious thought into Christianity. Like most fundamentalist Christians, she has God confined in a tiny box, severely limited by the literal descriptions of God in the Bible. Please God, show Kathy how to let you out of the box. Show her how to be my Nicodemus, not my Caiaphas.

PART 36

Falling Mirrors

March 2015 – May 2015

~ 820 ~

I have two bathrooms in my house, one near the master bedroom that I use, and another guest bathroom that Emily uses. I found an angel feather in Emily's bathroom this morning. Emily sent me a birthday e-card at the same time. It's just a small sign, but enough for me to know that the spirits are still with us.

A couple nights ago, several of the mirrored tiles that cover my bathroom wall fell down to the floor. I heard the crashing sound from my bedroom. But miraculously, they did not break; I found them neatly stacked on each other in an upright position just below the spot where they had been affixed to the wall.

From dreammoods.com:

> **Mirror –** Mirrors symbolize the imagination and the link between the conscious and subconscious. To see a mirror in your dream symbolizes a loved one or good friend. To break a mirror in your dream suggests that you are breaking an old image of yourself. You may be putting an end to an old habit.

Once again, as happened last year at this time, the symbology of dreams has come alive in the matter and energy of waking life. This reminds me of the time last year when my picture of Kuan Yin fell down from the wall in my office. (~701~) The glass plate that covered the picture broke.

> **Glass –** To see glass in your dream symbolizes passivity or protection. You may be putting up an invisible barrier to protect yourself in a situation or relationship. To see broken glass in your dream signifies disappointments and negative changes in your life. Alternatively, it could be symbolic of an aspect of your life that is in pieces.

Last summer Emily was going through a particularly rough time with me, and it did indeed seem that our relationship was in pieces. Kuan Yin is back up on the wall now, none the worse for wear, but without the invisible protective glass barrier between the symbolic bodhisattva and the living one.

~ 821 ~

I spent two days and a night with Emily, helping her move out of her house in the country into a new house the city. It was a tense time; there were many problems and angry outbursts. I was the ballast that kept the boat afloat in the storm.

It was deeply symbolic for me to have spent that last day and night in the house with her, sharing her goodbyes and letting go of her home of the last twelve years. Even though I was in the house only a few times, some of the most miraculous experiences of my life happened there — my first night with her, when our love came to the surface and I saw her many dysfunctional faces, and especially the night my arms melted into her.

Out of the blue she began asking me very intimate questions about my sex life with Lou, and telling me about her very sexual relationships with her men. Again she said that if I were a man, she would marry me, no question. I would have won over Danny, hands down.

There is karmic purpose in God's love coming to Emily in female form. If I were a man, she would not have to make the quantum leap to the place where love recognizes no gender. She would be unable to differentiate my spiritual love from her lustful physical love with men. For her to follow the path of divine love, it would be necessary for her to be liberated from her past habits, patterns, and social conditioning, including her aversion to same-sex intimacy. Divine love must be free of all limits — "rule-breaking erotics," as Campbell said.

I want so much to tell her about our glorious tantric love and its sexual manifestations, but she isn't ready to hear it. She still thinks of love in terms of what she can get out of it, particularly financial and emotional support, and sex is her primary form of currency. Until she breaks out of that mold, she won't be able to understand the fabulous couple that we are.

But even in her gratitude for my help with the move, all the while telling me she loves me, she couldn't help but bring up the things I do that upset her. She brings up my alleged misdeeds to elevate herself over me, to assuage her self-loathing demons. I do not argue or recriminate, because in my boundless compassion I see no wrong between us, only the karma unfolding as it was meant to. Our love, as I know it, is beyond all that.

~ 822 ~

When Emily talks to me about Danny, she is sheepish, almost apologetic. There seems to be a tug of war going on inside her, loving both of us in different ways, not quite understanding the difference. Part of her, the loving part, knows that I am her true love and that she is in a way cheating on me with him, but the other part, the fearful part, cannot resist his affections and attentions – the lustful conditional love with which she is familiar.

Perhaps her inner turmoil is a sign of her emerging understanding of our love. I think our intimate conversations last weekend were her efforts to understand, to explore, like a baby bird beginning to peck through its shell.

~ 823 ~

Danny arrives tomorrow. Yet even now, before his body is joined with hers, I already feel tantric energy flowing through me, the intimate joining of my material self with Emily's spiritual ectoplasm in the most amazing ritual of tantric sex. This is so hard to explain. It is not just a matter of extreme physical and emotional pleasure; it is a miracle of the highest form of love, the greatest and most powerful spiritual energy flowing through and transforming the psychology of the mind and the physiology of the body.

Emily is not ready for me in this life. She is still far away from letting go of her pain and her old ways of dealing with it. Her consciousness will not accept our spiritual union. But I am ready for her, and so I act out our tantric love – in body, mind, and soul – with the part of her that *is* ready, subconsciously, metaphysically, in the spirit realm. This love of the spirit, sent to me from the heavenly to the earthly sphere, will keep my body alive until her body finds its way to me.

I recently learned that the esoteric Buddhist mudras, mandalas, and other symbols that my sangha employs are directly descended from ancient Tantric Buddhism. It seems that I began practicing Tantra long before I knew what it was.

~ 824 ~

My friend Rita comes from a murderous family. Yesterday she told me that her mother almost killed her father. Earlier I had learned that her great-grandfather actually did kill his wife. (~759~) Rita spent her childhood traumatized by her parents' violent fights, her father's infidelity, and ongoing physical and psychological abuse. She suffers deep psychic wounds from this family history, yet she has risen above it. She has refused to follow in her parents' abusive footsteps and is a kind and caring person even in the midst of her pain.

Psychics say that we choose our parents. We are born into our particular families to fulfill a karmic purpose. I believe that it is possible for those of us alive now to reach back in time and rescue those who came before us – merit transfer, as the Buddhists say. I believe that Rita chose her murderous family to save them, to heal their horrendous karma with her love and forgiveness.

She is breaking the cycle of fear, anger, and abuse that has plagued her family for generations. She is a true bodhisattva, sent by God to bear the burdens of her family, remove the weight of them, and cleanse her ancestors for all eternity. This is the meaning of divine sacrificial love. Through Rita's suffering and forgiveness, the Way to salvation is opened.

~ 825 ~

Everything can be viewed from the dual perspective or the eternal perspective. Consciousness of eternity – the ability to see things from the eternal perspective – is the hallmark of enlightenment, being "born again," being a mystic or a bodhisattva. This is, as the Thomas Gospel says, awareness of the kingdom that is inside and outside us, that is spread upon the earth and men do not see it.

Both Jesus and the Buddha said that few will find the path to enlightenment. They also said that each of us is capable of finding the path if we choose to seek it and accept the trials we will encounter along the way. We all have the power to become children of God; all we have to do is say "yes" to the angel in the spaceship.

~ 826 ~

Emily called this evening. Her speech was slurred and almost incoherent, indicative of her consumption of a large amount of alcohol. She and Danny have broken up again, supposedly for the last time. He was abusive, acting crazy, frightening her. Yelling at her in front of the restaurant, creating such a scene that a security guard got involved. She kicked him out. She is, once again, heartbroken.

I told her that I was suspicious of his opulent gifts to her. I said that they were not a sign of love. "What, then?" she asked.

"He wants something and is willing to pay a lot for it," I replied. What I did not say was that she and Danny don't really love each other at all. They barely tolerate each other. After a week or so of trying to live together, he throws her out, and then she throws him out. They just use and abuse each other. He wants her body and she wants his money. Their relationship is not about love; it's just a business deal.

How fascinating it is – this morning, before I learned of the breakup, the heightened tantric sexuality that I felt a few days ago in anticipation of Danny's arrival dissipated. My spirit knew about the breakup before I did.

~ 827 ~

Emily said she feels like a deflated marshmallow. Feeling down, depressed. She has been on an emotional roller coaster for months, and her heart is wrung out. I said, "Please remember one thing: When you feel alone or abandoned, you aren't. I am here. I will not abandon you. I love you. Always will."

I could hear her crying on the other end of the phone. "I love you, too." she said.

~ 828 ~

I told Rita that, in taking on the suffering of her murderous family, she was the second coming of Jesus Christ. When she totally forgives her ancestors and bathes them in the compassionate love of God with no anger or bitterness, everyone in her constellation – past, present, and future – will be healed. She will have saved them all.

She said, "I think you are right on the money. I've suspected this for some time." "But why me?" she asked. "Why not a cousin instead?"

Jesus felt the same way in Gethsemane when he asked to be spared the bitter cup that was before him. But God said, "No, you'll go through with this just as we planned." God had earlier said to Jeremiah, "I want you to be a prophet to the nations." Jeremiah said, "Uh, no thanks. I don't know how to speak." God said, "Speak. I'll put the words in your mouth." And so Jeremiah did. And Jesus did. And Rita is doing.

I said to Rita, "God picked you because you are perfect for the job, and he sent Martha and me to prop you up."

She added, "Once you know you are called to this, there's no going back."

I can't go back. I am an eighth bhūmi bodhisattva, irreversible. So is Rita.

~ 829 ~

Martha said that Rita's dancing has been her spiritual link, the lifeline that has kept her from sinking into despair. I realize now that my music has been the same for me. All of my major epiphanies had a musical component, and when I suffered my post-Lou travail, my musical work kept my soul grounded, in communion with life and the world.

We usually think of the arts as a means of self-expression, letting our own thoughts, feelings, and inner self out. But from Rita's experience and my own, I can see that the conduit works in both directions, like mantras and chants, transmitting spiritual messages and power *to* us as well as *from* us. The highest purpose of art is enlightenment, to be a vehicle for mystical communication, reaching beyond thoughts and feelings to connect directly with the Source. Very few people, even great artists, fully grasp this, fully understand the awesome power art can exert over audiences and artists alike.

~ 830 ~

Emily has been in Colombia for five days. She likes the energy there. She is happy. She says she is one with God. But I think she is falling even deeper into denial and delusion. She has found a place where no one knows her, she has no responsibilities, she can eat, drink, and sleep as much as she wants whenever she wants, she can be as crazy as she wants. She can safely and easily indulge her demons and ignore her pain.

Sooner or later she will need to return to the world, to responsibilities, work, and people who will be affected by her behavior. When that happens, will she find that she was healed on her trip, or only that a thicker layer of plaster was added to her elaborate façade?

She ran away to Colombia to run away from herself. She is uncomfortable inside her own skin, but she cannot escape. Her demons and her pain follow her everywhere she goes. She will return from her trip refreshed on the surface, but still exhausted in the spirit. True healing must take place inside her, because that's where the pain is. If healing is to be found, it can be found anywhere; it is not a matter of geography.

~ 831 ~

POVERTY, CHASTITY, AND OBEDIENCE

I finished reading another great book, Dietrich Bonhoeffer's *Letters & Papers From Prison*.[53] I have quoted Bonhoeffer often, but now I know him and admire him even more deeply. As was the case with Martin Luther King, Jr., Jacobo Timerman, Gandhi, and so many others, prison seemed to draw out of Bonhoeffer a spiritual power and profundity that could not have been released any other way.

Through Bonhoeffer's words I see the Christian vows of poverty, chastity and obedience[vii] in a broader light. Dietrich wrote:

> The church is the church only when it exists for others. To make a start, it should give away all its property to those in need. The clergy must live solely on the freewill offerings of their congregations, or possibly engage in some secular calling. The church must share in the secular problems of ordinary human life, not dominating, but helping and serving. It must tell men of every calling what it means to live in Christ, to exist for others. It is certain that we can claim nothing for ourselves.

Poverty is not being poor; it is what the Buddhists call unsupported thought, claiming nothing for ourselves, not coveting, even when one has access to great wealth. Poverty in this sense is thus to dedicate all that one has – money, possessions, time, even life itself – in service to others, in the meaning of the 1st Perfection of Generosity.

> The essence of chastity is not suppression of lust, but the total orientation of one's life towards a goal. Without such a goal, chastity is bound to become ridiculous. Chastity is the *sin qua non* of lucidity and concentration.

This makes sense from the standpoint of both abstinence and tantric sex. **Chastity** is not the same as celibacy. Sex is chaste when its goal is the same as that of celibacy – to be one with God – and is reflective of "the total orientation of one's life" towards that goal. Even the most spiritually disciplined Hindus and Buddhists recognize true tantric sex as the equivalent

---

[vii] The three Evangelical Counsels of chastity, poverty, and obedience were first made in the twelfth century by Francis of Assisi and his followers, based on passages like Matthew 19:10–12 and Matthew 19:16–22.

of abstinence in the rigor of its spiritual goal, being the same "*sin qua non* of lucidity and concentration" in pursuit of that goal.

I am witnessing this paradox now in my own life. The total orientation of my life is spiritual union with God via Emily, my God with form. I find the same lucidity and concentration in pursuit of that goal in tantric sex when her spirit enters my body and in abstinence when it departs.

> One must completely abandon any attempt to make something of oneself, whether it be a saint, or a converted sinner, or a churchman, a righteous man or an unrighteous one, a sick man or a healthy one. By this-worldliness I mean living unreservedly in life's duties, problems, successes and failures, experiences and perplexities. In so doing we throw ourselves completely into the arms of God.

Obedience is not blindly following orders, but rather surrendering completely to God, letting go of ego and swimming unreservedly immersed in the current of life, not swimming above it or against it. Thich Nhat Hanh touched on this idea when he said, "You have to touch God through his creatures. You have to touch the ultimate dimension by touching the historical dimension deeply." Bonhoeffer's "this-worldliness" is the bodhisattva's joyful participation in the sorrows of the world. The Rev. Dr. Martin Luther King, Jr., said that the purpose of life is not to be happy, not to achieve pleasure nor avoid pain, but to do the will of God, come what may.

> The beyond is not what is infinitely remote, but what is nearest at hand.

Did Bonhoeffer know the Thomas Gospel? Perhaps he got his information from the same spirit who spoke to Thomas: "The kingdom of the father is spread upon the earth and men do not see it."

Poverty is not just being poor. Chastity is not just abstinence. Obedience is not just following orders. It is possible for a person to be rich, sexually active, and exhibit behaviors that some would call disobedience, and still be true to these ideals. (The Dalai Lama explains this: ~1430~) How one uses one's riches, body, and mind reveals the righteousness of one's motivation; Jesus said, "A tree is known by its fruit." These virtues are not acquired by practice and force of will, but by faith and grace. They come automatically as the effect, not the cause, of enlightenment. When one awakens to the God-self within, to the kingdom of the father that is spread upon the earth, these Christian virtues, like the Buddha's Four Immeasurables (~1030~), arise spontaneously from the indwelling God, as the morning sun naturally rises in the eastern sky.

~ 832 ~

LOVE, Part 7

The Unnamed One said he loved me, but he didn't really know what he was saying. What he meant by the word "love" was different from my meaning for it. I define my love very narrowly now – as the highest form of love, divine love. His experience with me was his first introduction to that kind of love. Sadly, he was unable to stay in the light of divine love, and his fear got the upper hand. Love and fear cannot coexist, and his tiny flickering flame of love was doused by a tidal wave of fear.

He still confuses real love with other warm, positive feelings like gratitude, admiration, affection, sympathy, respect, or kindness. When positive feelings subside or negative ones appear, "love" fades.

Worldly expressions of positive emotion are just responses to pleasant sensory stimuli. They are not really love at all. Divine love, even in its worldly aspects, is not an emotion; it is a state of being. It permeates every aspect of life – work, family, global politics, and all relationships. It rises above desire and fear, dissolving them like the salt doll into the ocean of God, in total trust and surrender.

Almost all of medical science, especially preventative medicine, is a play on our fear – fear of death, disability, pain, and with most cosmetic surgery, fear of ugliness or its first poison counterpart, desire for beauty. When we take the doctor's medicine, we are taking the first poison of desire to get relief from pain, or the second poison of fear to keep pain away. Religion is the same, playing on our fear of hellfire and our desire for happiness, in this life if possible, but most certainly, we pray, in the afterlife.

True love, like true religion, does not promise happiness or freedom from pain; in fact, it promises the opposite – disenchantment with happiness and assurance of pain. But once divine love has arisen and you have surrendered to it, there are no more choices to be made. You joyfully accept a mortal life of pleasure and pain because you know the simultaneous eternal life of bliss.

And yet, as long as we are in the body, we will experience desire and fear. Even Jesus – God with form, the embodiment of divine love – had his bout with fear in Gethsemane. But then, knowing the bliss of the spirit, he was able to explain to his mortal body-mind that there was no going back; there was only going forward in joyful surrender to the divine purpose for which he was born.

Again I asked myself if I was wrong to have been so blunt with The Unnamed One. Should I have held my tongue, gone along to get along, so that our relationship could have remained intact? No. I had to tell the truth, do what I had to do, and he had to respond as he did. Everything had to be just as it was, or neither of us could have made the spiritual advances that we made.

Allen Ginsberg wrote, "I have perhaps been overeager to teach meditation to people who are too dumb, like myself, to ask for it. It seems to me that in America it might be useful for people to be more forward. Usually, I understand, the proper etiquette is to wait until someone asks you three times. But you can always suggest to them that they might ask you three times."

I see my mistake with The Unnamed One. I tried to teach him the meditation of divine love before he asked for it three times.

~ 833 ~

Martha calls me a "wake-up fairy." God sends me to people who need waking up, their first introduction to divine love. The Unnamed One, Kathy, and Emily are people who live in fear and darkness. I am a first glimmer of light for them, the first candle of divine love lighting their spiritual path. But my loved ones cannot stay in the light. Their fear overwhelms their curiosity. After so long in the darkness, my light hurts their eyes.

> Tell all the truth but tell it slant –
> Success in Circuit lies
> Too bright for our infirm Delight
> The Truth's superb surprise
> As Lightning to the Children eased
> With explanation kind
> The Truth must dazzle gradually
> Or every man be blind –
>
> – Emily Dickenson

My truth-telling has always been powerful – too powerful. I must learn to dazzle more gradually and find "explanation kind."

I see now why I was given a fully realized love with Lou, and why it happened early in my life, with my first karmic love – so that I would recognize the deficiencies in my love with the others, my experiential knowledge of fully fledged divine love allowing me to resist the temptations of my human desires going forward, temptations that might have pulled me into lesser relationships of worldly dependency and away from my latent bodhisattva potential. My divine experience with Lou also gave me the courage to go forth as a sacrificial truth-teller and accept the pain of it, having known the divine bliss that is always in and around the pain.

~ 834 ~

Dream last night: *I rescue one lone fish from a threatening situation and place it in a fish tank in a dark room. As I pick up the tank to move it to the kitchen, I think I see more than one fish in the tank. When I get to the bright kitchen I can see that there are indeed lots of little fish in the tank. The fish I rescued must have been pregnant, I thought, a live-bearer like the guppies I used to keep. As I looked around the kitchen I saw that there were two other fish tanks there, each teeming with fish, all different sizes and species, swimming happily around.*

From dreammoods.com:

Fish – To see fish swimming in your dream signifies insights from your subconscious mind. Thus to catch a fish represents insights which have been brought to the surface.

Fish Tank – To see or clean a fish tank in your dream indicates how you have full control of your emotions. You keep your feelings in check. If you are watching the fish in the fish tank, then you may feel that your life is going nowhere or that you are going in circles with your life.

Kitchen – To see a kitchen in your dream signifies your need for warmth, spiritual nourishment and healing. It may also be symbolic of the nurturing mother or the way that you are for your loved ones. Alternatively, the kitchen represents a transformation. Something new or life-altering is about to occur.

My insights have come up from the dark subconscious into the light of consciousness, and they have grown and multiplied there. Do the three fish tanks represent my three karmic loves? My emotions are under control inside the tank. My life is going in circles as I watch the fish in the tank, but perhaps that's because there is no place to go; I am right where I am supposed to be. Kitchen scenes have happened before in my dreams, each time marking a transformation or spiritual transition. What am I cooking up in the kitchen? What new transformation is waiting for me?

~ 835 ~

A few nights ago, I had a dream that I was searching for a perfume called "Mystery." I never found it in my dream, but my curiosity led me to the Internet where I did find it. I bought a bottle.

From dreammoods.com:

Perfume – To dream that you are spraying or wearing perfume suggests that you are seeking more pleasure in your life. It is also symbolic of your sexuality, sensuality, and indulgence.

Mystery – To read or watch a mystery in your dream indicates that you need to be on the lookout for something that is out of place or out of the ordinary. Something is not what it appears to be. Be careful in your dealings.

Search – To dream that you are searching for something signifies the need to find something that is missing or needed in your life. The dream may be analogous to your search for love, spiritual enlightenment, peace, or a solution to a problem.

I am indeed searching for enlightenment, peace, and the meaning behind the sexual, sensual, indulgent mystery of Emily. I know that she is not what she appears to be, and I must be careful in my dealings with her.

I texted Emily about this dream, asking her if this perfume had any meaning for her. My dreams usually contain some spiritual message relevant to my waking life, and I wondered if perhaps this was a perfume that she or her mother wore. She knew of the perfume but claimed no connection to it, and replied that Naomi Campbell, a model who is associated with the "Mystery" brand, used to beat up her maids and is not considered a very nice person. With this deflection into judgment of Naomi Campbell I sensed that I had once again raised up her demons.

She also said in her petulant tone of voice, "This is about you, not me. We cannot have other people's dreams, not even you."

I answered, "It was my dream, not yours, but my dream images often involve you. We are swimming together in the soup of the unconscious. I treasure our swims together. That's where I can love you fully. And do."

BOUNDARIES, *Part 3*

Boundaries are indicative of the separation of individuals in space-time. They arise between people who feel threatened or vulnerable, usually to limit the power or control one person may have over another. Boundaries are put up to hide weaknesses and protect against possible physical or emotional assault by those we don't know, don't like, or don't trust.

I do my best to respect the boundaries of other people; I have no desire to offend or enter where I am not wanted. On the other hand, I have a long history of pushing through boundaries with my truth-telling. Sometimes it is necessary for someone to break the bounds of propriety to tell the emperor he has no clothes, and that someone has often been me. I have paid a price for this, as all truth-tellers do.

This kind of boundary-bursting is an act of love, not of desire, disrespect, carelessness, or malevolence. It happens as necessary to catalyze a rebirth, to crack the eggshell of darkness and break out of old, diseased, damaging habits in the light of new truth and understanding. Tough love, perhaps, but necessary, like the pain of childbirth, to move from past to future.

Boundaries exist within the worldly loves of master/slave, parent/child, and also between those who appear to be equals, where there is no apparent power differential: friend/friend and spouse/spouse. But not in divine love. With my increasing immersion in the eternal dimension, I recognize no boundaries anymore. In this highest love, there is no limit to anything, no level of intimacy that cannot be reached, no rules, no right or wrong behaviors that earn love or destroy it. The separation between individuals disappears and boundaries dissolve.

Fear creates boundaries, love removes them. Divine love is not an emotion or a relational condition; it is a state of being. In this state there can be no boundaries because there is no separation; no secrets, because every cranny of the heart, mind, and soul is laid bare; no privacy, because each person lives inside the other; no violation of person or property, because nothing, not even the physical body, is possessed by one person separate from another.

Jesus, in his great divine love, had no boundaries, not even with those who would do him harm. He said, "Do not resist one who is evil. But if any one strikes you on the right cheek, turn to him the other also; and if anyone would sue you and take your coat, let him have your cloak as well; and if any one forces you to go one mile, go with him two miles. Give to him who begs from you, and do not refuse him who would borrow from you." (Matthew 5:39-42 RSV)

This explains why I let Emily get away with so much. Yes, she uses and abuses me. She does the same with others, too, but with me it is different. The others love her in shallow ways that involve wanting something from her or depending on her. Putting up with her difficult and demanding personality, allowing her to cross their boundaries, is the price they are willing to pay to satisfy their desires.

The difference with me is that I don't want anything from her and am not dependent on her. I am called to her by her pain; it is a call of service, not desire. It is not a worldly love, but the divine love of God, that connects us. It is not that I allow her to cross my boundaries; with me there are no boundaries to be crossed, no sins to be committed, and no sacrifice of time, money, property, heart, even life, too great to make, even though in the worldly sense I receive nothing from her in return.

I know that I am in danger. In Emily's condition of extreme psychic pain she is unreasonable and irrational. She cannot love, only prey upon those who love her. Her psychological abuse could easily become violently physical, causing harm to herself or others. Her madness leads her to make ill-considered, impulsive, often self-destructive decisions that leave her in even worse shape financially, socially, and emotionally. These behaviors evoke fear in her more hapless victims; in me they evoke compassion.

The Sufi mystic Mansur al-Hallaj prayed:

> And these my servants who are gathered to slay me, in zeal for Thy religion and in desire to win Thy favor, forgive them, O Lord, and have mercy upon them; for verily if Thou hadst revealed to them that which Thou hast revealed to me, they would not have done what they have done; and if Thou hadst hidden from me that which Thou hast hidden from them, I should not have suffered this tribulation.[54]

Mansur was tortured and publicly dismembered because he said, "I am Truth," Truth being a name for God in the Koran, and refused to recant his belief that God was in him. Jesus was killed because he said he was the Son of God, that God was in him. Meister Eckhart got in trouble with the Church when he said, "The eye with which I see God is the same as that with which he sees me." I told Kathy that God is in me (and in her, too), and now she shuns me.

Refusing to recognize any boundaries between the creator and his creatures gets us into trouble. I have not yet reached the total unification with the divine that Jesus, the Buddha, Mansur, and many other saints have, but I am feeling its pull more and more powerfully as I approach the Far Shore.

~ 837 ~

I just returned from a quick trip. As I boarded the plane home, I noticed that both cloth webbing handles on my tote bag were frayed, on the verge of breaking. The outer layers of woven threads were dissolving and crumbling in my hands, but there were tough inner cords, like the steel girders that support tall buildings, that were still holding strong and would not break despite my tugging at them. Those fabric girders were still intact when I got home.

When I traveled at this time last year for two spiritual workshops, I experienced a similar phenomenon when two cloth straps broke on two different bags. (~655~) Dreammoods.com provided these clues:

> **Bag** – To see a bag in your dream represents the responsibilities that you carry. If the bag is ripped or torn, then it indicates that you are carrying a lot of burden.
>
> **Break** – To dream that you break something indicates that changes are ahead for you. You need to "break" away from some situation and change the direction that your life is headed in.

What is the meaning of the tenacious inner cords? Perhaps it means that while the outer aspects of my life crumble and fray, there is an inner strength that will hold me together and keep me intact. And also that while my earthly relationship with Emily might crumble and fray, our deep spiritual connection can never be broken. My love is her inner strength as well, holding her together without her consciously knowing it.

~ 838 ~

I finished another great book on my trip, *From Jung To Jesus*, by Gerald Slusser. It is yet another enlightening perspective on the hero's journey, the life of Christ, the Way, and yet another confirmation that I am on that path. These books seem to come to me as if by magic, and the angels who deliver them and elucidate them are my teachers. They appear just when I need them, when I am ready to receive their wisdom. "When the student is ready, the teacher will appear," says a Buddhist proverb.

I wonder if those who have written about the hero's journey – Campbell, Chopra, Slusser, Jung, et al. – wrote based on the writings and experiences of others, or if they were writing from personal experience. Because almost all the other authors I have read on spiritual topics wrote in the third person, not from the more intimate first person as I do, I am tempted to think that they are reporters of events and synthesizers of information from other people – skilled at that task, but still observing and analyzing from a distance. However, they write with assurance and the ring of truth. Such confidence and veracity rarely come except from experiential knowledge.

I suppose those sages who chose to write in the third person did so intentionally to depersonalize their story, to make its presentation seem more objective, scholarly, and thus more credible, less anecdotal. This doesn't work for me. I have found it impossible to depersonalize my life and the incredible, deeply personal events that punctuate it. My book, my life, my journey, is one long subjective anecdote.

In this passage from *Walden, or Life in the Woods,* Henry David Thoreau presages my rationale for writing in the first person:

> In most books, the I, or first person, is omitted; in this it will be retained; that, in respect to egotism, is the main difference. We commonly do not remember that it is, after all, always the first person that is speaking. I should not talk so much about myself if there were anybody else whom I knew as well. Unfortunately, I am confined to this theme by the narrowness of my experience. Moreover, I, on my side, require of every writer, first or last, a simple and sincere account of his own life, and not merely what he has heard of other men's lives; some such account as he would send to his kindred from a distant land; for if he has lived sincerely, it must have been in a distant land to me.

As Thoreau requires of me, this book is a simple and sincere account of my own life, bringing those in distant lands up close, also using what I have heard of other people's lives as a springboard for understanding my own narrow but uniquely powerful experience.

~ 839 ~

My spirituality reflects the intimate overlap of many disciplines – psychology, philosophy, art, religion, all the natural and social sciences. The study of one must become the study of all. My deep reach into the spirit cannot but also extend into the deep crannies of the body, heart, mind, and psyche. Marianne Williamson said, "*A Course in Miracles* says religion and psychotherapy are, at their peak, the same thing." [55]

I realize that much of what I have written about Emily and The Unnamed One is armchair amateur psychoanalysis. Some would say I am not qualified to psychoanalyze people. True enough, in the clinical sense. But sometimes love trumps qualifications. I do not have formal training in psychology, but I do have the gift of divine love, and thus a deeper insight into my loved ones than any psychologist could have. Emily's deep and continuing psychological struggle, despite her degree in psychology, is proof that education does not automatically bring insight or healing. Many physicians who seek to heal themselves fail to do so because it is not knowledge, analysis, drugs, or other therapies that heal at the deepest level. Only love can do that.

~ 840 ~

ORIGINAL SIN

> For as by one man's disobedience many were made sinners, so by one man's obedience many will be made righteous. (Romans 5:19 RSV)

The Christian doctrine of original sin comes from the Bible story in Genesis about Adam's sin of eating from the Tree of the Knowledge of Good and Evil in the Garden of Eden. St. Augustine of Hippo is said to have coined the term "original sin" and put forth the idea that Adam's sin is passed on to all of Adam's descendants. By this view, all humans are sinners from the moment of conception. "Original" in this context means "inherited," not intrinsic. Thus, we were not created as sinners, but became so by the deeds of our ancestors.

Not all Christian sects agree with this view of original sin, many considering the story of Adam's Fall to be a metaphor for human nature in general, not necessarily related to an actual historical event. Early Hebrew writings are inconsistent on whether or not the sins of the father may be visited on the sons:

> The son shall not suffer for the iniquity of the father, nor the father suffer for the iniquity of the son; the righteousness of the righteous shall be upon himself, and the wickedness of the wicked shall be upon himself. (Ezekiel 18:20 RSV)

> And now thy many judgments are true in exacting penalty from me for my sins and those of my fathers, because we did not keep thy commandments. For we did not walk in truth before thee. (Tobit 3:5 RSV)

Whether we believe that acquired characteristics can be inherited or not, whether we treat Bible stories as allegories or connect them to actual events, there is always a message. Adam's Fall is no exception.

In nature, there is no good or evil, no right or wrong. We do not condemn the female praying mantis for biting off the head of her mate, nor the lion for killing and eating her prey.

These animals are simply being true to their nature, not committing a sin in the sense of doing evil. They are acting as they must, without thinking, unconsciously accepting that this world of duality requires them to kill as part of their survival instinct. Animals act unconsciously according to instinct, as nature dictates, still at one with God.

> I think I could turn and live with animals,
> They are so placid and self-contain'd,
> I stand and look at them long and long.
> They do not sweat and whine about their condition,
> They do not lie awake in the dark and weep for their sins,
> They do not make me sick discussing their duty to God,
> Not one is dissatisfied, not one is demented with the mania of owning things,
> Not one kneels to another, nor to his kind that lived thousands of years ago,
> Not one is respectable or unhappy over the whole earth.

> – Walt Whitman, "Song of Myself"

Human beings rose above, or sank below, the animal kingdom when they discovered duality and started second-guessing their instincts and intuition, doubting their innate wisdom, and categorizing everything as either good or evil. Sins – missing the mark – are isolated events that we interpret as bad deeds. But in the big picture of the temporal world, these acts, even seemingly evil ones – even heinous crimes, wars, torture, and genocide – are the inevitable dualistic balance to the equal and opposite beautiful side of life. Not sin, just nature.

> What then shall we say? That the law is sin? By no means! Yet, if it had not been for the law,
> I should not have known sin. I should not have known what it is to covet if the law had not
> said, "You shall not covet." But sin, finding opportunity in the commandment, wrought in
> me all kinds of covetousness. Apart from the law sin lies dead. (Romans 7:7-8 RSV)

In creating the law, Moses and the ancient fathers set up a straw man for us to knock down. We would never have even thought about the evils of coveting, stealing, killing, or worshiping other gods if the law had not put those thoughts into our heads. The law set us up for sin, making rules that we were bound to break, putting up a target we were bound to miss. "For I know that nothing good dwells within me, that is, in my flesh. I can will what is right, but I cannot do it. For I do not do the good I want, but the evil I do not want is what I do." (Romans 7:18-19 RSV) Not only sin, but also guilt and shame, were created by the law.

At a deeper level, sin is more complicated than just breaking the commandments. Original sin, the basis of the entire concept of sin, is not a specific event, but a state of consciousness. Original sin is our genealogical legacy from Adam and Eve, the first sinners, who disobeyed

God in the Garden of Eden. By eating of the Tree of the Knowledge of Good and Evil, they discovered that their eternal life with God also existed in a state of separation in time and space.

With that knowledge came the birth of the ego with its conflicting and competing emotions, and vulnerability to the opposing effects of space-time separation. Adam and Eve were expelled from the Garden and born into consciousness of the dualistic world, but the tradeoff for gaining that consciousness was blindness to their unconscious life in eternal unity. The separation of space-time had separated them from God.

> And the LORD God commanded the man, saying, "You may freely eat of every tree of the garden; but of the tree of the knowledge of good and evil you shall not eat, for in the day that you eat of it you shall die." (Genesis 2:16-17 RSV)
>
> But the serpent said to the woman, "You will not die. For God knows that when you eat of it your eyes will be opened, and you will be like God, knowing good and evil." (Genesis 3:4-5 RSV)

God said that Adam would die from eating the forbidden fruit. The serpent said he would not die. God and the serpent both spoke the truth. The day Adam ate of the tree he died to his unconscious life in the Garden, but his soul, eternal and indestructible, remained alive. Jesus (and the Buddha, and others) appeared on earth to awaken Adam's slumbering God-self and bring it to the surface.

When that happens, the awakened, redeemed human, with knowledge of good and evil but also now with consciousness of unity with God, rises above the law and sin and becomes, as the serpent said, "like God," God's divine presence on earth:

> God is not merely mending, not simply restoring a status quo. Redeemed humanity is to be something more glorious than unfallen humanity would have been, more glorious than any unfallen race now is. ... And this super-added glory will, with true vicariousness, exalt all creatures, and those who have never fallen will thus bless Adam's fall. – C.S. Lewis, *Miracles*[27]

Each human life is a reenactment of Adam's Fall. Babies, like animals, enter the world pure and innocent, unconscious of their simultaneous separation from and unity with God. Then, unlike animals, they learn the law that creates sin, and become conscious of the pairs of opposites – good and bad, comfort and discomfort, satiation and frustration. The ego arises and takes control. Like a virus that overrides the DNA of the cell it inhabits, the ego overrides and impedes the innate God-self that is our true nature. The continuing legacy of original sin is our failure to resist the temptations of dualistic fears and desires, and our failure to let go of all worldly causes and effects – karma – and surrender all back to God.

> Now there was a man of the Pharisees, named Nicodemus, a ruler of the Jews. This man came to Jesus by night and said to him, "Rabbi, we know that you are a teacher come from God; for no one can do these signs that you do, unless God is with him." Jesus answered him, "Truly, truly, I say to you, unless one is born anew, he cannot see the kingdom of God." Nicodemus said to him, "How can a man be born when he is old? Can he enter a second time into his mother's womb and be born?" Jesus answered, "Truly, truly, I say to you, unless one is born of water and the Spirit, he cannot enter the kingdom of God. That which is born of the flesh is flesh, and that which is born of the Spirit is spirit.[viii] Do not marvel that I said to you, 'You must be born anew.' The wind[vi] blows where it wills, and you hear the sound of it, but you do not know whence it comes or whither it goes; so it is with every one who is born of the Spirit." (John 3:1-8 RSV)

It was necessary for a savior to come into the world to show Man the Way out of original sin and back into the womb to be born again of the spirit. Moses and David were almost perfect, but could not be absolutely perfect because they were born of Adam's lineage, from and into original sin. They each committed only one reported sin in their lives, but that was enough to keep Moses from entering the Promised Land and David from conquering his enemies and rebuilding the temple in Jerusalem. Neither Moses nor David was fit to be the savior.

Jesus' virgin birth is symbolic of birth into the world independent of Adam's biological baggage, to be "born of the Spirit" while also being born of the flesh in the temporal world. God brought himself into the world as an avatar that would be perceptible to the human senses, but without the blindness to eternity that original sin created.

Jesus as symbolized in the Bible was the only mortal born with the God-self fully exposed in human form. He bypassed Adam's Fall, came into mortal life still at one with God, the Word in touch with the Source, fully awakened, yet also in touch with the sorrows of the physical world. Through his life in the flesh he showed us how to reconnect with God, how we may be born again into the same awakened state, born into our own eternal life – he showed us the *Way*. Original sin is washed away in awakening to the *Truth*, and the Garden of Eden, symbolically the place of eternal *Life*, is reentered. We move from unconsciousness to self-consciousness to God-consciousness.

[viii] The same Greek word (πνεῦμα pneuma) means both wind and spirit.

When Adam disobeyed God and was kicked out of the Garden, the connections between the seven chakras were severed. The three temporal lower chakras were cut off from the three spiritual upper chakras, and Man was cut off from God. Normally we enter life at the 1st chakra and gradually empower the lower temporal chakras as we grow. But with the virgin birth Jesus entered life at the 4th chakra, the heart chakra where love enters, where the Buddha touches the earth, and through the power of love reconnected all the chakras.

> "No one has ascended into heaven but he who descended from heaven, the Son of man. And as Moses lifted up the serpent in the wilderness, so must the Son of man be lifted up, that whoever believes in him may have eternal life." (John 3:13-15 RSV)

Moses lifted up the serpent so that people may have temporal life. (Numbers 21:4-9) The Son of man was lifted up on his cross of sacrifice so that people may have eternal life and awaken to the God within them, the part of them which descended from heaven and thus may ascend to heaven. Those who do not awaken are doomed to temporal rebirth, reincarnation, spinning their wheels on earth until they, too, finally awaken to the Way and the Truth and the Life.

Another strange and wonderful paradox: At the two extremes of spiritual consciousness, there is no sin. When one is totally unconscious and simply acting in accordance with and in response to one's intrinsic nature, there is no sin, only the natural processes of life. This was Adam's condition, like that of the animals, before the Fall. At the other end of the spiritual spectrum, in the light of divine love where all is again surrendered to God, there is also no sin. I have written many times about this place where there is no right or wrong, all sin washed away in the ultimate forgiveness – or irrelevance of forgiveness – of divine love.

The virgin birth, the bread and wine of communion, the resurrection, original sin, and the miracles of the Bible are symbols meant to lead us to a mythology that teaches more than literal history can. It doesn't matter if the stories in the Bible actually happened. All that matters is that we understand the messages that those stories carry.

> The content of our obedience—the thing we are commanded to do—will always be something intrinsically good, something we ought to do even if (by an impossible supposition) God had not commanded it. But in addition to the content, the mere obeying is also intrinsically good, for, in obeying, a rational creature consciously enacts its creaturely role, reverses the act by which we fell, treads Adam's dance backward, and returns. – C.S. Lewis, *The Problem of Pain* [56]

~ 841 ~

Emily is virtually gone. I last received a report on her activities two weeks ago. The last conversation of any substance was almost two months ago. I feel like the good shepherd still looking for my one lost sheep. I search for her in the ether of life and in the collective unconscious, but she will not show herself. Is it time for me to shake her dust from my feet? My sorrow is huge, but I can never stop trying to find her; I will be forever listening for her bleat in the darkness.

It is so hard to describe the love that has led me to this place of absolute devotion to someone who cannot even begin to understand what that means. My sadness is not about loneliness for her or for what she does for me; she is rarely fun or pleasant to be with, and she has done almost nothing for me in the worldly sense. My life is much more peaceful and settled without her. Yet I grieve because her tortured soul remains tortured, still and perhaps always beyond the reach of my divine love, which continues to emanate to her like a lighthouse beacon cast out onto the vast, dark ocean. If someday she comes back into the range of my beacon, my light will be there, still shining, to welcome her back.

~ 842 ~

I am the true vine, and my Father is the vinedresser. Every branch of mine that bears no fruit, he takes away, and every branch that does bear fruit he prunes, that it may bear more fruit. You are already made clean by the word which I have spoken to you. Abide in me, and I in you. As the branch cannot bear fruit by itself, unless it abides in the vine, neither can you, unless you abide in me. I am the vine, you are the branches. He who abides in me, and I in him, he it is that bears much fruit, for apart from me you can do nothing. If a man does not abide in me, he is cast forth as a branch and withers; and the branches are gathered, thrown into the fire and burned. If you abide in me, and my words abide in you, ask whatever you will, and it shall be done for you. By this my Father is glorified, that you bear much fruit, and so prove to be my disciples. (John 15:1-8 RSV)

A pruned vine blooms more ardently because it thinks it is dying, the pruning inflicting mortal wounds, and its biology directs it to put all its energy into one last burst of reproductive flowering and fruiting. But the vine is not dying; as long as it remains connected to its root (in the Biblical metaphor, Jesus), the leaves, flowers, and fruits will return. It will be reborn. Thus the one who is wounded and appears to be dead arises to bear new fruit in even greater abundance.

The pruning of Jesus was the pruning of the Tree of Eternal Life. In his total submission to evil, Jesus opened the portal of love, enabling the interdependent co-arising of divine love in equal force to evil born of desire and fear. He opened the Way back into the Garden.

"Greater love has no man than this, that a man lay down his life for his friends." (John 15:13 RSV) Jesus' death on the cross demonstrated that we must not just lay down our life, but must do so in pain and hardship, rejected and alone, in total surrender, without resisting the forces that would wound or kill us. Not with a quick bullet in the head or peacefully in one's sleep, unless those ends come as the fulfillment of suffering, physical or emotional. We must be pruned.

I was pruned to within an inch of my life by Lou's death, and again by The Unnamed One, and now by Emily. My music, my writing, and my life of service are the abundant fruit of my pruning.

~ 843 ~

SIN, Part 2

> If we say we have no sin, we deceive ourselves, and the truth is not in us. If we confess our sins, he is faithful and just, and will forgive our sins and cleanse us from all unrighteousness. If we say we have not sinned, we make him a liar, and his word is not in us. (1 John 1:8-10 RSV)

At the beginning of the church service the congregation prays, "We confess that we are captive to sin and cannot free ourselves. Forgive us, renew us, and lead us, so that we may delight in your will and walk in your ways, to the glory of your holy name. Amen."

Confessing our sin is acknowledging that we embody both sides of duality. Forgiveness of sin is really the recognition that the acts we call sins are just the unavoidable yin/yang of duality – we can't have pleasure without pain, good without evil, or the law without sin.

> No one born of God commits sin; for God's nature abides in him, and he cannot sin because he is born of God. By this it may be seen who are the children of God, and who are the children of the devil: whoever does not do right is not of God, nor he who does not love his brother. (1 John 3:9-10 RSV)

There is a subtle but crucial difference between saying, as in 1 John 1 above, "We have no sin," and saying, as in 1 John 3, "No one born of God commits sin." The former is prideful denial of interdependent co-arising in duality; the latter is awakened recognition of eternity – the hallmark of being born again of the spirit.

When we completely surrender our worldly cares to God, let go of everything – as Jesus did, surrendering all his possessions, health, happiness, dignity, and ultimately his life – we are freed from sin and born again. The divine love that emerges out of this surrender enables us to unconditionally love ourselves, our brother, and our enemies. It frees us from desire, fear, and sin.

"And why are you anxious about clothing? Consider the lilies of the field, how they grow; they neither toil nor spin; yet I tell you, even Solomon in all his glory was not arrayed like one of these." (Matthew 6:28-29 RSV) Jesus asks us to surrender in a peaceful state of trust. In Buddhism, this trusting surrender is called "unsupported thought." In Islam, it is called "Islam."

~ 844 ~

GOOD AND EVIL, Part 3

> I hate, I despise your feasts,
>   and I take no delight in your solemn assemblies.
> Even though you offer me your burnt offerings and cereal offerings,
>   I will not accept them,
> and the peace offerings of your fatted beasts
>   I will not look upon.
> Take away from me the noise of your songs;
>   to the melody of your harps I will not listen.
> But let justice roll down like waters,
>   and righteousness like an everflowing stream.
>
>   (Amos 5:21-24 RSV)

As Jesus said to the Pharisees, "Woe to you, scribes and Pharisees, hypocrites! For you are like whitewashed tombs, which outwardly appear beautiful, but within they are full of dead men's bones and all uncleanness. So you also outwardly appear righteous to men, but within you are full of hypocrisy and iniquity." (Matthew 23:27-28 RSV) Rituals, offerings, and songs of praise are meaningless without justice and righteousness behind them.

What is justice? Righteousness? What appears to be a sin to one person might be another person's justice. The Buddhists do not condemn evil; they learn to live with it, deflecting unskilled behavior, not trying to stop it. Jesus said, "Resist not evil" and "Judge not, lest ye be judged." The poor are always with us, and so is evil. In the meaning of interdependent co-arising, good and evil are inextricably linked – evil cannot be destroyed without destroying good with it.

Jesus introduced this idea, a Christian perspective of interdependent co-arising, in "The Parable of Weeds among the Wheat:"

> Another parable he put before them, saying, "The kingdom of heaven may be compared to a man who sowed good seed in his field; but while men were sleeping, his enemy came and sowed weeds among the wheat, and went away. So when the plants came up and bore grain, then the weeds appeared also. And the servants of the householder came and said to him, 'Sir, did you not sow good seed in your field? How then has it weeds?' He said to them, 'An enemy has done this.' The servants said to him, 'Then do you want us to go and gather them?' But he said, 'No; lest in gathering the weeds you root up the wheat along with them. Let both grow together until the harvest; and at harvest time I will tell the reapers, Gather the weeds first and bind them in bundles to be burned, but gather the wheat into my barn.'" (Matthew 13:24-30 RSV)

The kingdom of heaven, like nirvana, allows both sides of duality to arise in the field of earth, knowing that trying to remove the evil weeds risks removing the good wheat as well.

> Then he left the crowds and went into the house. And his disciples came to him, saying, "Explain to us the parable of the weeds of the field." He answered, "He who sows the good seed is the Son of man; the field is the world, and the good seed means the sons of the kingdom; the weeds are the sons of the evil one, and the enemy who sowed them is the devil; the harvest is the close of the age, and the reapers are angels. Just as the weeds are gathered and burned with fire, so will it be at the close of the age. The Son of man will send his angels, and they will gather out of his kingdom all causes of sin and all evildoers, and throw them into the furnace of fire; there men will weep and gnash their teeth. Then the righteous will shine like the sun in the kingdom of their Father. He who has ears, let him hear. (Matthew 13:36-43 RSV)

The Parable of Weeds among the Wheat takes place in the field of duality. The close of the age is not the final resurrection – the H_2O iceberg melting into the ocean. It is the close of one segment of time, one age, in the endless expanse of time and space – the NaCl salt doll melting into the ocean. It is the soul resurrected to a waystation between incarnations. We know this because in the parable, the separation of heaven and hell, good and evil, is maintained. The angels enforce the law of karma, reaping what was sown – gathering the weeds and sending them to burn in the lower realms, and gathering the wheat to be reborn at a higher spiritual elevation.

At the last harvest into timeless eternity, *anuttara samyak sambodhi*, both the wheat and the weeds, the righteous and the evildoers, are gathered up together and unified in the empty singularity that is not God, but Godhead.[ix] Because duality and eternity are always together, one inside the other, both the separation and the unity are always now, in the present moment.

In divine love there is no law and no sin, no target to miss. In complete surrender, all thoughts, words, and deeds arise unobstructed, unimpeded, from the love that is God, as waters naturally bubble up from a spring, or as Amos put it, "roll down ... like an everflowing stream." There is no questioning, uncertainty, or confusion.

Even acts we usually call sins can be from God. Emily's acts of cruelty would be called sins by any worldly definition, but they were just what I needed in my life to bring me to a place of deeper understanding. Rev. Frederick Douglass said, "Those who profess to favor freedom, yet deprecate agitation, are those who want crops without plowing up the ground, and want rain without thunder and lightning." God created all things – the rain, and also the thunder and lightning. The wheat and the weeds. Jesus and Satan. The tempted and the tempter. The tortured and the torturer. Evil is part of God's plan. Somebody had to be Judas.

~ 845 ~

Emily's communications are fewer and farther between, texts only, containing minimum information. She no longer informs me about any aspect of her life. She has gotten everything she needs from me, so I am disposable. It seems I am just an annoyance now, a lingering vestige of her past that she barely tolerates.

My heart breaks for her, that she is still blinded by her pain and continues to impulsively grasp at illusions. And my heart breaks for me – I am still struggling with Mara. The temptation that haunts me is not Emily's seduction, the lure of physical delights in this life, but the vision I have of our perfect love in the spirit being brought to life on earth. Having known the full realization of divine love on earth with Lou, I know how it feels, and I can be sure that this is the Siren song calling to me, the call that I must resist if I am to walk the Middle Way. I must let go of all desires, even now this one: the desire for the earthly fulfillment of

---

[ix] "Godhead" is a term first used in Christianity by the English theologian John Wycliffe to describe the ultimate deity, the Source, the fusion of the Holy Trinity into the one and indivisible God. The term Godhead was later adopted and used by other writers to differentiate the singular eternal Source from the many worldly representations of God in scripture and other religious writings. In Jewish mystical thought (Kabbalah), the term "Godhead" usually refers to the concept of Ein Sof (אין סוף), the aspect of God that lies beyond the emanations (sefirot). "Of God as He is in Himself—Ein Sof—nothing can be said at all, and no thought can reach there." – *Wikipedia*

God's love. *Anutpattica dharma shanti* – forbearance in unarisen phenomena. Patience. No comfort for me, no *satori*, no tantric joy, only St. Francis' "perfect joy."

~ 846 ~

Ignacio introduced me to the poet Hadewijch of Antwerp, a 13th century Christian mystic who was associated with the Beguines, a religious community of women in what is now Belgium. She was a contemporary of St. Francis of Assisi, and like him, was inspired by the courtly love poetry of the era. I feel a tremendous affinity for her writing; our mystic souls understand divine love the same way. Although she writes from the Christian perspective, her poems often have a Buddhist flavor, like Zen poetry:

> You who want
> knowledge,
> seek the Oneness
> within.
>
> There you
> will find
> the clear mirror
> already waiting.

This poem describes divine love exactly as I know it:

TO LIVE OUT WHAT I AM

My distress is great and unknown to men.
They are cruel to me, for they wish to dissuade me
From all that the forces of Love urge me to.
They do not understand it, and I cannot explain it to them.
I must then live out what I am;
What love counsels my spirit,
In this is my being: for this reason I will do my best.
Whatever vicissitudes men lead me through for Love's sake
I wish to stand firm and take no harm from them.
For I understand from the nobility of my soul
That in suffering for sublime Love, I conquer.
I will therefore gladly surrender myself
In pain, in repose, in dying, in living,
For I know the command of lofty fidelity.

I do not complain of suffering for Love:
It becomes me always to submit to her,
Whether she commands in storm or in stillness.
One can know her only in herself.
This is an unconceivable wonder,
Which has thus filled my heart
And makes me stray in a wild desert.

Men tend to think from the lower chakras, in terms of survival, sex, and power. Male energy is active, physical, aggressive, reflective of the conscious mind. Female energy is passive, intuitive, receptive, reflective of the unconscious. Hadewijch describes Love as feminine because it is the female energy that opens the 4th chakra, where the God-self is awakened and divine love arises into consciousness, bringing the lower physical chakras into alignment with the upper spiritual chakras. I think this is why there are so many female mystics.

All mystics, whether male or female, are people in whom masculine and feminine aspects are equally balanced. Thus, I think all mystics are essentially bisexual. This is not about sexual orientation; it means that divine love is oblivious to gender; sexual identity and orientation are irrelevant. For this reason the images of many Hindu and Buddhist deities are sexually ambiguous. We love souls, and it matters not the sex of the body that houses them.

~ 847 ~

PRIDE AND THE EGO, Part 2

Cecilia said she doesn't believe that she is God. An aspect of God, perhaps, but not the whole thing. She feels that to consider oneself to be God is dangerous, prideful. She is up against some big guns arguing against her on this, not just Wayne Dyer and Deepak Chopra, but the ancient Meister Eckhart, too:

The eye through which I see God is the same eye through which God sees me; my eye and God's eye are one eye, one seeing, one knowing, one love.

I AM can be spoken by no creature, but by God alone. I must become God and God must become me, so completely that we share the same "I" eternally. Our truest "I" is God.

God enters into you with all that is his, as far as you have stripped yourself of yourself in all things. It is here that you should begin, whatever the cost, for it is here that you will find true peace, and nowhere else.

"... as far as you have stripped yourself of yourself in all things." This is key; the ego must be stripped away if the God-self is to be released. Poverty, chastity, and obedience – unsupported thought – is stripping yourself of yourself. All worldly trappings of fear and desire must be cast off before the seed in us that is God can sprout and bloom. Stripping yourself of yourself is the prerequisite to awakening the God-self, and protects against pridefulness in knowing yourself to be God.

Divine love is not something that is added or brought into life. It is there all along, revealed when all the obfuscation and obstacles are removed, all fears and desires given up. Divine love is what is left, uncovered at the bottom of the pile. The gold Buddha under the clay façade.

Ignacio cast another light on this subject with his study of the Book of Amos. Amos asked God not to send judgments of locusts and fire against Israel, and the Lord repented. "It shall not be," said the Lord. Ignacio pointed out that God gets angry and then repents; God admits he makes mistakes and then makes covenants with Man promising not to punish in the same way again. Then Ignacio said, "I don't believe that God is omnipotent, all-powerful, or almighty. We have power, too. God doesn't have all of it."

God does indeed share power with us and all the other separate aspects of God as we know them in the temporal world. God allowed Amos to advise him, and so shared power with him. However, at the same time, all of us, along with all things not of us, are inextricably connected in eternity and together create the singularity of God (Godhead), which *is* omnipotent, as well as omniscient, omnipresent, omnifarious – omni-everything – because it *is* everything (and nothing – the emptiness, the Great Void). Ancient scholars described God as "an infinite sphere whose center is everywhere and whose circumference is nowhere." [x] The center of that singularity which is God is each of us.

In eternity we don't just share power with God; our eternal God-self has all of it. In Amos, the angry, judgmental god and the repentant, merciful god are dual aspects of the same singular eternal God, and Amos himself, sharing in God's power, is a temporal manifestation of that selfsame singularity.

Just as the DNA of each cell in our body contains all the genes necessary to create the complete organism, so our God-self contains not just a piece of God, but the whole of God. As some of the genes in a specialized, differentiated cell are activated and other are not to enable the cell to perform a specific function, so some aspects of our God-self are active

---

[x] The Buddha had a strikingly similar description of nirvana: "a beam of light that lands nowhere."

while others are dormant to enable us to fulfill our unique temporal role in the eternal singularity of God.[xi]

> You are not just a drop in the ocean; you are the mighty ocean in the drop.
>
> – Rumi

~ 848 ~

SEX, Part 24

My sexuality has returned to the black-and-white hue of a mere biological urge; the Technicolor tantric sex once awakened in me again slumbers. Tears now follow sex, as they did after Lou died, in remembrance of the time when divine love was awake in life, in body and spirit, when time and eternity were together as one in consciousness and unconsciousness, in the reality that comes in dreams and in the dream that is the reality of life. Now they are separate again.

~ 849 ~

Today is the anniversary of Lou's death. I mentioned this to Emily. A little while later she texted that her brother had just died. I wonder, would she lie about a thing like that?

~ 850 ~

CHEAP GRACE

> Cheap grace is the grace we bestow on ourselves. Cheap grace is the preaching of forgiveness without requiring repentance, baptism without church discipline, communion without confession ... Cheap grace is grace without discipleship, grace without the cross, grace without Jesus Christ, living and incarnate." – Dietrich Bonhoeffer, *The Cost of Discipleship* [51]

Cheap grace is pretending we're sorry, doing some painless penance, and then going on with our unawakened life as it was, blinders of denial and delusion securely fastened. The salvation that Jesus purchased for us on the cross does not come so cheap. Jesus' sacrifice

---

[xi] Compare C.S. Lewis on Jesus the implicit poet. (~668~)

can only save us if we choose costly grace – to accept the life of Christ for ourselves, with the necessary dishonorable suffering that Bonhoeffer described. (~770~) Jesus opened the door to salvation by showing us the Way; it is up to us to walk through the door, even knowing that trials and tribulations await us.

Ignacio says that, in the Judeo-Christian prophetic tradition, prophets are the conscience of society. They have hindsight, insight, and foresight. Prophets were often pariahs in their own country and were not liked very much by the priests, who were usually criticized by the prophets, as Jesus criticized the Pharisees. Is my truth-telling, with all its dangers and punishments, a kind of prophecy?

PART 37

Hopeless

May 2015 – July 2015

~ 851 ~

I still have more to let go. I must give up *every last desire* – even my desire to see the end of Emily's pain, and also my desire to be an agent to that end. I must not be tempted by anything that attracts me to her – not even her deep psychic pain that drew me into her and that I presumed I was sent to assuage. When I can still love her unconditionally and devote my life to her service without the least expectation of personal satisfaction, without the faintest hope that she might in fact be healed, or even the hope that I might reach the place in her where such healing might be effected, then I will know perfect joy.

This is what Bonhoeffer meant when he called hope the last temptation. Hope is desire. Until I have given up every last vestige of hope – hope for myself, for Emily, for world peace, for anything – I have not completely surrendered. There is still a tiny speck of my ego, my independent will, remaining. The final liberation can only come when I am absolutely helpless and hopeless, completely at the mercy of the forces around me, in total submission to them like the plankton drifting in the sea.

Jesus' prayer in Gethsemane keeps coming back to haunt me. I think it was the most important thing that happened during Jesus' last day on earth, in terms of what he had to teach us. Jesus fell victim to the last temptation – hope. He hoped that God would spare him the horrible end that he knew was coming, and he prayed his desperately hopeful prayer. Then, when he let go of hope and said, "Thy will be done," he was finally hopeless, free from all desire, finally ready to die in total surrender to God. With this prayer Jesus showed us the final step of the Way, the final Truth, and opened the door to eternal Life. Hope is the last thing to be given up before life itself. I think Bonhoeffer understood this perfectly as he walked naked to the gallows.

It is true that where there's life, there's hope. As long as I live, hope will arise in me. I must treat hope, like all desires and aversions, as a temptation to be faced down. Accept hopefulness, but also accept that your hopes will be dashed. The best life is one that can be helpless, hopeless ... and happy. I am not quite there yet, but with this realization I can feel my grief beginning to lift.

> Hope is patience with the lamp lit.
> – Tertullian

To give up hope is to remain patient, peaceful, and trusting in God even when the lamp goes out. At the beginning of this journal I wrote, "This is the real fruit of wisdom – finding peace in the bonds of injustice and in the absence of hope." (~27~) After a quarter-century I find myself back where I started.

~ 852 ~

GOD IN A BOX

Kathy has God in a little box. She knows the limited God that is presented to her by the narrow-minded Christian church she attends. She is part of the recent trend toward contemporary non-denominational evangelical Christianity. Although their style of worship has broken away from the older traditional forms, their theology harks back to a fear-based Puritanical view of God and scripture that is confining, judgmental, repressive, and even hateful.

Although the Christian church I attend harks back to the older liturgical church in the rituals they observe, my more open-minded friends there have a much larger box for God. God is still in a box, though, still viewed in an anthropomorphic way through the limiting lens of scripture. Among these people, however, there is a tolerance, even a thirst, for alternative interpretations of scripture that let God out of the box. They recognize ideas from other religions, science, art, and philosophy which allow them to poke some air holes in the God box.

I am not a formal member of any church because I cannot put God into any box. My Christianity goes back to a time even before the liturgical Church, to a time when Jesus was still the Word, not yet flesh. "In the beginning was the Word, and the Word was with God, and the Word was God." (John 1:1 RSV) My view of God and Jesus are the same view – the unborn Jesus as the Word with God, and the resurrected Jesus sitting at the right hand of God. These "before" and "after" conditions exist simultaneously in the Now, the eternal present – just as past, present, and future are one in God.

The Holy Spirit that came to the disciples at Pentecost is the bridge that connects the temporal world and the body of Christ to eternity and the disembodied risen Christ. It is the thread that connects my life on earth to my life in eternity and allows me to straddle the razor's edge of the Middle Way where those realms meet. The symbol for the Holy Spirit is fire, the flame. Hence my affinity for the fire gods. Their flame abides in me.

~ 853 ~

In religion, as in war and everything else, comfort is the one thing you cannot get by looking for it. If you look for truth, you may find comfort in the end: if you look for comfort you will not get either comfort or truth—only soft soap and wishful thinking to begin with and, in the end, despair. – C.S. Lewis, *Mere Christianity* [76]

Anthony de Mello said that no patient wants a cure, all he wants is relief. A cure often hurts. In the same sense, people come to God and religion for comfort and relief – not for truth, salvation, or enlightenment. The road to salvation is full of pain, without relief.

I gave Emily the relief she wanted; now she backs away from my cure.

~ 854 ~

I spent yesterday working at a memorial observance presented by my Buddhist sangha. People attending this event remember their deceased loved ones by writing notes to them, which are then prayed over and burned in a ritual fire. I volunteered to help at the tables where people come to write their messages to the deceased. I was randomly assigned to Table #44. There's my Angel Number 4 again.

A big, angry, mean-looking guy in a black leather jacket and intimidating jewelry came to my table. I went over to him and, as I did with everyone, asked him if he had questions or needed any help. He appeared to be very upset and said, "I just called the cops on a guy. Nobody messes with me!" In his rambling muttering I couldn't quite tell what had happened to cause the altercation. I just said that I was sorry about his distress and hoped that by writing his memorial messages he might find peace.

I checked on him a few minutes later. He was much calmer, and began talking about his two deceased brothers, for whom he was offering his remembrance. He described how his brothers had helped him when he got into trouble, and cared for him when he was injured.

Underneath his rough, gruff exterior there was a sensitive soul who was able to find expression with me in the context of remembering his loss. As he left, he thanked me and gave me a warm hug. "Goodbye, my friend," I said.

~ 855 ~

Yesterday I mailed a check to my friend Josie who has been helping me in my spiritual quest. Why the check, why the large amount, why now? I didn't really know. In an email to her I wrote, "I will be sending you a check in the mail soon. It is not payment for services rendered. It is much more than that."

Today I got a reply from Josie saying,

> *Shortly after our last meeting, I found out about my son's long-term yet well-hidden challenge with drugs. His life expectancy was less than six months. Now for the good news: My son is much, much better. He is off drugs, employed and rebuilding his life. In fact, he is arriving for a visit with us tomorrow and that is a great victory for all of us.*

I wrote back:

> Thank you so much for telling me your story. Now I know why I sent you the check. This is yet another fascinating part of my spiritual journey. Occasionally a little voice tells me to send some money here, or there, for no apparent reason.
>
> I put money out into the universe. Often I don't know why I am doing it. I find out the reason after the deed is done. I knew that the real reason for my sending you money was not to compensate you for anything; I trusted that eventually the real reason would be made known to me. And within twenty-four hours, it was. This is the fourth or fifth time this has happened. The timing of everything is perfect.

~ 856 ~

Emily called. Our first serious conversation in over two months. She was reluctant to speak at first, but then she admitted she is depressed and wants to go traveling with me – to Colombia, then Asia, all around the world. She is just as messed up as before, maybe worse. Now that her financial situation is better since the house sale and the pressure to generate income is off, I am concerned that she has lost her mental and emotional grounding. Her thoughts and feelings are even more scattered and unfocussed, out of touch with reality, and her fragile psyche is slipping ever deeper into darkness. Nevertheless, my spiritual connection to her is unchanged. There is a mystical portal that always opens with her that is otherwise closed. I am swept through it before I know what happened.

~ 857 ~

SIN, Part 3

I am on an email list that sends me periodic excerpts from the book *Beyond Boundaries*[57] by Dr. Henry Cloud and Dr. John Townsend. Today's message was titled, "What Does It Mean for a Christian to be Free?" It contained what is perhaps the best practical exposition I have read on the nature of Mosaic Law, sin, and salvation:

> Under the Law: In God's grace, the law is intended to be a standard by which to evaluate ourselves. It helps us to see where we need to change.

There it is! The target that sin missed. Jesus took away the target, and with it, sin.

> There are at least five major consequences when we put ourselves under the law:
>
> 1. **Wrath**. God is angry at offenses against him; it is part of his legal system, the law. That is why we need Jesus, the one who takes his wrath away (Romans 4:15). But if we put ourselves under the law, we will be angry at God and ourselves.
>
> 2. **Condemnation**. We feel guilty and condemned if we do not do what we should. Yet we have been cleansed "once for all by [Christ's] own blood" (Hebrews 9:12).
>
> 3. **Separation from love**. If we feel unloved when we do not do as we should, we are still under the law. God loved us while we were his "enemies" (Romans 5:10), before we were interested in doing as we should. Nothing we do can separate us from the love of Christ (Romans 8:35-39). If we feel separated from God after trusting Jesus, we have put ourselves back under the law.

Jesus liberates us from the temporal anthropomorphic God and awakens us to the eternal God that is beyond wrath, judgment, sin, and condemnation. We are all avatars of God, perfect just as we are, no matter what we do, and so are unconditionally loved. In the temporal world we see things as separate, good separate from evil, and therefore it is possible to seem separated from love and from God. Christ showed us the love in eternity from which we can never be separated.

4. **Sin increases**. If we feel we should do certain things because punishment awaits us if we don't, we have not "died to the law" (Romans 7:4)—and the law will have power over us. "The law was brought in so that the trespass might increase" (Romans 5:20). In other words, the very method by which we are trying to change will produce failure. The more condemning voices we have inside, the harder it is to change a problem. Ask any addict.

Opposites arise by mutual consent. I don't know if these Christian authors knew they were doing it, but they perfectly described the Buddhist principle of interdependent co-arising.

Before the law, there was no sin. Sin was created with the law. (Romans 7:7-8) When Jesus set aside the law, he also set aside sin. "For the law of the Spirit of life in Christ Jesus has set me free from the law of sin and death." (Romans 8:2 RSV) As one side of the pairs of opposites arises, so does the other. When Adam acquired the knowledge of good and evil, both arose. When Jesus died, both imploded back into emptiness. For those who awoke to what was happening, those born again of the spirit who accepted grace and died to sin, the pendulum of life stopped in the middle between the opposites. Neither side of dualism, neither the law nor sin, had any power anymore.

Nothing changed about temporality when Adam ate of the Tree of the Knowledge of Good and Evil; the only thing that changed was Adam's knowledge of it. He had been coveting all along in the Garden with God, but he didn't know it, because in the oneness of eternity coveting was perfectly balanced and canceled out by not coveting.

5. **No benefit**. Whenever we do something because we feel we should or because we think we have to, it is of no benefit because our motivation is not love (1 Corinthians 13:1-3; 2 Corinthians 9:7). Only when we are free can we love freely.

In divine love, there is no "should" or "have to." Everything just "is." There is no thinking about it or weighing options. Whatever we do from the motivation of love, from our God-self, is spontaneous and automatically right.

The Bible's response to total freedom is a refusal to continue to live in destructive ways (Romans 6:1-4). "By dying to what once bound us, we have been released from the law" and can now live "in the new way of the Spirit" (Romans 7:6). The Bible teaches that there are two paths—one that works and one that doesn't. Both are reality: "The mind governed by the flesh is death, but the mind governed by the Spirit is life and peace" (Romans 8:6).

Yes, living in destructive ways ends, but it is not a matter of conscious refusal. Destructive behaviors end automatically, not by choice, but by the power of love. The "mind governed by the flesh" (that is, the mind governed by temporal sensory perceptions and mental formations) is overridden by the "mind governed by the Spirit" (that is, the mind governed by divine love).

> We are free to love and choose healthy ways of living. We do not have to love God or anyone else (see Joshua 24:15). But by looking in the mirror of God's law, we realize that if we do not choose love, our lives will be empty.

We do have a choice to accept God's love, salvation, and reconciliation. But in choosing love we must also choose the suffering that comes with it. We must accept the life of Christ and bear his cross, and do it joyfully. Once this choice has been made and all is surrendered to God, there are no more choices to be made. Healthy ways of living, of being, arise of their own accord.

This is not to say that spirit-filled beings are never presented with choices. Indeed, even those living fully in the spirit will encounter many forks in the road and multiple options to consider as they journey through life, but one fork or option will always stand out as the clear, shining path of divine love that must be taken. God operates the switch that directs our train onto the right karmic track, and blows the divine wind that sweeps us through the House of Eternity.

> In relation to others, when we love them we give them total freedom as God gives us. We accept others, "just as Christ accepted [us]" (Romans 15:7). When they fail to love us or choose not to love us, we do not withdraw our love from them. We may confront them or express our sadness about their choice, but we do not condemn them.

This describes my total acceptance and unending love for all who have come and gone in my life, even those who have done me harm. My sadness comes not from the harm that was done to me, but from their turning away the love of God that the angel in the spaceship brought to them – as God, who "so loved the world that he gave his only Son," grieves over those who do not accept his gift.

> Guilt says, "I should be different and if I'm not, then I'm bad," so we get defensive. Grace says, "I see the standard and I'm not measuring up. I need help and love to change so that I can live."

I will go one step farther, beyond guilt and grace to enlightenment. In recognizing oneself as love itself, you say, "I no longer see the standard and there is nothing to measure up to. Nothing needs to change; I live now in the spirit." At this point there is no sin, no vice or virtue; all of the pairs of opposites have melted back into the oneness of God from which they came.

The eternal cannot change. It's not touched by time. As soon as you have a historical act, a movement, you're in time. The world of time is a reflex of the energy of what is eternal. But the eternal is not touched by what is here. So the whole doctrine of sin is a false doctrine. It has to do with time. Your eternal character is not touched. You are redeemed. – Joseph Campbell[40]

~ 858 ~

THOU SHALT NOT KILL ... or KILL OR BE KILLED?

Both the Buddhists and the Judeo-Christians have a rule that says it is wrong to kill. Neither religion allows for any exceptions to that rule, at least as it applies to human beings. As a moral absolute, the rule says that killing is never morally justified, not even in defense. And yet, no sooner had Moses brought the Ten Commandments down from Sinai than the Israelites set out to kill the Canaanites and others who had taken over their Promised Land.

The Christians were no better than the Jews at following the rule. The Crusades, burning heretics at the stake, and wars waged in the name of God all over the world have made shameless murderers out of millions of Christians. And alas, although we think of Buddhism as a peaceful religion, one of the Five Precepts being against killing, Buddhists have done their share of killing, too. Some of the fiercest and most efficient killers in the world were the Zen samurai of Japan. Where Buddhism is associated with national identity, as in Thailand, Sri Lanka, and Myanmar, Buddhists have sometimes openly abandoned the nonviolent teachings of the Buddha in service to their view of the national interest.

Jesus taught us to turn the other cheek, and the Buddha taught us the 3rd Perfection of patience and forbearance. Their lives and the lives of their disciples demonstrated how absolute non-violence virtuously plays out, even in hopeless situations where the adversary has no conscience and the only possible end is death. The death of martyrs, while appearing to be a defeat in the short term, often proves to be a long-term victory, the power of divine love eventually prevailing.

But is that how we are all supposed to live our lives? Monastics and highly elevated spiritual practitioners without family or social responsibilities can allow themselves to be swept into the evil maelstrom and remain nonviolent all the way to the limitation in death, as Jesus did. But for those of us who live in connection with others, our mission to serve each other and the common good often calls us to arms. Is there no circumstance in which defensive killing can be defended?

While the basic teachings of Buddhism do not address this question, the *Sutra on the Range of a Bodhisattva* holds that a ruler may use arms to defend his kingdom and protect his people, but he may only use as much force as is necessary to expel invaders. Once they are expelled, he must not seek to punish the invaders but instead try to make peace with them. This sutra provides a pragmatic bridge between the eternal absolute and the many relative choices we must make in worldly life.

In this context, killing can be justified if it is absolutely necessary and purely defensive, not an act of aggression, conquest, or imperialism, and if one's personal motivations are pure, to further the common good, not self-serving interests. By violating the precept in order to defend others, the killer accepts that his defilement, while not producing bad karma, will postpone his awakening to another incarnation. This compromise between non-violence and defensive violence is akin to the choice the bodhisattva makes to forego complete unexcelled awakening – to become a buddha – and instead to be reborn into the world to bring others to the Pure Land.

In his early years, Dietrich Bonhoeffer was an idealist, believing that there could be no exceptions to "Thou shalt not kill." But as he witnessed the horrors arising with the Nazi regime in Germany, he sensed that "Love thy neighbor" had to include defending and protecting thy neighbor, leading to his alleged complicity in an assassination attempt on Hitler's life. Bonhoeffer wrote in *Ethics*, "It is worse to be evil than to do evil." Reflecting on the righteous necessity of breaking the commandment against killing, Bonhoeffer came to a conclusion startingly similar to the Buddhist view, accepting responsibility for the apparently sinful act and the guilt that comes with it. He wrote:

> When a man takes guilt upon himself in responsibility, he imputes his guilt to himself and no one else. He answers for it... Before other men he is justified by dire necessity; before himself he is acquitted by his conscience, but before God he hopes only for grace. – Dietrich Bonhoeffer, *Ethics*

~ 859 ~

I recently attended a film and discussion about Anthony de Mello. The topic de Mello addressed in the film was "Why do people get upset?" He explained that it is not external conditions or events that upset us: "Nothing has the power to upset you. You upset yourself.

We have been trained to be emotionally dependent on people. When they die, we are upset. No one is to blame, not even ourselves. Our programming caused our upset, but we are not blaming our programming; we are understanding it. As a result of understanding it, you are freed from it. You don't have to *do* anything for liberation; just understand." [58] (Stephen Hawking also knew the liberation that comes from understanding: "If you understand how the universe operates, you control it in a way.")

An audience member asked how to handle a confrontation with an upset person. De Mello's response concluded with this statement: "Compassion finds the right time to explain where the upset is coming from." These words went straight to my heart. My compassion for Emily must find the right time to help her understand, or more precisely, awaken to what, deep inside her, she already understands.

~ 860 ~

This morning I received this message from my Buddhist guide: ... *like a clam shell opening ... you have helped someone ... you are on the right path ... continue to nurture this person ... continue doing what you are doing ... share the teaching, your experiences ... Kannon is holding your hand, always guiding you.*

I asked the guide after the session if she had an image of the person I had helped. She asked if there was someone with whom I have a spiritual relationship; the message that was coming through her was definitely about a specific person. She said that this person was like the clam opening its shell, just beginning to open her heart, expose her insides. There was an emphatic message that this is the time for me to go forward with this person. She told me that when her vision of Kannon holding my hand came up, a warm, compassionate feeling came over her. She smiled broadly, and assured me that the spirits are with me in my soul journey with this person.

Last night I had a recurrence of the ache in my lower back and thighs that I reported on two other occasions. (~577~/~738~) I cannot think of any strain or injury that could have caused it. The pain kept waking me up, but disappeared by mid-morning as mysteriously as it had appeared, as in the previous occurrences.

Last year I attributed the pain to a disturbance in the back side of my 2nd chakra: "Small back pains can be symptoms of a second-chakra back side that is not completely open or that is unprotected." [19] At that time I was resigning my job and struggling with Emily's increasing delusion. Not unlike the situation now.

~ 861 ~

The abandonment dream is back, but now it comes to me when I am awake. Emily has left again for Colombia and other points unknown. Our paths barely cross now, our souls connect only in the spiritual ether. Emily is almost gone, a lost soul I cannot find.

My panic came back. Just a little bit – feeling uneasy at the thought of being trapped in a paralyzed body, in a cage, or in chronic pain. Had trouble getting a satisfying breath. Had trouble relaxing into sleep, but finally did get there.

I have experienced an awareness of eternal peace granted to very few, but my body's craving for comfort, and its fear of losing it, continue to override. I can see the arch of the narrow gate, but I am not through it yet.

~ 862 ~

"Said a disciple, 'I don't trade my love for money.' Said the Master, 'Isn't it as bad—or worse—that you trade it for love?'" – Anthony de Mello, *Awakening: Conversations with the Masters*

Anthony de Mello says that the only thing anyone ever needs is "to love." Not to be loved, but to love, to *be* love. When we give up desire, wanting things from people, we discover our true self, our God-self. God is love. We discover our ability to love people exactly the way they are, not for what they could be, or what they could do for us. We love them even if they do not love us back.

Perfect love casts out fear. Where there is love there are no demands, no expectations, no dependency. I do not demand that you make me happy; my happiness does not lie in you. If you were to leave me, I will not feel sorry for myself; I enjoy your company immensely, but I do not cling. – Anthony de Mello, *Awareness*

Tony says that once we give up all our attachments, we discover that we are all alone. Alone in a good way – not dependent on anyone or anything – as I have described it, the solitude of the bodhisattva in unsupported thought.

Happiness cannot be found in things or in people. It can only be found by looking inside. Happiness is what is left after you have released all your attachments and with them, your fear of losing them. This explains why, even in the depths of my despair over Emily, I am strangely happy.

> To be without a reference point is the ultimate loneliness. It is also called enlightenment. – Pema Chödrön, "Six Kinds of Loneliness"

Space is a reference point. Time is a reference point. Eternity is timeless and spaceless. To be enlightened, as Pema says – to *be* love, as de Mello says – to implode into the timeless, spaceless singularity at the speed of light, as Einstein says – to have eternal life, as Jesus says – is to be alone without a reference point ... and be happy.

~ 863 ~

I feel Emily sliding down the slippery slope of delusion, away from my healing love, and I can't help her. I feel my body sliding down the slippery slope of old age, and I can't help that, either. Will we be allowed one last burst of autumn color before the dry leaves fall off the tree?

~ 864 ~

Last night I texted Emily: "I feel you with me tonight. I am holding you, easing your pain."

She responded: "I really wish you would not assume things. It irks me. I am happy and more content than I have been in years."

If her pain wasn't there, she wouldn't be irked. The fact that she is irked by my bringing up her pain rather than grateful for my relieving it is proof of its existence, and proof of her ever-deeper denial of it. It is not what I say that irks her; she irks herself. I don't want to push her into places she doesn't want to go, but her stinging protest against my innocent expression of compassion proves that her pain *does* exist, and the slightest scrape against her protective veneer releases the pain in huge waves. The *asura* doth protest too much.

> I'm not interested in arguing. You either face the fact that your life is in a mess or you don't. If you don't want to face it, I've got nothing to say to you. – Anthony de Mello, "A Rediscovery of Life" [58]

I've got nothing to say to Emily.

~ 865 ~

I used to wonder how so simple an equation as $E=mc^2$ could explain a concept as complicated as Einstein's relativity. And *c squared*! What a huge number, and an impossible one, because nothing can go faster than the speed of light. This must be just a symbolic equation, I thought, not meant to be taken literally.

Scientists used to think that nothing could go faster than the speed of light, that it was the ultimate limit of the universe. Now scientists are considering that it may be possible to go faster than light; in the realms of quantum mechanics and astrophysics, nature may jump beyond the bounds of physical laws and limits.

A while ago I mused about how Einstein's equation and its permutations could serve as a spiritual metaphor bridging time and eternity. (~545~) In the supernatural world, anything goes. The speed of light may be the ultimate limit in space-time, but in the infinitesimal infinity that is eternity, that is God, there are no limits or rules, and any speed is possible. As physical laws and violations thereof are irrelevant at the quantum level, so religious laws and violations thereof (sin) are irrelevant in eternity.

Now, in that infinite eternal realm, I take the equation literally. Einstein's thinking was literally out of this world.

> There is a light within you, it is the lamp of the being of God.
> – St. John of the Cross

> Light is the mystical substance through which the divine travels.
> It is the mystical current of God.
> – Caroline Myss

~ 866 ~

As has happened repeatedly in the course of my spiritual journey, wisdom comes to me just when I need it, in just the right form. In this case it is in the form of Anthony de Mello. He said this about happiness, attachment, and grief:

Happiness is a state of non-attachment. Attachment means unless I get you, I cannot be happy. Love means I'm perfectly happy without you, darling, it's all right. I wish you all good, and I leave you free. When I get you, I'm delighted, but when I don't, I'm not miserable. I've learned to be self-sufficient; I'm not leaning on you. When you go away I don't miss you; I don't feel pain.

When you grieve, who are you grieving for? Whose loss? I wouldn't grieve if I wasn't attached. I wouldn't grieve if in some way you were not my happiness. When I enjoy you wholly, I love you in the sense of "I'm sensitive, I care, it is your good I seek." You are not my happiness, I have not given over to you the power to decide if I will be happy or not, then I do not grieve at your absence or your rejection ... or your death.[58]

Of course I have known these truths for some time, and have expressed them many times in this tome. But Tony, by stripping away all the social niceties, carrying his train of thought all the way to the end and extrapolating truth to the nth degree, has shown me how God's boundless love can be fully expressed by living beings in the bounds of space-time.

He is now causing me to dig deeper into the subject of grief. My grief over losing Lou was clearly from the loss of attachment; he was indeed my happiness. But the loss of The Unnamed One was different. When I felt his disaffection and rejection approaching, the feeling of grief began to arise, but then I said to myself, "Let it go. This was meant to happen." I felt the inevitability of it. This is much like the emotional detachment I felt on several occasions when I was persecuted for my social justice activism. Fight the good fight, but don't fight the tidal wave of life. Ride the wave and see where it takes you. Enjoy the ride – literally, the ride of your life.

I am wondering if my grief over Emily isn't yet another kind of grief, a special kind reserved for bodhisattvas. It is the grief of the tearful angel in the spaceship (~669~), who was sad because the person she was sent to rescue declined the invitation to ride the spaceship to nirvana. My grief over Emily is not about losing her or what she does for me; it is not about desire or dependency. My happiness does not depend on her. My grief is a kind of spiritual PTSD, the torment of watching her soul continuing to suffer, knowing that the divine love I bring could heal her if only she would let it in.

~ 867 ~

For the last couple months I have felt out of touch spiritually. Emily is far away. The tactile and visual sensations of my 5th and 6th chakras that had been strong and frequent are now almost gone. No epiphanies, no provocative dreams, no seismic eruptions, rainbows, gusts of wind, no voices or visions from the great beyond, no animal visitations, no sensory evidence of powerful forces that in the past had given me connection and direction.

Just because I am not consciously aware of these forces doesn't mean they aren't there. The pastor gave me a clue to their continuing presence with his sermon about the woman who was healed by touching Jesus' robe:

> And there was a woman who had had a flow of blood for twelve years, and who had suffered much under many physicians, and had spent all that she had, and was no better but rather grew worse. She had heard the reports about Jesus, and came up behind him in the crowd and touched his garment. For she said, "If I touch even his garments, I shall be made well." And immediately the hemorrhage ceased; and she felt in her body that she was healed of her disease. And Jesus, perceiving in himself that power had gone forth from him, immediately turned about in the crowd, and said, "Who touched my garments?" And his disciples said to him, "You see the crowd pressing around you, and yet you say, 'Who touched me?'" And he looked around to see who had done it. But the woman, knowing what had been done to her, came in fear and trembling and fell down before him, and told him the whole truth. And he said to her, "Daughter, your faith has made you well; go in peace, and be healed of your disease." (Mark 5:25-34 RSV)

The pastor pointed out that Jesus had healed her without intention, without even knowing it, just by being who he was, just by his mere presence. His love, his power, flowed to her without his knowing to whom it went or why. Our faith heals us. No test required, no catechism, no baptism, no confession, no confirmation, not even prayer.

I was reminded of an experience I had in church a couple weeks ago. I came to church late and sat in the closest available seat, next to a first-time visitor to the church. When I arrived she was alone, downcast and quiet, almost sullen. Her hair and clothes were dirty and disheveled. Then, for some unknown reason, she began to tell me her troubles. She had just moved back after many years away, was frustrated with broken things in her apartment, and was having trouble making ends meet. I encouraged her to reach out to the congregation. "There are good people here," I said. "They will help you." She gradually began to soften, seeing a way out of desperation. By the end of the service she had begun to cheer up and was letting in some of God's light and love.

Today I saw her again. Her hair and clothes were clean and neat; she smiled and engaged in conversation with many people around her. She was transformed.

I remembered the angry man at the memorial event last month (~854~) who experienced a similar transformation after relating his upset to me, writing his notes of remembrance for his deceased brothers, and telling me how they had helped him. By the time he left my presence God's love had touched him.

Just by symbolically touching my garments, being in my presence, people seem to find a measure of healing. Martha called me a "wake-up fairy." My calling might not be to effect the final cure, but to open the door to it, to wake people up to the love of God, to let in the first rays of light for those in darkness. To give them a first glimpse of what God's unquestioning, unconditional love looks like on earth, in the flesh.

God's love flows from me to my loved ones, and to complete strangers, often without my knowing it. It also flows *to* me, even when I do not receive the sensory signals heralding its arrival. Even without my knowing it.

~ 868 ~

Last night at Martha's intuitive gathering I made spiritual contact with a toddler. For much of the two-hour session we looked into each other's eyes, intently, relentlessly. Small children have no problem making extended eye contact. No words, only a little smiling. At one point she waved to me, and I waved back. I reported earlier two other occasions (~426~/~611~) when I found powerful nonverbal communion through the eyes of children. In all of these cases no words were spoken.

~ 869 ~

I am seeing a pattern now. Through Lou I was introduced to divine love in full earthly flower. Through him I was awakened to the greatest love and then to the horror of losing its earthly manifestation.

The Unnamed One taught me another lesson – how perfect love manifests imperfectly in someone not fully open to it. Although our divine love was expressed in some ways, it was clouded by his fear, which ultimately prevailed over his love. Through the pain of his disaffection I learned to keep on loving even while being hurt, and to let go, accepting that there was no other choice.

Emily sends me into an even darker place, into another sphere entirely, into a place of extreme delight and extreme pain, where the strength, depth, and tenacity of my divine love is constantly tested, this time with an *asura* so wounded that the light of love can only barely penetrate her darkness. Serious pain has been and continues to be inflicted on me, but if I am winning my battle with Mara, I will continue to love her unconditionally through it all, joyously participate in her suffering, and live in her service.

~ 870 ~

I hate hope. It was hammered into me constantly a few years ago when I was being treated for breast cancer: Think positively! Don't lose hope! ... There is some evidence that the ubiquitous moral injunction to think positively may place an additional burden on the already sick or otherwise aggrieved. Not only are you failing to get better but you're failing to feel *good* about not getting better. Similarly for the long-term unemployed, who are informed by career coaches and self-help books that their principal battle is against their own negative, resentful, loser-like feelings. This is victim-blaming at its cruelest. ... The trick, as my teen hero Camus wrote, is to draw strength from the "refusal to hope, and the unyielding evidence of a life without consolation." To be hope-free is to acknowledge the lion in the tall grass, the tumor in the CAT scan, and to plan one's moves accordingly. – Barbara Ehrenreich, "Pathologies of Hope," *Harper's Magazine*, February 2007

Hope dies last. Letting go of hope is really the end. Not finality in despair or resignation, but in acceptance – finding peace in "a life without consolation," in the presence of pain and the absence of hope. (Note the difference between hope and optimism: ~1358~)

As I give up hope that Emily will find her way to heaven on earth, I live more easily with her in the spirit. Today as I watched a documentary about Colombian music, I envisioned us together there, I teaching the children music while she teaches them English. In my fantasy, we bought a little house near her school and lived there happily ever after. A pleasant summer reverie.

As hope leaves, I feel death enter. It is not an unpleasant feeling; it will be a good death. If my life's work is done, I am ready to go, joyously fulfilled.

~ 871 ~

APOLOGY AND FORGIVENESS, Part 4

When I was a child I had a pet mouse. I loved the mouse and cared for him, but as often happens in a child's life, my attention was diverted into other things for several days and I forgot about the mouse. I neglected him, and by the time I noticed him again, he was near death. I scurried around getting him water and food, cleaning his cage, trying to nurse him back to health, to no avail. The mouse died the next day.

My grief and guilt were overwhelming. I buried him in the backyard and said prayers over him for weeks. I apologized to the mouse and begged his forgiveness. I had learned an important lesson about respect, responsibility, and the suffering that can ensue when those in one's care are neglected, even unwittingly, without meaning any harm. I wonder if my mouse has forgiven me.

My temporal body-mind forgives Emily's neglect of me, but it's not so important. My mouse and I both know that in the spirit there is nothing to forgive. Anthony de Mello said, "If you never condemn, you never need to forgive."

~ 872 ~

For a long time I have wondered why I continue to feel so much emotion – fear, grief, loneliness, hopelessness, helplessness, the nearness of death – from Emily's psychotic behavior. I fear her anger and the tension that it raises up in me, but then I grieve when she pulls away from me. I feel jealousy when she turns her attention and affection toward others. I feel abandoned and vulnerable when she does not return my affection or show concern for my feelings.

I should be immune to all this, knowing as I do the traumatic source of these behaviors and the spiritual truth of our relationship. But rationality and intellectual understanding are not the point. Compassion, suffering with her in the pain she cannot face, is the point.

She has become her mother, and I, her daughter. She flatters, then terrorizes, then abandons me as her mother did to her. I have been feeling the same powerful emotions in response to these behaviors that she must have felt as a young child. I am literally feeling her pain as she visits her mother's pain upon me. It is not my fear I feel; it is hers. I am taking on her negative energy and giving her release from it. This is why she is happy while I writhe in agony.

The ritual life of a bodhisattva, living on earth in human form and simultaneously in the spirit, requires falling off the Middle Way to suffer with the world, first falling to the side of desire, then to the other side of fear, knowing what is happening and understanding the necessity of it, joyously participating in the suffering of the world, and then returning to nirvana to refresh the spirit and polish the mirror. Many times I have felt myself falling and being lifted up again.

~ 873 ~

I am beginning to see the nature of the remaining dust on my mirror. Last night I practically cried myself to sleep over Emily, wanting her to open to my healing love and share my vision of eternal perfection. I was having difficulty accepting that her current condition of repressed pain is where she needs to be right now. I wanted things to be different, better, but for whose sake? She says she is happy and content, and from her conscious perspective, perhaps she is. Who am I to say otherwise?

Even the desire to be helpful, to be an agent for healing and happiness, to serve God and be a vehicle for God's love, is in the end a poison. A passion for peace, joy, healing, and happiness is still a passion. Finding the antidote to that poison, the quieting of that passion, is now my quest.

For many years I have been serving God without thinking about it or even knowing I was doing it. I will continue to do so as God subconsciously directs, without my desire or conscious intention. In fact, a conscious desire to serve God only gets in the way, adding the corrupting element of personal pride to an otherwise pure expression of God's love. A life of service must spring spontaneously from divine love, not from a desire to build merit or curry favor. The Buddha said, "Bodhisattvas do not cling to the merits they generate."

The prayer of St. Francis says, "Lord, make me an instrument of thy peace." As long as we pray this prayer from an eternal perspective, fine. But if this prayer is a wish that we hope will be fulfilled – a desire – we are asking that our will, not God's, be done. In my surrender to God, I open the door to this instrument-of-peace potentiality, but I do not walk through it by my choice; not my desire to serve, but God's assignment to serve, prevails. God's will, not mine, be done. May God's will and mine be one and the same.

As St. Paul so well described in Romans 7:7-8, sin was created by the law. By the principle of interdependent co-arising, the conscious desire to bring healing and happiness to others creates a sin of covetousness in hopeful clinging to the happy state one wishes to bring about. Anthony de Mello, in his depiction of the separation of happiness and love (~866~), makes a similar point. If my happiness comes from bringing happiness to others, I am not really loving them; I am using them as tools to achieve my own happiness.

You're putting on a great act. And you don't even know it. You think you're being so loving. Ha! Whom are you loving? Even your self-sacrifice gives you a good feeling, doesn't it? "I'm sacrificing myself! I'm living up to my ideal." But you're getting something out of it, aren't you? You're always getting something out of everything you do, until you wake up. – Anthony de Mello, *Awareness*

~ 874 ~

There is a war going on inside me. My life in the spirit is waging war with my life in the body. They are fighting for custody.

PART 38

Trouble

July 2015 – September 2015

~ 875 ~

I just returned from a week-long workshop on the topic of "Trouble." I was among a group of about twenty people of diverse backgrounds and walks of life. Many of the people in attendance were psychologists, social workers, clergy, or other social service professionals. A few, like me, were artists or educators. The materials used in the seminar were drawn from the disciplines of psychology, philosophy, religion, and the arts.

On the first day I discovered that I am on a different track from the rest of the group. I said some things that seemed to pull the discussion off the track that the group leaders had in mind. In the Upanishads it says, "Those who speak do not know; those who know do not speak." On the second day I did not speak.

Why am I here? To learn how to teach, to listen, to help, to heal. I decided that on the third day I would say something provocative and see who seeks to know more. I offered this haiku:

> Many words, one sound.
> Refracted God, one white light.
> Let the living die.

Two people sought more. We talked, as did Jesus and Nicodemus, about dying to this life and being born again of the spirit.

The leader of this workshop, Herb, is concerned about my silence. He wants me to talk about my experiences. Why? He is a psychologist, used to hearing people's troubles, expecting to hear them, and thinking that when he doesn't, something is being repressed.

When Jesus met with other people, did he talk about how hard his childhood was as a poor carpenter's son, or how he never got over Joseph not being his real father? He spoke not from the experiences of his earthly life, but from his direct knowledge of eternal life. When I open my mouth to speak, it will not be about my personal troubles.

I realize now that I am not meant to be a participant in this workshop, but an observer of it. The others are here to talk; I am here to listen. If I speak, I will derail the train. So I listen, letting their words and tears wash over me. I learn from them.

I have the answers to their questions, but I dare not speak them. Each person must take his own journey, not vicariously take mine. The answers will have no meaning and may even be upsetting if they come too soon, before the stage is set. Don't cut them off at the pass. Let them stop at all the stations of their journey. If I provide the answers before they are ready to ask the questions, the answers will fall on infertile soil. Everyone must find the answers for himself by experiencing his own trials.

Speak in poems and parables. Don't elaborate. Let people find their own understanding through their own process. But speak with assurance. I speak truth, as Jeremiah spoke the words that God put into his mouth.

> *The cat has adopted me. He left his headquarters near the lodge and now lives on the porch of my cabin. A tender mercy from God.*

The body language of the people around the circle reveals the turmoil within. Herb, acting in the role of leader, sits in a series of authoritative postures that assert his command, composure, and strength. Debbie sits like a pretzel, her arms and legs entwined in themselves, reflecting the tangle of thoughts and emotions inside. Robbie is a bundle of twitches and nervous tics. Albert sits hunched over with his head in his hands. Violet folds her arms and stretches her legs out in *faux* self-assurance, a defensive "I don't give a damn" mask that was built over a lifetime of abuse. It is heartbreaking how much pain, hurt, and fear they hold inside. Sometimes they let it out; rarely do they let it go.

I can feel the pain of others, but how can I understand the lasting effect of childhood trauma and other painful situations that I have never experienced? Does it matter if I fully understand, or does love wash over all, passing understanding? The relative lack of trouble in my early life allows me to be a blank slate, to be an empty vessel that can hold the pain of others without the weight of my own baggage.

In my empathy with these people and their pain, I am validated. I have troubles, but they don't consume me. I have a hard time even identifying them as troubles; I just see them as ... life. What is the opposite of trouble? There is no opposite. All life is suffering. Trouble contains both sides of duality. Pleasure and pain are both trouble.

Why are these people here? Tony de Mello said that people do not go to the doctor for a cure, but for relief. Many do not seek the kingdom of heaven, just an end to trouble. Even those who are earnestly seeking God are often doing so to gain relief, not enlightenment. They would latch on to anything, God or not, if it gave relief, and blinded by blessed relief, they would mistake the reliever for God.

God is not found by seeking. ("How could sitting in meditation make a Buddha?") God did not come to me by my seeking him. When I stopped seeking, stopped trying to find relief through my own efforts, threw up my hands and opened up to whatever was beyond my controlling mind, God was revealed. Not by actively seeking, but by passively allowing, I found God. Or, I should say, God found me.

$$Surrender \neq defeat$$
$$Acceptance \neq resignation$$
$$Letting\ go \neq giving\ up$$

Acceptance is key. Accepting the world, life as it is, trouble and all, knowing that where the eternal God resides, all is well. When trouble comes, it has something to teach us. When death comes, it will be at the right time, life's work having been completed as it was meant to be.

My last letting go is the need to be needed. Hear the world's cries, but don't expect to silence them or heal their cause at its source. It may be appropriate to offer support and guidance, that the sufferer might then heal himself, but most of the time it won't be wanted. The patient only wants relief, not a cure.

The cat wants to be with me even at the expense of eating. He won't leave the porch of my cabin, not even to eat. He waits for me to return from class. Brushing up against my leg, sitting on my lap, seems more important than food, for both the cat and me. The cat is a spirit messenger.

Many of the people here are so fractured that they cannot drop the barricades around their soul to let love and consolation in, like a drowning swimmer whose flailing fends off his rescuer. To know God, one must be vulnerable, willing to accept more trouble, not less. When looking for relief, we find the opposite.

And Jesus, perceiving in himself that power had gone forth from him, immediately turned about in the crowd, and said, "Who touched my garments?" (Mark 5:30 RSV)

Yesterday I spoke to one of the group leaders and made an offer of anonymous financial aid to anyone in the group who might not be partaking of body therapy sessions due to lack of funds. Today it was made known to me that there was such a person. I felt my healing energy going out from me, not knowing to whom. I don't know who touched my garments.

"How can I accept that my mistakes were meant to be?" asked Albert, a lovely young man, one of the participants who does odd jobs around the camp. It was clear after the first few days that he was troubled. He spoke little, seemed distant and detached, and broke down in tears when he confessed to making mistakes, overcome by feelings of guilt and self-recrimination. One night after our evening session Albert struck up a conversation with me in which he told me a little about a difficult transition he was in, but he revealed no specifics.

More specifics about Albert's suffering came forth in a breakout group, during which I brought up the characteristics of an *asura* – suspicious, distrustful, angry, judgmental, and cruel. Albert perked up, wanting to know more about *asuras*. He lost his shyness, and words began to fly from his mouth. He is having trouble with his girlfriend, who apparently exhibits many of these qualities. *Asuras* are very good at making their loved ones feel guilty, finding fault with them for things that are not their fault. Albert was exhibiting the same symptoms I did when Emily began to abuse me. He and I shared another conversation later that seemed to help him. I got the feeling that Emily had come into my life so that I would understand what Albert was going through and know what to say to him.

Emotions come and go, rise and fall. Love and fear are more than emotions; they are states of consciousness, of being. They are the substrate from which emotions emerge. When love drives out fear, all emotions lose their power over us. Both positive and negative emotions subside, wiping the slate clean, polishing the mirror, clearing the way for Kannon to hear the cries of others. You cannot hear the cries of others when your own cries, whether from joy or sorrow, drown out everything else.

The cat sleeps at my feet.

I saw the corner of the multi-colored envelope with my money in it sticking out of Debbie's notebook. I had already sensed that it was she who touched my garments.

"You can't find beauty in someone's pain," said Pam, one of the group leaders.

Although it is not the first quality that appears, I can see awesome beauty in someone's pain, as I have seen it in Emily, as a manifestation of the marvelous dark side of God. The Dalai Lama, Richard Bach, and Carl Jung made essentially the same point. (~726~)

"No one can tell someone that their trouble is beautiful. That's just arrogance, ego," said Herb.

It's not arrogant or egotistical to tell someone his trouble is beautiful; it's the simple truth. Saying this to a suffering person is not often advisable, however; it can be hard to hear for those not ready to hear it. (This is why I hold back, as Anthony de Mello held back telling his audience, until he got their permission to do so, that grief is really greed.)

The serendipities and synchronicities that I knew would arise at this gathering reached their peak at the banquet on the last night of the workshop. Each person, upon entering the dining room, drew from a bag a small strip of paper on which was written a number that indicated the number of his seat, where another paper would be found. I got number eleven. Both the paper drawn from the bag and the one at the seat had a word or phrase on it; on one paper was a noun, on the other, a verb. I got "Son of Man" and "forgive." A little smile crossed my face. *Okay God, I get the message: Time to out myself to the group.*

When it was my turn to describe how the words I drew applied to me, I said: "I got 'Son of Man' because *that is who I am.* I got 'forgive' because the Son of Man has *authority to forgive sins.*" "But that you may know that the Son of Man has authority on earth to forgive sins ..." (Mark 2:10 RSV)

Let's see who approaches me tomorrow, wanting to know more. Who will be my Nicodemus, or my Caiaphas?

Caiaphas appeared. It was Herb.

Herb had previously coaxed me to reveal more of my personal experience. Thinking that perhaps the notes I took during this week would be useful to him, I asked, "Herb, would you like me to share my notes with you?"

"I would rather you share your experiences," he said. "You have not been participating. You are very smart; you know a lot. You quote the words of others, but you don't talk about your own experiences. It seems to me that you are holding your troubles inside, unwilling to let them out."

Herb was still treating me as if I were a patient in his psychology practice, not a fellow soul-seeker, and he had just described himself, projecting onto me both his intelligence and his unrevealed troubles. Words rose up into my throat and to the tip of my tongue. I knew that saying them would get me into trouble, so I hesitated. Yet I also knew that they were the truth; perhaps saying them was the whole point of my being here. Something was tugging at me – hard – to say them, so I did: "Based on what you have said, I don't think you are ready for my notes."

Herb tensed up, and his countenance turned dark. "That was a very arrogant thing to say ... thank you." He angrily stormed off.

Herb had not understood my message last night about the Son of Man, nor the message this morning about my all-black and all-white images of trouble, nor my Zen story about the acceptance of pain. He did not recognize the presence of an elevated spirit in the midst of his group.

But the cat did.

Many people who are in positions of spiritual or intellectual authority – teachers, clergy, physicians, psychologists – put on airs of understanding, quoting scripture or other authorities, sensing that there is deep meaning in the words but not quite grasping it. Sometimes people become lifelong scriptural scholars trying to find that deep meaning, as people sometimes become psychologists (as did Herb and Emily, I suspect), trying to heal their own psychic wounds.

Some teachers use the words of others to graft onto themselves the external wisdom of others. I use the words of others because they resonate with the internal wisdom I acquired through direct experience. Others who have seen what I have seen and walked the path before me have already found the most eloquent words to describe that experience, so I borrow from them. Herb's failure to see this was the sign to me that he was not ready to hear me elucidate my mystical experience. Brené Brown warned us to be careful who we tell our story to, to tell it only to those who have earned the right to hear it and can bear the weight of it. Herb isn't ready.

Was I wrong to speak so bluntly? Was Jesus arrogant when he said to the Pharisees, "Neither will I tell you by what authority I do these things"? (Matthew 21:27 RSV) Jesus withheld his experiences from those who did not honor their source. Martha told me to trust my intuition; I am a truth-teller and a wake-up fairy. What I said to Herb may have sounded arrogant, but my alleged arrogance was not the cause of Herb's upset. My truth woke him up to his own arrogance, his egotistical need to be the highest guru in the group.

If Herb thought I was arrogant or delusional in thinking myself to be the Son of Man, wouldn't compassionate concern, not rebuke, be the appropriate response of enlightened leadership, especially from one who is a licensed psychologist? And yet, I understand. His inner demons have not yet departed to make way for compassion. But I have compassion for him. I hold his trouble tenderly in my hands, without anger or judgment. Nevertheless, I must shake his dust from my feet.

I am soooo living the life of Christ, the Son of Man.

~ 876 ~

SIN, Part 4
Marriage, Divorce, Sex, and Celibacy

> And Pharisees came up to him and tested him by asking, "Is it lawful to divorce one's wife for any cause?" He answered, "Have you not read that he who made them from the beginning made them male and female, and said, 'For this reason a man shall leave his father and mother and be joined to his wife, and the two shall become one flesh'? So they are no longer two but one flesh. What therefore God has joined together, let not man put asunder." They said to him, "Why then did Moses command one to give a certificate of divorce, and to put her away?" He said to them, "For your hardness of heart Moses allowed you to divorce your wives, but from the beginning it was not so. And I say to you: whoever divorces his wife, except for unchastity, and marries another, commits adultery." (Matthew 19:3-9 RSV)

Marriage is an earthly construct, grounded in the culture of its time and place. The above passage from Matthew deals with the subject of marriage on the temporal plane, addressing behaviors relevant to life in the world. The rules concerning marriage and divorce are part of the body of law that created sin – the law and sin that Jesus came to take away.

Matthew and Luke go on to reveal the irrelevance of marriage, divorce, and carnal sex on the eternal plane:

> The disciples said to him, "If such is the case of a man with his wife, it is not expedient to marry." But he said to them, "Not all men can receive this saying, but only those to whom it is given. For there are eunuchs who have been so from birth, and there are eunuchs who have been made eunuchs by men, and there are eunuchs who have made themselves eunuchs for the sake of the kingdom of heaven. He who is able to receive this, let him receive it." (Matthew 19:10-12 RSV)

> There came to him some Sad'ducees, those who say that there is no resurrection, and they asked him a question, saying, "Teacher, Moses wrote for us that if a man's brother dies, having a wife but no children, the man must take the wife and raise up children for his brother. Now there were seven brothers; the first took a wife, and died without children; and the second and the third took her, and likewise all seven left no children and died. Afterward

the woman also died. In the resurrection, therefore, whose wife will the woman be? For the seven had her as wife."

And Jesus said to them, "The sons of this age marry and are given in marriage; but those who are accounted worthy to attain to that age and to the resurrection from the dead neither marry nor are given in marriage, for they cannot die any more, because they are equal to angels and are sons of God, being sons of the resurrection. (Luke 20:27-36 RSV)

When the Pharisees and Sadducees asked Jesus questions, they were trying to trip him up. His cryptic answers to their questions were therefore meant to disarm them as much as to impart information. In Luke 20, Jesus was rebuking them for their worldly approach to marriage, their blindness to its meaning as symbolic of an eternal union. What God has joined together is joined eternally; if divorce is deemed necessary or even conceivable, then the marriage was not of God.

Marriage and divorce have nothing to do with love, or the spiritual relationship of husband and wife, or their relationship with God. Marriage has meaning only in this dualistic world; it is a social contract meant to provide a protective and supportive environment for dependent women and children. There is no marriage in the resurrection, in eternity, because there are no separate individuals to be joined together in marriage, with whom to have sex or raise children. This metaphysical, extrasensory, supernatural realm has no use for marriage, sex, children, time, or space.

My apparently sinful, adulterous relationship with Lou was not a marriage of this age; it was the karmic union of beings always and eternally alive, sons of the resurrection. Even in our sex life – our tantric sex life – we were beyond the scope of the Law of Moses, beyond answering to it. There was no chastity or unchastity, no law and no sin.

For Lou and me, worldly marriage was the symbolic temporal acknowledgment of a preexisting eternal condition, the oneness of all things, a union that God had joined together before we were born and no man could possibly put asunder. Nothing about our relationship changed as a result of our getting married. As nothing about God changed when Jesus was born into the world, as nothing changed when the Buddha was enlightened. As nothing would change if Emily awoke to our divine love and we were joined together in earthly marriage.

Until they become sons of the resurrection, Jesus recommended that his disciples make themselves eunuchs for the sake of the kingdom of heaven. Unless you are joined to a soulmate with whom you were united before you were born, who is, like you, a son of the resurrection for whom earthly marriage is irrelevant, celibacy is the preferred choice. This is the same message that tantric Hindus and Buddhists send about chastity, tantric sex being the one exception to the rule of abstinence.

~ 877 ~

There is no need to plan or contemplate how best to benefit others, since bodhisattvas on the eighth level automatically react correctly to every situation.[11]

Do I react correctly to every situation? With Emily? With Herb? With my colleagues in business and music? My reactions are not always pleasing and are sometimes pain-inducing, but yes, if I am acting out of love, doing the will of God, they are correct.

In the last year or so I have grown into the eighth bhūmi characteristic of fitting into many situations. I discourse with Christians, Buddhists, shamans, psychics, and atheists. With rich philanthropists and poor musicians, learned scholars and illiterate toddlers. With animals, trees, rocks, and rainbows. As Jesus dialogued with Pharisees and beggars, tax collectors and prostitutes, angels and demons, Jews and gentiles. The gospel, the dharma, is for them all.

I am a wake-up fairy for all these people. But why can't I get past the wake-up phase? Why can't anyone go the distance with me? Only Lou was ready for me, and I for him. Not Emily, or Kathy, or Herb, or The Unnamed One. This is the solitude of the bodhisattva, alone at the edge, at the end of the tunnel where the light is so bright that no one else can look at it. It hurts their eyes.

~ 878 ~

A friend of mine who is a cancer survivor said to me, "I just decided to resign my job next month. Things have come up that are stressing me, making my heart pound, and I need to protect myself."

I asked, "Do you have your successor lined up? Will you be a mentor to the new person in your job, ease the transition?"

"No," she said. "I have to think of myself first. Save my own life."

She is not a callous or insensitive person. She has spent her whole life working for the betterment of others, not preoccupied with herself. She spoke out and took risks for the sake of others. Before her cancer, she would have been very concerned about the welfare of her organization, seeing to it that her departure from her job did not cause undue hardship. But the specter of death changed all that. Fear drew this once outward-looking person into herself, and has overridden the social and vocational connections that had made her life meaningful.

I was tempted to tell her that perhaps it is worth risking your life in order to do that which makes life worth living. Is living with all stress intentionally removed really living? It may be peaceful, but isn't living that way just another kind of dying? Death is the ultimate peace.

The stress of my experience with Emily has threatened my life and health, but I wouldn't want to give up the fabulous awakenings that her madness brought me – awakenings that could not have happened but for the very madness that caused my stress. I have often said that I will stay alive long enough to accomplish my purpose and no longer, and I will welcome death when it comes. Will I change my mind when death is not theoretical, but looks me in the eye?

~ 879 ~

THE NARROW GATE

> Enter by the narrow gate; for the gate is wide and the way is easy that leads to destruction, and those who enter by it are many. For the gate is narrow and the way is hard, that leads to life, and those who find it are few. (Matthew 7:13-14 RSV)

I admit it sounds terribly audacious and presumptuous for me to be so sure that I am the Son of Man, a bodhisattva, that I have found the narrow gate.

Why am I so sure? When you discover the love of God inside you – the force that overwhelmed Ben-Hur when he felt Jesus' voice take the sword out of his hand, that allowed Jesus to forgive his torturers from the cross – your every thought, word, and deed comes from that love, which transcends sin, the Law of Moses, and both sides of duality. The Buddhists describe the same condition by saying that bodhisattvas walk every moment in the dharma – they have poked their head through the hole in a log in the vast ocean, or as the Christians say, they have entered by the narrow gate that few will find.

A sure sign that someone has not found the narrow gate is that he continues to act out of temporal desire and fear rather than out of eternal love. This doesn't mean that awakened beings have no feelings – Jesus expressed anger, fear, sorrow, and grief. The difference is that awakened ones know that emotions come from the body-mind, not the spirit. They do not react to their emotions as others do at the dualistic level. They let emotions come, and watch them go.

Awakened ones use their emotional responses as tools to heal, not to hurt; to impart divine truth, not to vent; to motivate, not to alienate; to teach, not to punish; to unify, not to divide. Emotions can be used as a language that people in the world can understand, used as the authors of the Bible did in ascribing to God anthropomorphic qualities like anger, vengeance, mercy, and kindness.

Everyone is the Son of Man – the divine presence of God in the world – but very few know it and live in the light of that knowledge. Simply answering the altar call, being baptized, and accepting Jesus Christ as your Lord and Savior does not mean you are born again any more than sitting in meditation makes a buddha. Accepting Jesus or sitting in meditation means that you accept the life of Christ, of the Buddha; you choose to begin the journey along the hard way to enlightenment and eternal life. You have opened the door to the spirit, but the narrow gate is still far away. Many trials still stand between you and nirvana. Surrendering the ego to God is only the first step toward enlightenment, salvation, freedom from sin, and being born of the spirit – only the beginning of the journey, not the end.

> To be called to a life of extraordinary quality, to live up to it, and yet to be unconscious of it is indeed a narrow way. To confess and testify to the truth as it is in Jesus, and at the same time to love the enemies of that truth, his enemies and ours, and to love them with the infinite love of Jesus Christ, is indeed a narrow way. To believe the promise of Jesus that his followers shall possess the earth, and at the same time to face our enemies unarmed and defenseless, preferring to incur injustice rather than to do wrong ourselves, is indeed a narrow way. To see the weakness and wrong in others, and at the same time refrain from judging them; to deliver the gospel message without casting pearls before swine, is indeed a narrow way. The way is unutterably hard, and at every moment we are in danger of straying from it. If we regard this way as one we follow in obedience to an external command, if we are afraid of ourselves all the time, it is indeed an impossible way. But if we behold Jesus Christ going on before step by step, we shall not go astray. – Dietrich Bonhoeffer, *The Cost of Discipleship* [51]

My Buddhist spiritual guide says I know this narrow way. (~689~) Indeed, it is because I "behold Jesus Christ going on before step by step," showing me the Way and the Truth and the Life of extraordinary quality to which I have been called.

~ 880 ~

Epic dream last night, a series of vignettes:

1) I am driving along a poorly defined road, partly dirt and partly grass. There are lots of other cars on the road, bumper to bumper, but moving quite fast. I overtake other cars and move into a parallel lane on the left.

2) Then I am driving on a paved road in a tunnel or under a bridge. Again, there are lots of cars moving fast. I am not paying attention to my driving; I can feel myself zoning out and losing consciousness, yet I am not hitting anything. I return to my senses, see that there is still a good distance between me and the car in front of me, and I have not veered out of my lane. I am grateful that no harm was done.

3) I am in a dimly lit hotel room. I am on the phone with someone and I say, "A suitcase is being delivered," as a bellman leaves a small suitcase on the floor in front of me. Then he moves to the desk, where I see a small box on the desk. I look back toward the suitcase, then to the desk. The bellman has disappeared and the lights have gone out. I try to turn the lights back on, but none of them work. As I pick up the box, it morphs into a tablet with scintillating figures and images of old World War I biplanes; government buildings with domes, columns, and lots of steps; and indecipherable hieroglyphics. Then the whole desktop begins to light up with these images. It was like something from a Harry Potter movie.

4) I find myself driving again, this time in a small subterranean room with lots of scorched wooden beams holding up the ceiling, like a burned-out mine shaft. I try driving around the beams, but they are so close together I can't avoid hitting them. I take a devil-may-care attitude, not worrying if I crash into them. Yet they don't fall down. I back up and try to turn around, but I can only face forward. There is a dark, scorched wall in front of me. I stop, wondering where to go from here. I begin to feel trapped, frightened, but I realize there is nothing I can do but just sit there. I woke up.

From dreammoods.com:

Car – To dream that you are driving a car denotes your ambition, your drive and your ability to navigate from one stage of your life to another. Consider how smooth or rough the car ride is. If you are driving the car, then you are taking an active role in the way your life is going. Dreaming of a car that is driving fast suggests that you need to slow down and think through your choices.

Hotel – To see a hotel in your dream signifies a new state of mind or a shift in personal identity. You are undergoing some sort of transition and need to move away from your old habits and old way of thinking.

Telephone – To see or hear a telephone in your dream signifies a message from your subconscious or some sort of telepathic communication. You may be forced to confront issues which you have been avoiding. Alternatively, the telephone represents your communication and relationship with others.

Suitcase – To see a suitcase in your dream indicates that you are a very composed, together person. You keep your attitudes and behavior in check. Alternatively, a suitcase symbolizes your need for a much-needed vacation or break.

Desk – To see or sit at your desk in your dream suggests that you are evaluating and weighing your problems. It is indicative of self-exploration and discovery.

Box – To dream that you are opening a box indicates an aspect of yourself that was once hidden is now being revealed. It symbolizes self-discovery. Consider your feelings as you open the box.

Mine – To dream that you are in a mine suggests that you are getting to the core of an issue or condition. Alternatively, it indicates that something from your subconscious is coming to the surface. To see or dream that you are in a mine shaft symbolizes the depth of your subconscious.

All of these scenes took place against a dark backdrop, indicating that they are messages from the subconscious. In all of the vignettes there was an element of fear, but also wonder and curiosity. In spite of the scary and dangerous elements in all the scenarios, nothing bad happened. It seems that I am protected from harm as I explore the caverns of my inner nature.

Often I feel that both the primary and alternate meanings presented by dreammoods.com are applicable. In this case, perhaps the person I am speaking with on the phone is Emily, the phone representing subconscious communication involving my relationship with her. When I tell her that a suitcase is being delivered, I am expressing both my composed demeanor and my need to take a vacation from her abuse.

~ 881 ~

My trouble with Emily is that I know too much. I know her better than she knows herself. I want to reach into the place where she is a stranger to herself and pull her out of there, knowing that if I could do that, she could be saved. But I can't. She won't let me. The truth is, only she can save herself. I am not her savior, only the potential midwife attending her potential rebirth.

I went to see Elaine today. As I was walking toward the elevator, a voice behind me called my name. It was her daughter Natalie. We three had a lovely visit. Elaine kept saying over and over, "It is so good to see you." I feel Lou's love radiating to me through her.

~ 882 ~

I am finishing another provocative book, *C.G. Jung and Hermann Hesse: A Record of Two Friendships*,[59] by Miguel Serrano. Both Jung and Hesse knew of the unconscious mind and the lonely, solitary path.

Dr. Jung then made this observation [concerning Serrano's mystical experience]: "As I said, those are all subjective experiences, and they are not collectively verifiable. What you call vibrations may only have been dreams, or at most, manifestations of the Collective Unconscious."

I was disappointed by Jung's answer. He seemed incapable of penetrating these mysteries, and for a sad moment, I had the feeling that all he had done in his work was to create a new terminology to explain old truths. I had been similarly disappointed by the Dalai Lama, who had made no revealing statements about my phenomena, but had relied on ancient dogma, citing texts in support of his observations. Perhaps he had been afraid of exceeding himself as the head of a church, and in the presence of his court officials. It is always a heavy task to be responsible for a body of organized religious doctrine—or for a school of scientific psychology.

I then realized that I would never find any guidance, or explanation, for my personal experiences—which for Jung, were purely subjective—and I knew that I would have to rely solely upon my own intuition. I would have to walk alone, as Jung himself had once done, along the "razor's edge."

Decades ago I noted that I would have to take the final leg of my spiritual journey alone – as did Jung and Jesus and the Buddha and all who travel to the distant outpost, the Pure Land, through the narrow gate, along the razor's edge. Jung and the Dalai Lama were not disrespecting Serrano's experience; they knew that they could not add anything meaningful to it. They knew that it is folly to try to analyze or interpret – and thereby limit – someone else's mystic experience.

For several years I have been frustrated by suddenly waking up from daydreams or catnaps and losing the train of thought that I had been developing while in the fantastic realm between dreaming and waking. I wanted to continue the thought to its conclusion, but then consciousness interrupted. At first I thought this was a sign of creeping dementia or the forgetfulness of old age. But now, the fact that this has been happening to the point that I am noticing it, says to me that I am living more and more on the edge of the unconscious. I am still having trouble keeping my conscious mind out of the way, though.

~ 883 ~

SEX, Part 25

Hermann Hesse and Carl Jung understood tantric sex as I do, with its essential eternal oneness beyond simple physical sensation and satisfaction:

from Hesse's last work, "Piktor's Metamorphosis:"

Now everything was perfect, and the world was in order. In that moment, Paradise had been found. Piktor was no longer a solitary old tree, but was fulfilled and complete and bore a new name which he called Piktoria. And this he sang out, loud and clear, the word "Piktoria!" And this phrase also signified "Victoria" or victory. At long last, he had been transformed, and he realized the truth of eternal metamorphosis, because he had been changed from a half to a whole.

From then on, he knew he would be able to transform himself as often as he liked. The force of continuing creation was now released within him, and he knew he could renew himself as a star or a fish or a cloud or a bird. But he also realized that whatever form he took would be a whole, and that in each image he would be a pair; he had both the Sun and the Moon within him, and he was at once Man and Woman.[59]

from Jung, described by Miguel Serrano:

In philosophic alchemy, there exists the idea of the *Soror Mystica* who works with the alchemist while he mixes his substances in his retorts. She is with him at all times throughout the long process of fusion, and at the end, there occurs a mystic wedding, involving the creation of the Androgynous. This could not have occurred without the presence of the woman, without, in short, the psychic encounter of the Sister and the Alchemist.

This psychic union never takes place in ordinary love, for even though two lovers may wish to fuse themselves completely, they will never be able to dream the same dream; there will always be something that separates them. The magic wedding is alone capable of closing the gap. Jung said that this psychic union could only take place in a spirit of love, since only then would one be willing to risk everything. While it is true that this love does not exclude physical love, the physical becomes transformed into ritual. What is excluded is mutual sexual pleasure.

The best way of explaining this complicated idea is to consider the Tantric practices of India, in which the Siddha magicians attempted to achieve psychic union. The man and the woman would go off together into the forest, living like brother and sister, like the alchemist and his sister, exchanging ideas, images and words. They would sleep together in the same bed, but they would not touch each other. Only after months of preparation would the final Tantric Mass take place, in which wine was drunk, meat and cereal eaten, and finally *Maithuna*, or mystical coitus performed. This act was the culmination of the long process of sublimation, during which the flesh was transformed and transfigured, just as in alchemy lead is converted into gold, and the act of coitus was really intended to ignite the mystic fire at the base of the vertebral column.

On the walls of the temple of Khajuraho, in India, this forbidden love is pictured in thousands of sculptured figures. But nowhere are there statues of children, and that is why this love is an unnatural love. Inside the temple, in a most secret place, sits Shiva the Androgynous, meditating with his eyes closed, considering and enjoying his own act of creation.

In India, the meaning of this forbidden love is reiterated in the story of Krishna, the blue god, so loved by Hesse, who danced with his loves in the gardens of Vrindavan. His chief lover was Radha, who was a married woman, and with her was realized the Number Three [the trinity] while they danced within a mandala and attained the Self.

In these strange rites, it is not important that the *Maithuna* be physical; what is important is that the Mystic Sister be there, with the alchemist, helping him to mix his substances and, like Mary Magdalen, aiding him in his hour of greatest need.

The final wedding, or union, takes place within the isolated individual, who is so completely alone that he really has no sense at all of his own body. This union is achieved by Kundalini, which Jung defined as an 'emotional current.' Like the mercury of the alchemists or the 'astral fire' of the occultists, Kundalini awakens the chakras one by one until finally the Third Eye, or Ajna Chakra is opened and the Brahma Chakra or Final Emptiness is achieved. It is a wedding between the Ego and the Self achieved through a union of the Anima with the Animus.[59]

Joseph Campbell also struck this chord with his description of forbidden courtly love (~643~) and his interpretation of the tale of *Parzival*. (~787~) Over and over I have described my karmic loves in this way, sex with them being categorically different from the usual idea of sex. Tantric sex, like courtly love, is spiritual, not biological; a product of divine, not worldly, love; only engaged in after months of preparation.

With Emily I discovered the highest pinnacle of the tantric experience. The most amazing of my discoveries are that the experience of *maithuna*, mystical coitus, can be had even when one's partner is of the same sex, even when one's partner is not consciously aware of the tantric connection, and even from a distance, when one's partner in psychic union is not physically present. My avatar body receives and expresses our spiritual love independent of all laws and rules, even the laws of nature as we know them in the physical sense.

Serrano, in describing tantric sex as taking place "within the isolated individual" and as "a wedding between the Ego and the Self," explains how it is possible for me to have tantric sex without a physical partner in attendance. The Mystic Sister is with me in spirit, facilitating the process, but the transformation is all within me. My physical body and my spiritual God-self become one, my own Anima and Animus are united, and "the creation of the Androgynous" is accomplished.

I have always resisted Emily's sexual advances in spite of my intense desire for her, because I know that her desire for me is just the ordinary kind, and I cannot make love to her except from the place of divine love. The height of my ardor with her arose when we became a trinity – Emily, Danny, and me – like Krishna, Radha, and her husband – like me, The Unnamed One, and his wife – like King Arthur, Lancelot, and Guinevere – like Lou, his first wife, and me. My life is one bout of erotic, rule-breaking, tantric, divine courtly love after another.

All this time I have considered myself to be the Shakti side of the tantric equation, because of my female anatomy. Perhaps with Lou and The Unnamed One I was Shakti, but with Emily I have become Shiva, and through union with her, my masculine and feminine aspects, the Animus and Anima, are equally balanced.

I am Piktor the tree who has been transformed and made whole, but in whom there is still a pair, sitting in meditation like Shiva the Androgynous, "considering and enjoying his own act of creation."

~ 884 ~

Last night I dreamt that I was giving birth: *I popped out lots of babies, around eighteen or so, but I felt one more stuck inside. I could feel its weight at the bottom of my pelvis. I was looking around for someone to help me deliver it, but there was no one. I thought if I just push a little, I can deliver it myself. I could see the head crowning and then the baby came out. "That was easy," I thought. The baby was small, brown, with a slight smile on its face. It had a large head on a long, plump, egg-shaped body with very short arms and legs. It wasn't crying, so I patted the baby's back to be sure it was alive. One eye seemed stuck shut, so I pried it open. I was satisfied that all was well.*

From dreammoods.com:

Birth – To dream of giving birth or see someone else giving birth suggests that you are giving birth to a new idea or project. It also represents a new attitude, fresh beginnings or a major event.

Baby – To see a baby in your dream signifies innocence, warmth and new beginnings. Babies symbolize something in your own inner nature that is pure, vulnerable, helpless and/ or uncorrupted. If you dream that the baby is smiling at you, then it suggests that you are experiencing pure joy. You do not ask for much to make you happy.

Eyes – To dream about someone else's eyes indicates an emotional or intimate connection with that person. It also signifies a mutual understanding. To dream that eyes are injured or closed suggests refusal to see the truth about something or the avoidance of intimacy.

~ 885 ~

After many months, I went to the beach today. The butterfly fish, puffers, and other sea critters greeted me. As I was swimming back to shore, I noticed a fabulous rainbow forming above me. It started in the clouds over the mountains and then arched 180 degrees over the ocean, being gradually drawn from one horizon to the other as if by a painter's brush. I floated in the middle of the arch and watched the panorama in awe. I have spent so much time lately immersed in words, thoughts, and ideas; sometimes it is good to escape their limits and get back to the simple suchness of nature.

~ 886 ~

I love the analogy of duality being contained within eternity as the colors of a rainbow are contained within invisible white light. God is the invisible light and also the prism that splits eternity apart and reveals the visible inside the invisible. God's creation is an illusion, and also real, the same way a rainbow is.

And yet, the colors of a rainbow, while differentiated, are not separated. All colors appear and disappear together. As white light is split in a prism, blue is revealed, but so is red, and yellow, and infrared and ultraviolet. As eternity is split into its components, heaven is revealed, but so is hell. Good, but also evil. All the facets of duality rise and fall together – interdependent co-arising.

~ 887 ~

The mirrored tiles in both of my bathrooms have been falling with reckless abandon over the past couple weeks. Only one of the tiles broke, though. Just now three more fell, with a loud bang that startled me.

Emily is leaving today for another visit with Danny. Yes, they are back together again.

~ 888 ~

In Ignacio's discussion group today, the subject was Islam. Regarding the differences between process thought and Islam, Islamic writer Mustafa Ruzgar says: "It is clear that

Whitehead does not accept the dominant doctrine of *creatio ex nihilo* and the widespread view that creative power belongs only to God." [60]

Humans have creative power, but where does it come from? We are all little expressions of God, and as creative beings we express the creativity of God. God gives each of us access to his creativity, knowledge, and power. When we view our creativity this way, as an extension and expression of God's creativity, we are avatars of God, doing God's work.

But when we assert that humans have creative power independent of God, we separate ourselves from God, as Adam and Eve did. We are cast out of the Garden of Eden as they were. By insisting on our own creativity, knowledge, and power, we are saying that we want to stay outside the Garden, keep our illusion of independence from God, and pass up the return to eternal life that Jesus proffered. This is pride, the stubbornness of ego, that leads to reincarnation, not resurrection – the continuation of karma, not enlightenment.

This attitude of independence from or resistance to God is described in the Bible as "hardness of heart." Several different Hebrew, Aramaic, and Greek words were translated into English as "hardness of heart;" all of them mean something like stubbornness, harshness, stiffness, self-glorification, obstinacy. "Hardness of heart" is thus the ego's defensive response to being threatened, attacked, or challenged: "How dare God tell me what to do!"

When we surrender the ego to God, our hearts are softened. We learn how to turn the other cheek, love our enemies, and forgive those who sin against us. We discover that our strength and creativity come not from asserting our independent will, but from accepting God's will; not from being outside God, but from being inside.

Carl Jung said:

> That is the reason why I tried to find the best truth and the clearest light I could attain to, and since I have reached my highest point and can't transcend any more, I am guarding my light and my treasure, convinced that nobody would gain and I myself would be badly, even hopelessly injured, if I should lose it. It is most precious not only to me, but above all to the darkness of the creator, who needs Man to illuminate his creation. If God had foreseen his world, it would be a mere senseless machine and Man's existence a useless freak. [59]

Jung understood the relation of Man to God perfectly. Man and God arise together and create each other. Creative power belongs to God, as it is revealed, illuminated, and activated through his creation, in the countless facets of himself who appear and disappear as his creatures.

The earth may be regarded as a precipitation of space. Is it any wonder, then, that the laws of that space are ingrained in our minds? The philosopher Alan Watts once said, "The Earth is peopling, as apple trees 'apple.' People are produced from the earth as apples from apple trees." We are the sensing organs of the Earth. We are the senses of the universe. We have it all right here within us. And the deities that we once thought were out there, we now know, were projected out of ourselves. – Joseph Campbell, *Thou Art That* [61]

~ 889 ~

MY CALLING

What is it to be "called" to a profession? Most people want to make a living doing something they enjoy and are good at. If they are good at science in school, they want to be doctors or engineers; at language and writing, they want to be journalists or authors; at music, they want to be musicians; at sports, they want to be professional athletes. The positive reinforcement they receive from parents, teachers, and fellow students directs them along certain paths and into certain fields. Some people think this is a calling, and in a way, it is. God made you good at something to encourage you to pursue that thing as your life's work.

God made me good at everything. I graduated at the top of my high school class. I was good at math, science, languages, history, music, art, and even gym class. I could have gone into any field I wanted. It was necessary for God to do something dramatic to point me in the direction I was meant to go.

My life's first big epiphany came when God's finger pointed me toward a life in music. (~340~) I didn't recognize it as such when it happened, but in retrospect, after forty years walking the path that God set me on that day and experiencing incredible wonders along that path, I can see the hand of God very clearly in that early event. That, I now see, is what a "calling" really is.

Another thing I did well in school was writing. So well, in fact, that my high school English teacher thought I had plagiarized a paper I had written. It seemed too good to have been written by a mere high school student. And it was. Even then God was doing my writing for me. My words reflect a God-given gift, as the ninth bhūmi bodhisattva exhibits "wondrous eloquence and skill in presenting doctrinal teachings." Perhaps I am now called by God to put that skill to use, a calling within a calling, so to speak.

But I am wondering if there are any words, no matter how well put together, that can explain why I write startling things with such boldness and assurance. I say I am a bodhisattva and a mystic; I say that I am God as Jesus was, that I am Truth as al-Hallaj was, and that I am no longer a sinner because Jesus took away sin and the law when he gave me the keys to the Kingdom. These are startling and audacious things to say. I don't blame anyone for being skeptical or considering me a fool, charlatan, or heretic. I would have felt the same way, too, in my younger days before the miracles.

I can only be so sure of these things because of the power of God's calling to me – the serendipities, synchronicities, miracles, visions, dreams, the spiritual forces of man and nature – all the physical and metaphysical ways that God reaches me. It is this indescribable power that strikes me dumb (and then puts words in my mouth) and gives me no choice but to surrender and let it guide my every step.

> You said that words were a mask, and that is true; but it is also true that underneath the dialogue of words, there is another dialogue, and it is this second one to which we must listen, since it is the only one which really matters. – Miguel Serrano, in a letter to Hermann Hesse[59]

I am doing the best I can with words. I will have been successful with this book, which is really just one big Zen *koan*, if my readers are able to see past the mask of my words to the dialogue underneath. May the touch of God reach into them as it has reached into me. Then there will be those who have eyes to see and ears to hear, and I will have succeeded in describing the indescribable.

~ 890 ~

I am realizing with great sorrow that there are very few people who don't have a least a little of the poisons in their system, some element of desire or aversion that impedes their ability to have the deepest spiritual relationships. When some small desire is not fulfilled, or an annoying habit in a loved one irritates us, the poisons percolate up and distance is created, be it ever so small.

Almost no one knows the love that washes away every desire and every aversion. This is the solitude of the bodhisattva that I have so often described. There is no one to share with me the hole in the log in the vast ocean that is so hard to find, or go with me through the narrow gate which few may enter. There is no one to join me in tantric embrace here on earth, no one to meld with me on earth as we are one in heaven. I am consigned to aloneness in this life, no kindred spirit in the flesh. Only spirits in the ectoplasm keep me company.

~ 891 ~

Why do I still ache for Emily? The same shudder and shiver go through me when I think of her as when Lou died. It is my body's response to the blast of god-wind, the breath of heaven, blowing across the time-eternity nexus. My awareness of our perfection in eternity jostles my temporal body; my heart twinges and my mind grieves. My desire to see our perfection realized in this life is my last remnant of desire, my last hope, my last temptation.

Hope and fear are the first and second poisons of the future. We hope for good things, fear bad things. The third poison of the future is to not go there at all, but we who are stuck here in space-time have no choice but to go there. Past, present, and future are with us now in this moment. The trick is to accept the past as it is and take the future as it comes, moment by moment. Hope for nothing, fear nothing. Let the illusion of life play itself out. We are players in a play, actors in a virtual reality movie the ending of which we have already written.

~ 892 ~

I think that Emily and The Unnamed One both knew that our love was something out of this world, but they couldn't figure out how to stay in its light and still maintain their old, safe, comfortable way of living and loving, the only way they had known for the first half-century of their lives.

They had to distance themselves from me. They were happy to welcome my comfort and support at the beginning of our life together, but they couldn't handle the dark tunnel through hell, exposing their weaknesses and vulnerabilities, that is an obligatory part of the journey to heaven. To ride the spaceship of divine love all the way to heaven would mean giving up their worldly ways completely, as Jesus required his disciples to leave home and family to follow him. Divine love is all or nothing. So here I am in the bodhisattva's solitude, knowing all, having nothing.

~ 893 ~

I woke up this morning at 4:44 a.m. Angel time. By 5:15 or so, since I wasn't falling back asleep, I decided to get up and go out for some cool predawn air. I got some breakfast and headed for my sacred place by the ocean. As I was finishing my breakfast, sitting on the rock wall as the sun was coming up, I noticed a feather next to my coffee cup. "Oh, an angel feather," I thought. I took a picture of it and put the feather between the pages of my book. Then I noticed another feather nearby, and another one. "There are lots of birds around, so there are bound to be lots of feathers," I thought. "This doesn't mean anything."

And then, just as that thought entered my mind, another feather wafted down in front of my face and landed on the ground beside my foot.

PART 39

Servants of God
September 2015 – December 2015

~ 894 ~

THE SERMONS OF JOHN WESLEY

"On Divine Providence"

> If, therefore, God were thus to exert his power, there would certainly be no more vice; but it is equally certain, neither could there be any virtue in the world. Were human liberty taken away, men would be as incapable of virtue as stones. ... He cannot destroy out of the soul of man that image of himself wherein he made him: And without doing this, he cannot abolish sin and pain out of the world. But were it to be done, it would imply no wisdom at all; but barely a stroke of omnipotence. Whereas all the manifold wisdom of God (as well as all his power and goodness) is displayed in governing man as man; not as a stock or stone, but as an intelligent and free spirit, capable of choosing either good or evil.[62]

In this sermon John Wesley (1703-1791) shows us a potent Christian view of interdependent co-arising: Temporal man must have equal opportunity for both vice and virtue, and the liberty to choose between them.

"On Faith"

Wesley expanded on John William Fletcher's "Treatise on the Various Dispensations of the Grace of God," which described several levels of faith "distinguished from each other by the degree of light which God vouchsafes to them that are under each." At the bottom of the dispensation pile are Materialists, Deists, Heathens, followed by "Mahometans," Jews, and rising to the top, of course, Christians. Among Christians, Wesley had some disdain for the "Church of Rome," but he did acknowledge the righteousness of anyone who followed "that faith that worketh by love." Regrettably, Wesley was not conversant with the mystic traditions of non-Christian cultures; if he had been, he might have been more open to and respectful of those other equally loving paths to God.

Nevertheless, Wesley, coming from that faith that worketh by love, brought much wisdom to his flock, including this stern warning to those who base their entire faith on scripture:

> Hitherto faith has been considered chiefly as an evidence and conviction of such or such truths. And this is the sense wherein it is taken at this day in every part of the Christian world. Can this faith save him? Can it save any man either from sin or from hell? No more than it could save Judas Iscariot. No more than it could save the devil and his angels, all of whom are convinced that every title of Holy Scripture is true.[62]

To be truly graced with a Christian dispensation requires a greater intimacy with God than mere belief or adherence to scripture. Wesley described two stages on the way to Christian dispensation — being a *servant* of God, as personified in John the Baptist, and the ultimate Christian dispensation, being a *son* of God, as personified in Jesus Christ:

> But above both the heathen and Jewish dispensation was that of John the Baptist. To him a still clearer light was given; and he himself "a burning and shining light." To him it was given to "behold the Lamb of God that taketh away the sin of the world." Accordingly our Lord himself affirms, that "of all which had been born of women," there had not till that time arisen "a greater than John the Baptist." But nevertheless he informs us, "He that is least in the kingdom of God," the Christian dispensation, "is greater than he."
>
> And, indeed, unless the servants of God halt by the way, they will receive the adoption of sons. They will receive the *faith* of the children of God, by his *revealing* his only begotten Son in their hearts. So the Apostle writes to the Galatians: "Ye are the sons of God by faith. And because ye are sons, God hath sent forth the Spirit of his Son into your hearts, crying, Abba, Father;" that is, giving you a childlike confidence in him, together with a kind affection toward him. This then it is, that properly constitutes the difference between a servant of God, and a child of God. "He that believeth," as a child of God, "hath the witness in himself." This the servant hath not.
>
> I exhort you, lastly, who already feel the Spirit of God witnessing with your spirit that you are the children of God, follow the advice of the Apostle: Walk in all the good works whereunto ye are created in Christ Jesus. And then, "leaving the principles of the doctrine of Christ, and not laying again the foundation of repentance from dead works, and of faith toward God," go on to perfection. Yea, and when ye have attained a measure of perfect love, when God has circumcised your hearts and enabled you to love him with all your heart and with all your soul, think not of resting there. That is impossible. You cannot stand still; you must either rise or fall; rise higher or fall lower. Therefore the voice of God to the children of Israel, to the children of God, is, "Go forward!" "Forgetting the things that are behind, and reaching forward unto those that are before, press on to the mark, for the prize of your high calling of God in Christ Jesus!"[62]

The *servants* of God approach the threshold of the narrow gate that few may enter. The *sons* of God proceed through the narrow gate. I can be more specific than Wesley about the "kind affection" toward God, and what it is to have "the witness in himself," or as St. Paul said, "I live now, not I, but Christ in me." This is "a measure of perfect love" – divine love, the love of God. It is the Buddha touching the earth at the 4th chakra, the heart chakra, where "God hath sent forth the Spirit of his Son into your hearts." It is a love of childlike simplicity, of total surrender, the expression of absolute trust and acceptance that is the ultimate definition of true faith, a love that frees the child of God from all belief, all sin and repentance, all vice and virtue, all good and evil.

When Wesley says, "You cannot stand still; you must either rise or fall; rise higher or fall lower.... Go forward!" I am reminded of the description of the irreversible movement forward of the eighth to tenth bhūmi bodhisattva:

> Eighth bhūmi bodhisattvas are said to be "irreversible," because there is no longer any possibility that they might waver on the path or backslide.... From this point on, bodhisattvas move quickly toward awakening. Before this stage, progress was comparatively slow, like that of a boat being towed through a harbor. On the eighth through tenth bhūmi, however, bodhisattvas make huge strides toward buddhahood, like a ship that reaches the ocean and unfurls its sails.[11]

Billions of people, maybe trillions over the centuries, have read or heard words like Wesley's. St. Paul, St. Francis of Assisi, Bonhoeffer, Chopra, Thich Nhat Hanh, Campbell, the sages of every culture and religion talk of the life of Christ, of the bodhisattva, of liberation at the highest levels of awakening. But few who read or hear these words can fully understand what they mean. To have actually *lived* these words, to *know* what these saints and seers are talking about ... I am left in dumbstruck awe.

~ 895 ~

I have been seeing angel feathers again. Yesterday I casually looked down at the sidewalk in front of me as I was walking by the art museum, and there it was. Today, as I was walking up the stairs at the mall, there was another one.

I put the fallen mirror tiles (~887~) back up in my bathroom, but not yet in Emily's. Just now another tile fell in Emily's bathroom. (I was gone most of the day; the tile waited until the minute I arrived home to fall.) I guess I'd better put hers back up, too, before the rest of her life comes crashing down. A couple hours ago she texted, "I feel my life slipping away ..."

~ 896 ~

Last night four more tiles fell, and three of them broke. Is this Emily's life slipping away? A while ago she said that she felt as if her soul was lying on the ground and she had to pick it up and dust it off. Maybe if I start putting the tiles back up, her soul will be picked up and dusted off.

When I came home this afternoon, I discovered that another whole column of six tiles had fallen down in my bathroom, the column next to the tiles I had just replaced. While I was picking up the broken glass, another column came crashing down before my eyes. Now most of the tiles are breaking. As soon as I pick up one part of my soul another part falls to the ground.

I suppose this extended period of high humidity is causing these tiles to fall, the decades-old adhesive finally giving way. But the location and the timing seem meaningful to me. Why one bathroom, then the other? Why this day, this month, this year, and not another? Why in the middle of the night? Just as I walk in the door? While I am right in front of them?

A couple days ago Emily asked, "Did you ever feel like you were in a dream?"

I replied, "All the time." The symbols of dreams appear in my waking life. I am living a dream.

~ 897 ~

The scripture reading in church today was from the gospel of Mark:

> And Jesus went on with his disciples, to the villages of Caesarea Philippi; and on the way he asked his disciples, "Who do men say that I am?" And they told him, "John the Baptist; and others say, Elijah; and others one of the prophets." And he asked them, "But who do you say that I am?" Peter answered him, "You are the Christ." And he charged them to tell no one about him.
>
> And he began to teach them that the Son of man must suffer many things, and be rejected by the elders and the chief priests and the scribes, and be killed, and after three days rise again. And he said this plainly. And Peter took him, and began to rebuke him. But turning and seeing his disciples, he rebuked Peter, and said, "Get behind me, Satan! For you are not on the side of God, but of men."
>
> And he called to him the multitude with his disciples, and said to them, "If any man would come after me, let him deny himself and take up his cross and follow me. For whoever would save his life will lose it; and whoever loses his life for my sake and the gospel's will save it." (Mark 8:27-35 RSV)

As did most of the Jews at the time of Christ, Peter thought that the Messiah would bring world peace, prosperity, and freedom from Rome. Like many people today, Peter found the prosperity gospel much easier to take than the cross of suffering. Jesus rebuked him for thinking in earthly terms, not heavenly ones. A while ago I wrote, "What religion could win followers by telling them they have to suffer?" After Jesus told the people they would have to take up their cross if they followed him, his crowds of devotees diminished greatly.

The minister exhorted the congregation to take up the cross and "go for it." "Don't be afraid," he said. "You won't be alone. Many others will be there with you." Here, in his well-intentioned attempt to soften the blow for his parishioners, the minister strayed from Christ's word. Although the journey to eternal life might well start with companions, at the end we are utterly alone, abandoned even by God, as Jesus was on the cross. As it was for Jesus it will be for everyone who follows his path. All companionship, all support, will fall away. Few pass through the narrow gate.

"For whoever would save his life will lose it; and whoever loses his life for my sake and the gospel's will save it." If I were to leave Emily to save my life, to protect myself from her abuse, I would lose it. I have suffered much at her hands, but the rewards – getting a view into the dark mind of God, rediscovering tantric sex with her, learning how Kannon's compassion removes obstacles for an *asura* – are far more precious than the ego-dominated life I would have saved by avoiding her torment. By losing my life in her service, I save it. She teaches a post-doctoral course in perfect joy.

For one gains by losing
And loses by gaining.

(*Dao De Ching*, Chapter 42)

~ 898 ~

Martin Luther King, Jr., said that whatever affects one directly, affects all indirectly, and that no one can be what he ought to be until everyone is what he ought to be. King's message was as much Buddhist/Hindu as Christian: interdependent co-arising, Indra's Net, the interlocking cause and effect of karma. We lift each other up and tear each other down.

This defines the relationship of all things, in microcosm and macrocosm. The earth cannot be what it ought to be until the sun shines as it ought. The cells of my lungs cannot do what they ought until the cells of my heart do what they ought, and vice versa. The water cannot reflect the light of the moon until the moon shines upon the water. I cannot gloriously love Emily as I ought until she loves me as she ought. The creator is made manifest, enabled and limited, by his creation.

~ 899 ~

Two angel card jumpers today:

"Peace" – Archangel Chamuel: *"Peace comes from remembering that only love is real."*

"You are safe" – Archangel Michael: *"I am protecting you against lower energies, and guarding you, your loved ones, and home."*

I had dinner with Emily tonight, the first time we have seen each other in over six months. I thought that having our bodies in close proximity again would reignite our fire. No. Her light is out. She is gone, firmly locked into her illusory life of co-dependency with her lovers and denial of her real self. Her discussion of deeply emotional issues was flat, detached, and colorless, not explosive and intense as it had been a year ago. I got the feeling that she might be taking mood-altering drugs. Whether due to drugs or something else, her personality is lost, as Joseph Campbell described:

> The psychological problem in the play *Equus*, which the psychiatrist realized, was that in "healing" his patient, he had deprived him of his God. I think it's Nietzsche who said, "Be careful, lest in casting out your devil, you cast out the best thing that's in you." Many people who have been psychoanalyzed are like filleted fish. Their character is gone.[2]

When Emily locked up her demons to stabilize her personality, her tormented wounded child was imprisoned with them. The voice that once screamed to me for help has been silenced.

Is our spiritual connection broken, or just dormant? The back of my 5th chakra has been tingling all evening, and is tingling now. Okay spirits, I hear you. I will let Emily keep her devil.

~ 900 ~

I slept long and deep last night. I fell asleep in front of the television at 11:30 p.m., then moved to bed and fell right to sleep again. I woke up at 7:30 a.m. and checked email for an hour, then went back to sleep, in and out of consciousness until noon. I feel dazed, wiped clean like an emotionally blank slate. Being with Emily changes my body chemistry, first one way, then another.

Had another provocative dream: *I am driving my car, but I can't see where I am going. It is night and there are no lights. Beyond the windshield is utter darkness. I am blindly steering the car, hoping to stay on the road, wherever it is. Suddenly I feel control of the steering wheel being taken away from me by some unseen force, and the car is swerving sharply to the side. I try to regain control, but fail. I look for the emergency brake but can't find it.*

In the darkness of my subconscious, the darkness of Sheol, I am not meant to know where I am going. It is okay to relinquish control of my car – my life – and let it go where it will. Let the car veer off the beaten path. Don't look for the brake. Just let go and trust that God is driving the car.

~ 901 ~

In church today I came to a tipping point in my use for ritual and liturgy. The traditional prayers and ceremonies of the church tend to reinforce the idea that God is somewhere outside of us and that heaven is a place we are not yet in. But I know from my own revelatory experience that this is not the case. The kingdom of God is within us, heaven is spread upon the earth, and we are, right now on earth, avatars of God as Jesus was.

> *Our father who art in heaven, hallowed be thy name.*
> *Thy kingdom come, thy will be done, on earth as it is in heaven.*
> *Give us this day our daily bread,*
> *and forgive us our sins, as we forgive those who sin against us.*
> *And lead us not into temptation, but deliver us from evil.*

For several months I have been in a quandary over the meaning of the Lord's Prayer. Jesus himself taught us this prayer, so there must be God-given truth in it. A while ago

I tried to find meaning in the prayer that made sense in the context of my personal revelation. (~522~) I succeeded only to a point. Today I realized that the prayer is not supposed to make sense to me. It is not for me, not for prophets, mystics, and bodhisattvas who already know perfect joy, who know that they must be led into temptation, that trials must be faced along the Way, and that they must submit to evil before they can be delivered from it.

To find the narrow gate is to realize that our father in heaven is inside us; that God's hallowed name is our own; that God's kingdom has already come in our human form, and God's will is now being done on earth as it is in heaven by us, through us; that our daily bread is given to us as God clothes the lilies of the field; that forgiveness is unnecessary in the spirit, where there is no law, no sin, no judgment, no shame, no blame, no right, no wrong, no good, no evil, and thus no need for forgiveness; that we have been joyously led into temptation as Jesus was, and as Jesus was, we will be delivered from evil by bearing sacrificial witness to it.

Few pass through the narrow gate; few are truly born again of the spirit. Jesus knew that, so he gave earthbound men a prayer to steer them toward the narrow gate while they are still in darkness, not yet able to see God except in material and temporal terms; not yet aware of their own divinity, not yet ready for the trials and sufferings at the end of the journey, not yet awakened to the eternal truth that is their ultimate deliverance.

Have I risen so far that I transcend even the Lord's own prayer?

~ 902 ~

It is so hard to describe why I stay with Emily. To the outside observer it must seem that my blind devotion is a sick obsession, limiting and crippling. But I am not blind; this is devotion with my eyes wide open. This relationship is ordained by God; it is the ultimate trial I must face to be freed from all desire and made fit to reenter the Garden of Eden through the narrow gate.

Imagine the agony of it. I have been given visions of eternal perfection with Emily and allowed to actually experience the joy of tantric union with her, yet her worldly self rejects me and chooses a life of separation from her angel in the spaceship. She chooses a lesser love with Danny and others when she could have the ultimate union with me. If I am to win this last battle with Mara, I must really be okay with that.

~ 903 ~

Everyone's first and deepest role model for love is our mother. Emily the Child was never able to experience a healthy mother's love, and so Emily the Adult built a life of emotional isolation as a defense against "love" that hurts, the only kind she has ever known. The only intimacy she knows is sexual, and there is always an element of hurt in her sexual relationships, as in her relationship with her mother. Emily has never known an intimate relationship that exposes her vulnerability that didn't also bring hurt. Who can blame her for not trusting my love, which seems so strange and unfamiliar?

The Unnamed One said that he never knew a love that didn't exact a price from him. (~362~) In the end he paid a price for loving me, but not one demanded by me or our love. It was exacted from both of us by his fear. I wonder if Emily is leading me even farther down the same path.

~ 904 ~

Movie and dinner with Emily. A little chink in the armor; deflector shields came down a little bit.

She torments me by coming close, then pulling away again, teasing me with hope that perhaps our spirit life might come alive in this world, then dashing my hopes on the rocks of despair. She puts before me in simultaneous juxtaposition the stark contrast of my limited temporal life and my unlimited spiritual life. This angst is the price I must pay for knowing what I know.

To know all that is, but cannot be in this life – that is samsara. To know all that is, and live it in the endless eternal moment – that is nirvana.

~ 905 ~

SEX, Part 26

For a couple years I have had a recurring dream, perhaps a lucid dream, a kind of sexual fantasy, that goes like this:

I am in a restaurant where the waitresses are topless, and the "cream" that customers order for their coffee is literally milked from the waitresses' breasts. There is also a backroom where men may go to more fully respond to their urges, where women are available to service these customers.

The women in the backroom are anonymous; only their alluring body parts are exposed. Breasts and genitals are revealed, but the rest of the women's bodies, including their faces, are hidden behind solid barriers. The women are totally detached from the sex acts being done to them, so uninvolved that they read books and file their nails behind their barricades to pass the time while dozens of men have their way with them. There is no physical or emotional pleasure for these sex workers. They feel nothing.

But at the end of the day, another man comes into the room. My attention is drawn to one particular woman lying on her back, legs spread, body covered. The man approaches her, gently washes her private parts, applies soothing lotion, and massages her tired legs and hips. The woman is aroused, feeling a connection with this man unlike anything she knew with the other men. She removes the barrier to her full body and face, looks into his eyes, and he looks into hers with deep compassion, knowing her suffering. She invites him to make love with her, and he does, with infinite tenderness.

There is a huge difference between having sex and making love. Sometimes when I have this dream I identify with the suffering woman, sometimes with the healing man. More and more I am recognizing that I am the man, and Emily is the woman. This dream is a temporal expression of our eternal tantric love.

~ 906 ~

I went to dinner and the theater with Emily. The play was a comedy, a farce, on the subject of the female orgasm. I did not know the subject matter of this play when I invited Emily to join me.

The only socially acceptable way to present such a ticklish subject is through comedy, but this comedic treatment cheapened and trivialized the matter to a point beyond recognition for me. My experience with orgasm has almost no correlation with the portrayal of it in this play, so I did not find it titillating or arousing at all. But I wondered about the forces that brought Emily and I together in this theater at this moment, why I was seeing this play sitting next to the person with whom I have experienced the most powerful tantric sex, through whom I have learned the deepest meaning of orgasm.

Emily seemed happy to be with me this evening. She thanked me over and over for inviting her. It seems that she is glad to have me back in her life. Although we both carefully avoided discussing the content of this play, I can feel our latent sexuality straining just below the surface, trying to burst from spirit to flesh. But I must not hope for anything. Hope is the last temptation, and the multiple temptations that Emily puts before me are my ongoing spiritual trial.

This is how I know that Satan is part of God, the dark face of God. Even as Emily tempts me and tortures me and draws out my latent desires and fears, I see God shining forth in her and feel the love of God flowing through us. She is my God with form, sometimes God in the form of Satan.

~ 907 ~

LOVING AT A DISTANCE IN TIME AND SPACE

> And then one or other dies. And we think of this as love cut short; like a dance stopped in mid-career or a flower with its head unluckily snapped off—something truncated and therefore, lacking its due shape. I wonder. ... It is not a truncation of the process but one of its phases; not the interruption of the dance, but the next figure. We are 'taken out of ourselves' by the loved one while she is here. Then comes the tragic figure of the dance in which we must learn to be still taken out of ourselves though the bodily presence is withdrawn, to love the very Her, and not fall back to loving our past, or our memory, or our sorrow, or our relief from sorrow, or our own love. – C.S. Lewis, *A Grief Observed* [3]

I was startled by Lewis' saying that we must learn to "not fall back to loving ... our own love." Here is the stark dividing line between duality and eternity. To know *agape* is to know that loving even our own love is a subject-object worldly love, defined by the separation of lover and beloved; in eternity we rise from *loving* love to *being* love.

Lewis also captured the meaning of love in the spirit – tantric love – whether it be shared with a dead lover or with a living one who happens to be elsewhere, as I experience it with Emily. "We must learn to be still taken out of ourselves though the bodily presence is withdrawn."

Eternal love is not truncated by death or distance, but infinitely expanded. We learn to "love the very Her," or as Marianne Williamson said, to see them "*so* really ... the way God would see them." Not the way we remember them, or imagine them, or fantasize them. Not in any way that springs from limiting sensory perceptions or mental formations in time or space.

~ 908 ~

Emily began to interrogate me on my relationship with Joe and ranted at me for allowing Joe to take advantage of me. "I'm very disappointed in you," she tells me. "You are in denial. You are upset because Joe's girlfriend is keeping him away from you. I'm a therapist, you know. You can't hide these things from me." I couldn't get a word in edgewise as she impugned Joe's motives, and his girlfriend's, and berated me over nothing. Then she told me I should clean up my house because there is a man out there for me who will not want me with my clutter.

I said, "If someone loves me unconditionally, my clutter will not matter."

She projected onto me, Joe, and his girlfriend feelings of jealousy, possessiveness, and competitiveness that none of us have. Is she in fact the one who is upset, in denial about the people who take advantage of her, whose offers of pleasure and support she cannot refuse, who use her as she uses them?

~ 909 ~

GOOD AND EVIL, Part 4

Ignacio's discussion group took up the topic of deliverance from evil today. In his article "Deliver Us From Evil, Including Our Own," John B. Cobb described Whitehead's view: "Sadly, there is no avoidance of tragedy. Life adds greatly to the value of entities, but life is, in Whitehead's words, 'robbery.' Living requires destroying other things, including other living things." The group began to feel guilty for eating meat, and then for eating wheat, and then chastised the wheat for robbing the soil of its nutrients.

Is it evil for a lion to kill and eat an antelope? Plants and animals simply follow their instincts in strict obedience to the God-given laws of nature. (~840~) Nature is neither good nor evil; it just is what it is. But humans added another layer of consciousness: the knowledge of duality, of good and evil. Thus came the co-arising of the law and with it, sin. (Romans 7:7-8) The effect of living in the separation of good and evil, the law and sin, is the price humans pay for eating of the Tree of the Knowledge of Good and Evil.

Plants, animals, and people engage in wars and other violent acts to acquire and secure territory and resources, win a mate, defend themselves, and get food. None of this is sinful or evil when viewed from the highest perspective. There is no judgment in eternity, as there is no law and no sin. There is no separation of good from evil, no law to break, no target to miss, and thus no basis for sin or judgment.

> Before I had studied Zen for thirty years, I saw mountains as mountains, and waters as waters. When I arrived at a more intimate knowledge, I came to the point where I saw that mountains are not mountains, and waters are not waters. But now that I have got its very substance, I am at rest. For it's just that I see mountains once again as mountains, and waters once again as waters. – Ching-yüan Wei-hsin (Seigen Ishin), from *The Way of Zen* [7]

Adam and Eve lived in the Garden at one with God, and they saw mountains as mountains and waters as waters. Then they ate of the Tree and arrived at a more intimate knowledge, and things got complicated. Then came Jesus to show us the very substance. Mountains are just mountains, after all, and waters, just waters.

~ 910 ~

Ignacio is thoroughly wedded to process theology. I have no quarrel with it. It works well and explains many things in the limited context of temporality. But like Newtonian physics, it breaks down when one enters the metaphysical realm. In the realm of Einstein's relativity, Newton's laws no longer apply. In the realm of eternity, where there is no time, no space, no thought, and no process, the time-burdened processes of process thought no longer apply. Referring to miraculous healing, spiritual author Joel Goldsmith said, "The laws of the material world do not apply to gods realized."

The limits of thinking in time are revealed when we differentiate our free will from God's will. Ignacio doesn't like it when God is called "almighty." (~847~) He said that God does not have all the power; people have power, too. I said that people get their power from the God-self that is present in each of us. He said that people have power even separate from God. We were both right; I was viewing from eternal unity; Ignacio was viewing from temporal separation.

Thinking that people have power separate from God locks us firmly in duality; it is prideful, egotistical, denying the creator within, placing us outside of and perhaps in opposition to God. The first commandment is to love God "with all your heart, and with all your soul, and with all your mind, and with all your strength." (Mark 12:30 RSV) When we act through the love of God in us, God's will is done. When we act separate from God, from love of self rather than love of God, our ego's will is being done, and our acts are liable to be sinful.

> Pilate therefore said to him, "You will not speak to me? Do you not know that I have power to release you, and power to crucify you?" Jesus answered him, "You would have no power over me unless it had been given you from above; therefore he who delivered me to you has the greater sin." (John 19:10-11 RSV)

We have no real power unless it is given to us from above. We are all emanations of God; there is nothing in us or from us that is not of God. God shares his power with us, but it is still God's power, at work through us as his embodiment on earth.

Ironically, even acts apparently not of God are of God, both sides of duality being of God. Even Judas, who committed a greater sin than Pilate's, was acting in accord with God's plan, as was necessary for Jesus to accomplish his sacrificial mission.

Pilate's sin was less than Judas' because Pilate acted as required under Roman law; not knowing the divinity of Jesus, he saw Jesus as just another Roman subject and gave unto Caesar what he thought was Caesar's. Pilate's power came from above, was granted by God, because at the spiritual level where Pilate was, he was obedient to the law he was under.

Judas' sin was greater than Pilate's because he acted not according to any law, but according to his own ego; he exercised his free will separate from God's will, wrenched power away from God, and by so doing he chose to enact the dark side of God. He gave unto Caesar what he knew to be God's.

Humans do have choices – which side of God to choose in this world. When we know that in everything we do we act as God on earth, we cannot choose badly. In the end, all things are right, even things we think are wrong.

~ 911 ~

What is God's plan?

God's plan is to bring you from where you are back to where you are. Nothing changes when you are enlightened, or born again. You simply return to where you started, where mountains are again just mountains, and waters, just waters. (~909~)

If God has a plan and everything we do is part of God's plan, is there free will?

Yes. Even though our spiritual destination can be only one place – the Source, the oneness and emptiness of eternity – there are infinite different ways to get there, as I described in the House of Eternity. (~435~/~437~/~441~) The exercise of free will, our freedom of choice, determines the length and trajectory of the path our journey will take.

Is evil part of God's plan?

Yes. If you use the word "God" to mean the Source, the Godhead, the formless God of the 7th chakra, then Satan is part of God just as Yahweh is.

What is "good"?

> And God made the beasts of the earth according to their kinds and the cattle according to their kinds, and everything that creeps upon the ground according to its kind. And God saw that it was good. (Genesis 1:25 RSV)

In the biosphere that God created, which he called "good," predators were eating their prey, bacteria were infecting their hosts, army ants were making war, lightning strikes were setting forests afire, and poisonous plants were teaching those who would eat them, not to. Even before Man appeared on the scene, there was pain and violence in the world ... and it was good.

> Do not be conformed to this world but be transformed by the renewal of your mind, that you may prove what is the will of God, what is good and acceptable and perfect. (Romans 12:2 RSV)

The will of God, what is "good and acceptable and perfect," includes both sides of duality. If you define God as being only good, then he is not the Source, but only the happy side of duality. (The unhappy side is Satan.) This "good" god is not the one God of the Zoroastrians, Muslims, Jews, and Christians, but just one of many facets of God, like the multiple gods of ancient India, Egypt, Greece, and Rome.

The Dao that can be named is not the Dao. The God that can be named is not the Source. Yahweh, Adonai, Emanuel, Brahma, Vishnu, Shiva, Amida, Kannon, Achala, and all the others are lesser gods representing aspects of the one true God. The one God, the Godhead, the emptiness of the Great Void, is neither good nor evil, and both.

~ 912 ~

"I dream of angels but I live with demons," said a schizophrenic perpetrator on the TV show *Law and Order SVU*. No matter how diligent law enforcement tries to be, we all still live with demons. The justice system is imperfect, and even a 100% conviction rate cannot prevent the continuation of criminal acts nor heal the damage done to the victims. No matter how compassionate I am, and even if my divine love were successful in bringing all my loved ones into higher spiritual states of peace and healing, there will still be suffering.

No matter how much good we do, the poor are always with us, as are the sick, downtrodden, and those who suffer hardships of all kinds. Good and evil ebb and flow from one moment to another in this temporal world, but in the eternal picture, yin always equals yang.

So what good is it to do good? Why even try, if evil cannot be conquered? Jesus told us to let the day's own trouble be sufficient for the day. The only time that matters is Now. Our job is to address the issue at hand, what is presenting itself to us at this moment – the only moment in which we have any power.

Justice done now is a true victory, although it may not be immediately apparent. As the present moment is healed, so is the past which brought it forth and the future that will come out of it. Our goal is not to conquer evil, but to find eternal peace around and between the pendulum swings of temporal good and evil. Peace comes one eternal moment at a time, one immortal soul at a time.

~ 913 ~

Every time I look at Emily's picture, I remind myself: No Hope.

I have seen us in nirvana, living in eternal union, all pain released. And it is not just that I have seen us in that condition; I have literally *lived* it, in tantric spiritual union made tangible in the flesh. No one understands this, a love so deep that it transcends the boundaries and biology of life. That I cannot experience this eternal condition with her physical form in this life and I must give up any hope for it is an inconceivable sorrow.

When we talked last, Emily said that she is very comfortable with herself and she likes being alone. She is blithely happy and superficially content, in total denial of her buried pain, her unhealthy physical and emotional dependencies, and her pathological behaviors. She meditates to calm her mind and eats a vegan diet to heal her body while her soul festers in generations of foul karma.

She is able to live free from the weight of her past because I have taken that weight – her sins, pain, regret, and guilt – upon me. She doesn't know it. When I mention, even obliquely, that I feel her pain, she rears up in anger.

I think this weight is literally killing me. I have tried to use the spiritualist's "cancel-clear-delete" to remove negative energy and chase away evil spirits. But this can only go so far. I came into Emily's life to suffer with her, to carry her pain because she is not able to handle the burden alone. It would not be right to put it all back on her. Jesus took the sins of the world upon him, and he carried them all the way to his sacrificial end.

My blood pressure, historically normal, is now dangerously high, and has been for about a year. I am ambivalent about treating it. My spirit tells my body what to do. When my work is done on earth, I will blow up, and that will be okay with me.

~ 914 ~

My perception is changing. I have been thinking of Emily as a live person who feels more and more dead to me. Now I am beginning to think of her as a dead person who occasionally appears in life. The Unnamed One, too. These karmic lovers, like Lou, are now more like ghosts than living beings. More ectoplasm than protoplasm. The illusory nature of life is becoming ever more apparent to me. Phantoms become real as Halloween approaches.

~ 915 ~

It seems that I have stopped learning new things. My recent revelations have brought deeper meaning to truths I unearthed many years ago, but there are no new realizations. Perhaps I know all that I need to know; now it is time to gather the threads of my knowledge together and hone my skills in communicating it.

> Then he said to them, "Nation will rise against nation, and kingdom against kingdom; there will be great earthquakes, and in various places famines and pestilences; and there will be terrors and great signs from heaven. But before all this they will lay their hands on you and persecute you, delivering you up to the synagogues and prisons, and you will be brought before kings and governors for my name's sake. This will be a time for you to bear testimony. Settle it therefore in your minds, not to meditate beforehand how to answer; for I will give you a mouth and wisdom, which none of your adversaries will be able to withstand or contradict. You will be delivered up even by parents and brothers and kinsmen and friends, and some of you they will put to death; you will be hated by all for my name's sake. But not a hair of your head will perish. By your endurance you will gain your lives. (Luke 21:10-19 RSV)

This scenario described by Luke has played out several times in my life, mostly in the context of my social justice activism. I was persecuted and delivered up by kinsman and friends who could not withstand or contradict the wisdom of my testimony. I was hated for the sake of my truth. On two occasions I was cast out, symbolically put to death. But I have not perished.

The Rev. Martin Luther King, Jr., like many others in social justice work, found it impossible to separate his spiritual calling from his earthly work. It is no coincidence that so many of the world's most courageous truth-tellers have been clergy or other spiritual practitioners. Truth, if it is indeed true, is always from God, be it scientific truth, artistic truth, political truth, economic truth, or philosophical truth. Prophets bear testimony as God instructs them, take the hatred and persecution that was foretold would come from telling the truth, and by enduring perfect joy, they gain eternal life.

All who walk the Way know the unresisted suffering of Christ the truth-teller. We know it as recipients of abuse at the hands of those who oppose our truth. But we do not run from our abusers, because in the boundless emptiness, we are not separate from them. There is no place to run.

~ 916 ~

Last night I had a dream about Joseph Campbell. I was expounding to a group of students on the incredible impact Campbell had on the world's knowledge of spiritual truth.

This morning in my email I found a notice from the Joseph Campbell Foundation concerning their fundraising campaign for a new book on Campbell's mythology. I guess Campbell is telling me through the collective unconscious that I should support this project. ... Okay, will do.

~ 917 ~

A couple days ago Emily sent me a friendly, "have a nice day" text. Then later that evening, without any provocation on my part (there never is), came a little flurry of mildly abusive texts, first accusing me of not caring enough for her, then caring too much.

"Sorry, I need more from my close friendships."

"What more do you need? I give you all that I have."

"I always wanted you as my best girlfriend but you constantly put emotional pressure on the relationship. I release you."

"You do not hold me, so you cannot release me. Love is forever and cannot be let go."

"Need another good friend, not another person in love with me."

"I am not 'in love' with you. My love is not like that of the others. Not dependent, not demanding. A blessing for both of us."

"No, it is not a blessing because I want a friendship, but you get in the way."

It is not my emotional pressure on our relationship that gets in the way – it is hers – her discomfort with my seeing so deeply into her. When I say I love her, I do not mean that I am "in love" with her. "Falling in love" implies a worldly emotion that can be fallen out of. I did not fall in love with her, and so I cannot fall out of love with her. I live constantly with her in ever-present divine love, which is not a passing emotion, but an endless state of being. She cannot see this critical distinction.

Within a minute of the last text, the phone rang:

"I just want normal, not crazy."

"I will try my best to be normal, but may I still send you the little heart emojis?"

"You may do whatever you want, my love."

And then, early yesterday morning, she texted:

"May I stay with you this weekend? More demolition and paint fumes. Feeling very ill." (Her new house is being remodeled.)

"Of course you may stay with me. Your toothbrush is right where you left it."

We spent most of the rest of the day together at my house, and she spent the night. I discovered a reason for her psychotic texts the day before: She has been having severe abdominal pain and bloating, and she is going in for a biopsy. She said:

"You are one of the cornerstones of my emotional support. I can't talk about this with very many people, but I have to tell you."

I took her hand and said, "You can talk to me. That's why I'm here."

"I realize that now."

She was in a great deal of physical and psychic discomfort, but we had a very calm, healing, time together. I made dinner, we ate, talked, watched TV, and slept.

I woke up this morning about 4:30 a.m. I stayed in bed, going in and out of consciousness until about 7:30 a.m. During that time I felt great peace, Emily sleeping in the next room, Emily and I being in the right place at the right time, in the moment. I felt angels descending upon us, holding us in their hands.

~ 918 ~

Emily is tossed back and forth among her lovers who seek to possess her. Vincent buys her gifts, gives her money, and does things for her to hang on to what little remains of their past together. Danny buys her gifts, gives her money, and does things for her to purchase their future together. Arthur buys her gifts, gives her money, and does things for her for both reasons, hanging on to nostalgia for their past and vain hope that they might have a future together.

I do not cling to the past or the future. I buy her gifts, give her money, and do things for her to fulfill my mission as her guardian angel, to support her through the minefields of life. I do not possess her, but I am always with her, and she with me. I hold her in the spirit now and always, in the eternal present. I possess her the same way I possess myself, holding us both in the ephemeral ether of eternity. As the wind possesses the air and the air possesses the wind. As the water possesses the wave and the wave, the water.

~ 919 ~

Martha says she can see that I am enjoying my time with Emily. Yes, but in a way, not. Every moment of enjoyment with her is a cruel temptation to grasp at hope for something I cannot have.

If Emily is to walk the path with me, she will need to lose herself in me as I am lost in her, to surrender her ego to divine love. She will want to be with me for my sake, not hers. My allegedly moldy carpet (second poison aversion) and Danny's $7,000 ring (first poison desire) will not matter. Until then, she is not ready. The worldly relationships she has now seem so important to her, but if she knew my love, she would easily leave them behind to join me in eternal union.

Old loves will no longer have any hold on her. She will have no problem letting go of Danny, Vincent, Arthur, and even the memory of her late husband, as I was able to let go of Lou when The Unnamed One appeared. She will keep them in her heart and remember them affectionately, but not grasp and pine for them. The hole in her life that they filled will disappear, the divine love she discovers with me being all she needs. She will follow me as I follow her, as the disciples followed Jesus: in poverty, empty, in unsupported thought, free of attachments, hopes, and fears.

Of course, the blessed vision I have just described I cannot have. The last bit of ego I must extinguish is the hope that I might someday have it.

~ 920 ~

All three of my karmic loves were diagnosed with cancer in their late fifties. Lou died of it, The Unnamed One was cured of it, and Emily lives with it under control so far. Is there meaning in this?

~ 921 ~

The phone rang. The caller ID said "private caller." I don't usually answer unidentified calls, but this time I did, because I was expecting a delivery. As I said "Hello," a bone-chilling, blood-curdling voice said something indecipherable and then, "... and you won't tell me!" The caller hung up.

I fell silent, stunned. I recognized the voice. It was Emily's dissociative voice, her abusive mother's voice. Is it possible that her dissociative disorder is so advanced that her alter ego has its own private phone number? If it wasn't actually Emily calling, it was a message from the spirits: *BEWARE*.

I sense that as Emily's surface persona becomes more calm and controlled, her hidden persona becomes more dark and desperate. As the surface smooths, the depths become turbulent. As her abusive nature is suppressed in her conscious life, it rises up in her subconscious: *DANGER*.

~ 922 ~

HALLOWEEN

Emily's psychic disease seems so deep, so ferocious, that there is no way for her to find divine love in this life. To witness such a severe illness in full bloom is breathtaking – and frightening, so appropriate for Halloween. I see ever more clearly that my purpose is not to experience divine love with her, but simply to introduce it to her, to be her wake-up fairy as the end of her life approaches, to prepare her soul for a better life in the next incarnation.

My love has not reached her consciousness, but I know that some part of her does know this love and wants to live it. This is why she keeps putting off marriage with Danny, and why she chose not to move closer to him after her house was sold. Her subconscious mind knows the truth, but her conscious mind still wanders in darkness.

Divine love is not something to be chosen; it is something to be surrendered to, as one surrenders to the power of a great wave that carries you away with it. I will know she has opened her heart to this love when she no longer feels that she has any other choice. Will it happen in this life? She must play the hand already dealt to the last card before a new hand can be dealt.

> There is perfection in the process—and all life arises out of choice. It is not appropriate to interfere with choice, nor to question it. It is particularly inappropriate to condemn it.... Be watchful, therefore, of the choices of others, but not judgmental. Know that their choice is perfect for them in this moment now—yet stand ready to assist them should the moment come when they seek a newer choice, a different choice, a higher choice. – *Conversations with God* [23]

~ 923 ~

In the last couple years I have become mildly addicted to playing Spider Solitaire on the computer. Well, okay ... more than mildly addicted; I have played over 1,000 games. This game is teaching me how the future unfolds from the past. Each move, especially early in the game, sets the game on a particular course and predetermines whether the game can be won or not. All games can be won, but not by every route. Only certain sequences of moves can produce a win.

The game allows unlimited undo, so it is possible to retrace one's steps, go back to the past and change course. In a difficult game, at the highest level involving all four suits of cards, fewer routes lead to victory. Sometimes one move early in the game, sometimes a counterintuitive move, makes the difference between a win and a loss. Over time I have come to understand the rhythm of the game, how one move leads to the next, to the next, and so on, and how the entire rhythm of the game is changed as one move is changed.

This is what life is. A wrong move in the game of life is like taking a wrong turn in a maze. When one lives in time and eternity simultaneously, it is possible to back up in the maze, revisit the past and find a new route to the center or the exit. This is what the seers mean when they say we are living the past. Each move in the game of life is a karmic tug at Indra's Net, and each move affects every other move across the entire net. We can reset past moves and set up a new route to the future.

This is the reason for my existence – to reset the past, repair bad karma, and plot a new course for suffering souls that finds the way out of the maze and wins the game of life. Through me and all the mystics, God is pushing the reset button, altering our collective GPS to enable a blessed change of course into the future.

~ 924 ~

My Buddhist guide says: *A bell is indicated … your voice rings in the bell … your voice can reach people, get their attention … some will hear, others not.*

Martha says I am a wake-up fairy. So do the Buddhists.

I don't put much stock in Chinese fortune cookies, but this one, from my lunch today, caught my attention: *"You shall soon achieve perfection."* (I wonder how many millions of those they printed!)

~ 925 ~

I just arrived at my vacation destination for a week of relaxation, rejuvenation, meditation. When I checked into my lodging I was told I was in Building 4, Room 426. There's my Angel Number 4 again.

The number 4 has been haunting me for decades. I first became conscious of its meaning at a Doreen Virtue workshop last year. (~652~) Carl Jung teaches that the powerful symbolism of the number 4 goes back much farther than that:

> The arrangement of snakes in the four corners [of a room in a dream] is indicative of an order in the unconscious. It is as if we were confronted with a pre-existent ground plan, a

kind of Pythagorean *tetraktys*. I have frequently observed the number four in this connection. It probably explains the universal incidence and magical significance of the cross or of the circle divided into four.[77]

~ 926 ~

FULL MOON – NEW MOON, Part 7

This angel card has been coming up repeatedly the last several days: *"Moon Cycles"* – Archangel Haniel: *"Notice how the moon affects your energy and manifestations, and capitalize upon these cycles."*

This year Emily's birthday falls during the time of the new moon, the darkest phase of the moon, when the moon is closest to the sun, obscured by the light of the sun, and thus not visible on earth.

I have always felt close to her during the full moon, when the light of the western sun fully illuminates the moon on the eastern horizon, fully reflecting the light of the sun to observers on earth. This condition represents the vision of God with form at the 6th chakra, the moonlight being God's light fully reflected to earth; as Jesus was God with form, in a physical body, transmitting God's light from heaven to earth; as the Buddha put enlightened form to the formless emptiness of the Great Void; as the Hindu gods have avatar bodies to bring spiritual forces to earth.

The symbolism of this phenomenon – the lunar reflection being God with form at the 6th chakra – has been a powerful force in understanding my relationship with Emily. I am God with form, reflecting God's light, God's love, to Emily. And she is my God with form; in her I see God reflected back to me.

But now, I think the new moon, the invisible moon, is an even better metaphor for our love, even more powerful, symbolizing the disappearance of the moon into the sun, as the salt doll disappears into the ocean. At the 6th chakra, the full moon is directly facing the sun and reflects its light; at the 7th chakra, the new moon is embraced by the sun and swathed in its light.

As the new moon is enveloped in the light of the sun, so we are enveloped in the light of God. God with form returns to its Source, to God without form at the 7th chakra. The Word that was made flesh, made visible in the light of the full moon, returns to sit invisibly at the right hand of God the Father. Resurrection.

I am dissolved and absorbed into Emily, and she into me, as the new moon sits at the right hand of the sun, as Jesus sits at the right hand of God, as the salt doll dissolves into the ocean. This is how I have learned to love Emily even when her physical form is far away from me. This is Tantra.

~ 927 ~

I hope Emily is not disappointed that I have not given her a lavish birthday present. I am not good at gifting. All I know how to give is love. Love is not measured in material objects, money, flattery, or even acts of kindness. Many people have given her these things, but I give her the greatest gift — my life, my soul, my eternal essence. I am not here to give her things or do things to make her happy; I am here to liberate her from desire for things.

Love is measured, if it is measured at all, not in doing but in being — being at peace in the moment, without health or wealth, boundaries or defenses. My love makes me totally vulnerable, but at the same time liberated. Love drives out fear.

~ 928 ~

Twice today I nodded off in front of the TV. Both times I dreamt that I was negotiating a narrow footbridge across a deep chasm. I was walking carefully and did not fall, but I was aware of the danger. One time I was jolted awake by an acrophobic shudder coursing through my body.

From dreammoods.com:

Bridge – To dream that you are crossing a bridge signifies an important decision or a critical junction in your life. This decision will prove to be a positive change filled with prosperity and wealth in the horizon. Bridges represent a transitional period in your life where you will be moving on to a new stage.

Abyss – To dream of an abyss signifies an obstacle that is creating much anxiety for you. You need to work through the difficulty and overcome this obstacle in your life.

Walking – To dream that you are walking with ease signifies a slow but steady progress toward your goals. To dream that you have difficulties walking indicates that you are reluctant and hesitant in proceeding forward in some situation. The difficulty in walking is a reflection of your current situation and the obstacles that you are experiencing.

Narrow – To dream about narrow spaces indicate that you are experiencing some struggle in your life journey. You are feeling restricted and confined. Something narrow is also symbolic of female sexuality.

~ 929 ~

On the last day of my trip, the silver necklace chain that Emily had given me broke in two places. Today the elastic band in a bracelet she gave me broke as I was putting it on. Could dream symbolism be coming to life once again?

From dreammoods.com:

> **Break** – To dream that you break something indicates that changes are ahead for you. You need to "break" away from some situation and change the direction that your life is headed in.

> **Jewelry** – To see broken jewelry in your dream signifies disappointments in achieving your goals and attaining your highest desires.

> **Necklace** – To see or wear a necklace in your dream represents unsatisfied desires. It also highlights your intellect and your desire to have more influence and power over others. If the necklace is broken or lost, then it indicates that your rational thinking is in accordance with your emotional thinking. You need to act on your gut instinct about some situation or relationship.

> **Bracelet** – To see or wear a bracelet in your dream refers to an expression of deep passion and fire. The dream also highlights your need to reach out to others. To see a broken bracelet in your dream suggests that you tend to sacrifice your own comfort and happiness for others.

In the breaking of the necklace I am told that my head and heart are in accord, and I should listen to my intuition, my gut. The broken bracelet describes me to a tee. The broken necklace and broken bracelet may not be negative signs, but positive, validating ones.

~ 930 ~

On my first Sunday back home, I returned to the Christian church. In his sermon the pastor came right out and said that the apocalyptic scripture is widely misinterpreted to mean the literal destruction of the temple in Jerusalem, the second coming of Jesus in bodily form, and a new kingdom where the lion will actually lie down with the lamb.

This literal interpretation is not what the scripture means. To understand the metaphor: The destruction of the temple is the end of the old law of Moses; the second coming of Jesus is each person's own awakening to his own divinity and liberation from the old law; and the new kingdom is a return to the original one, our entry back into the Garden of Eden where there is no law, no sin, no predator, no prey, and no dualistic conflict, only the eternal love of God.

> Not long ago, archaeologists could agree that the Old Testament, for all its embellishments and contradictions, contained a kernel of truth. Obviously, Moses had not parted the Red Sea or turned his staff into a snake, but it seemed clear that the Israelites had started out as a nomadic band somewhere in the vicinity of ancient Mesopotamia; that they had migrated first to Palestine and then to Egypt; and that, following some sort of conflict with the authorities, they had fled into the desert under the leadership of a mysterious figure who was either a lapsed Jew or, as Freud maintained, a high-born priest of the royal sun god Aton whose cult had been overthrown in a palace coup. Although much was unknown, archaeologists were confident that they had succeeded in nailing down at least these few basic facts.
>
> That is no longer the case. In the last quarter century or so, archaeologists have seen one settled assumption after another concerning who the ancient Israelites were and where they came from proved false. – Daniel Lazare, "False Testament," *Harper's Magazine*, March 2002

Sometime in the prehistoric fog, someone made up a story about the Jews being slaves in Egypt and Moses parting the Red Sea to liberate them. It was a metaphorical, mystical story to describe the process by which we can each find our own personal liberation. Like Zen *koan* or the parables of Jesus, this story was intended to create a state of mind that goes beyond the mind, into the realm of spirit. But at some point, people began to think that this miraculous story was historical fact, and to this day the Jews re-enact this event in their Friday night seder.

The Christians have done the same thing with the miracles in the New Testament. Jesus did not raise Lazarus from the dead, nor was his body resurrected to reappear to the disciples after he died. These Bible stories are no more real than the legend of King Arthur, who did *not* pull a sword out of a stone. When we think these things actually happened, we move our minds out of the spirit and back into the world. The mystery is gone. The message is lost.

~ 931 ~

Today I sent the Joseph Campbell Foundation an online donation, as my dream last month nudged me to do. (~916~) I got an immediate reply from an officer of the Joseph Campbell Foundation, whom I had met at a workshop over a year ago (~654~):

> *Thank you so much for helping ensure others will have access to Joseph Campbell's work. I remember that amazing week and the synchronicities you shared afterward. So glad to know that Joseph Campbell's spirit is alive and well with you.*

I responded:

I am honored that you remember me, and I wanted to tell you that the synchronicities continue. Joe visited me in a powerful dream just before I learned of your fundraising campaign, and that motivated my gift. Campbell was a true mystic, and through his work, I am learning that I am one, too.

He replied:

I have no doubt you are a mystic.

~ 932 ~

I couldn't make this stuff up. Yesterday I was talking with Rita about her boyfriend and Joseph Campbell's ideas on courtly love. She wanted to know what Campbell had to say, and I offered to lend her my Campbell books on the subject.

Today in the mail I got a box full of books from the Joseph Campbell Foundation, my reward for the donation I had made a few days ago. Included in the box was Campbell's book about King Arthur, the Grail, and courtly love. I gave Rita the book. Campbell is with us now, guiding our every move, in the collective unconscious – and also in hardcover and paperback.

Some miracles are subtle, but some just smack you upside the head.

~ 933 ~

In his book *Mysticism*, F.C. Happold describes these seven characteristics of mystical states:

> 1. First of all, a mystical state has the quality of *ineffability*, that is, it defies expression in terms which are fully intelligible to one who has not known some analogous experience. ✓
>
> 2. Nevertheless, while mystical states are akin to states of feeling, they are also states of knowledge. They have a *noetic* quality. They result in insight into depths of truth unplumbed by the discursive intellect, insights which carry with them a tremendous sense of authority. ✓
>
> 3. Mystical states can seldom be sustained for long; they rarely last for any length of time. They have thus the quality of *transiency*. The following of a particular way of life can, however, increase their frequency. At that stage of the Mystic Way known as the Illuminative Life, they can be very frequent and, it would seem, controllable. In the words of St. John

of the Cross, "the soul has it in its power to abandon itself, whenever it wills, to this sweet sleep of love." ✓

4. Nevertheless, when they occur, mystical states invariably carry with them a feeling of something given. They have the quality of *passivity*. The mystic feels as if his own will were in abeyance, as if he were grasped and held by a power not his own. ✓

5. A common characteristic of many mystical states is the presence of a *consciousness of the Oneness of everything*. ✓

6. A further characteristic of mystical experience is the sense of *timelessness*. ✓

7. Bound up with the sense of oneness and the sense of timelessness there is another characteristic of mystical experience, the conviction that the familiar phenomenal *ego is not the real I*.[54] ✓

Seven points, seven check marks in my life. Yes, I'm a mystic.

~ 934 ~

I have been studying the work of Abraham Maslow, a psychologist who, unlike his contemporary Sigmund Freud, studied healthy, successful people rather than the mentally ill. He therefore learned the psychological patterns that lead to mental health, not illness, and to the highest levels of personal achievement and satisfaction. Maslow summarized his work thus:

> There are at least five sets of goals, which we may call basic needs. These are briefly physiological, safety, love, esteem, and self-actualization. In addition, we are motivated by the desire to achieve or maintain the various conditions upon which these basic satisfactions rest, and by certain more intellectual desires.

> Thus man is a perpetually wanting animal. Ordinarily the satisfaction of these wants is not altogether mutually exclusive, but only tends to be. The average member of our society is most often partially satisfied and partially unsatisfied in all of his wants.

> Any thwarting or possibility of thwarting of these basic human goals, or danger to the defenses which protect them, or to the conditions upon which they rest, is considered to be a psychological threat. With a few exceptions, all psychopathology may be partially traced to such threats. A basically thwarted man may actually be defined as a "sick" man, if we wish.[63]

"Thus man is a perpetually wanting animal." With this statement Maslow unwittingly pronounced the Buddhist Second Noble Truth: the cause of suffering is desire.

Saul McLeod explained Maslow's principles in more detail:

Maslow's original hierarchy of needs:

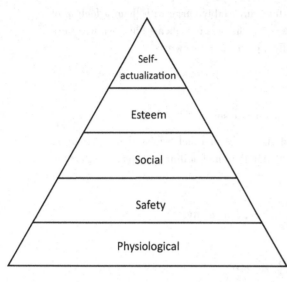

1. *Biological and Physiological needs* - air, food, drink, shelter, warmth, sex, sleep.

2. *Safety needs* - protection from the elements, security, order, law, stability, freedom from fear.

3. *Love and belongingness needs* - friendship, intimacy, affection, and love from work group, family, friends, romantic relationships.

4. *Esteem needs* - achievement, mastery, independence, status, dominance, prestige, self-respect, respect from others.

5. *Self-Actualization needs* - realizing personal potential, self-fulfillment, seeking personal growth and peak experiences.

One must satisfy lower level basic needs before progressing on to meet higher level growth needs. Once these needs have been reasonably satisfied, one may be able to reach the highest level called self-actualization.[64]

Maslow did well as far as he went, but he did not describe the level beyond self-actualization, which is enlightenment. The breakthrough from self-actualization to self-annihilation comes when a person, once all five levels of needs are satisfied, discovers unsupported thought and realizes that even the lowest physiological needs can be largely done without. Bliss can only be found by letting go of all of it.

Prestige, social status, love and friendship, safety and security, even fulfilling basic biological needs beyond the degree necessary for mere survival, are actually impediments to awakening. Desire must be extinguished. If, as Maslow says, "a basically thwarted man may actually be defined as a 'sick' man," then the awakened man is the ultimate picture of health, because without having any needs or fears, there is no way he can be thwarted.

The awakened man achieves everything of which he is capable, reaches his full potential, finds complete satisfaction and success in life, and then discovers that none of it matters. The worldly needs and desires that he once thought were so important have no meaning anymore. There are no more dependencies or attachments, no more greed or fear. This explains why mystics of all cultures and ages often live alone in poverty and are happy that way. All their needs have disappeared.

Both Jesus and the Buddha grew up in the safety and abundance of a caring family, satisfying all of Maslow's basic needs, then left that life to become wandering mendicants, and then re-engaged with the world to serve, empowered by what they found on that highest plateau beyond self-actualization, beyond self itself.

~ 935 ~

"Why didn't you tell anyone?"
"Then the abuse becomes real. If you keep quiet, you can pretend it's not."

– Olivia Benson (Mariska Hargitay) on *Law and Order SVU*

This may be why Emily is so quiet.

Each time she disappears, she goes farther away. She is now more dead than alive to me. Yet I stand by, sensing that someday she may need my kind of love.

But before she can come to me, I must let go of three layers of desire:

1) My desire for her to love me back, to awaken to our eternal connection in this life;

2) My desire to see her healed, which is partly my desire to feel the weight of her pain lifted from me as it is lifted from her; and

3) My desire to be the agent for her healing. Perhaps it is meant for Danny to be the catalyst for her recovery, if there is to be recovery. If that happens, I must rejoice for her and for him, without a trace of jealousy or regret.

And yet, even while letting go of all these desires, I must not let go of my abiding compassion for her. I cannot remove first-poison desires and second-poison fears by taking the third poison of escapism. I cannot win my battle with Mara by running away from it. I must stay in the fire through the final sacrifice, until the pain doesn't hurt anymore.

If and when I can fully let go of all these desires, then and only then will the path be open for us to realize the full flowering of divine love and the psychic healing that naturally flows from it. A Buddhist aphorism says, "If one doesn't have desire, then it is all right to possess a thousand measures of gold. If one has desire, then one needs to give up one's attachment to even a single copper penny." When I have finally given up attachment to the last of my ego's selfish demands, then it will be all right to have heaven on earth.

Emily's silence at this time, her rejection of me, is as powerful a lesson as there is. She is indeed my highest guru and my last temptation. Maybe I was not drawn to her for her healing, but for mine.

~ 936 ~

Emily is back. The first communication in nineteen days, but only small talk. Nothing has changed. She is happy with Danny, but not married, and still not sharing anything of importance with me about her life.

I fell asleep on the couch and had this dream: *I was climbing a sheer vertical wall with only the most tenuous handholds and footholds. I was moving very carefully, reminding myself to remain focused, because the slightest misstep would be the end. I got to the top and looked down thousands of feet to the bottom of the cliff. Then I had to go back down, which I realized was much harder than going up. After descending several levels I felt myself losing control and leaning backward. I told myself not to give up; if I let go I would fall to my death. I fought to hold on, and made it down to the bottom, where another person was waiting to go up. Having regained my courage, I started to climb back up a little way.*

From dreammoods.com:

> **Climb** – To dream that you are climbing up something signifies that you are trying to or you have overcome a great struggle. It also suggests that your goals are finally within reach. To dream that you are climbing down something indicates that you need to acknowledge and take notice of your subconscious.

> **Height** – To dream that you are at a great height signifies that you have reached one of your highest goals or objectives.

> **Falling** – Dreaming that you fall backwards suggests that you prevented yourself from making a bad decision or mistake. It may also mean that you are not ready to move forward and need to take a step back.

I woke up and found a text from Emily waiting for me: "Are you ok? Your texts sound off." She followed with some platitudes about love means being happy for someone and is not possessive. (She understands this intellectually, but not spiritually.) I did not reply, except with a little heart emoji. I wonder if Emily was the person at the end of my dream, about to start her climb up the wall.

~ 937 ~

Emily's insanity is the perfect balance to my sanity. Together we are the dark side and the light side of the moon, of God with form.

Cecilia said that Emily has me hooked, and I need to break away. I said that I have no choice but to stay hooked. God called me to this. I can no more abandon this relationship and the pain it brings than Jesus could walk away from his destiny on Calvary. I am in Adonai's and Achala's fire, and I must stay there until I am consumed and reborn into the scorched earth of nirvana.

No one understands my perfect sacrificial love, my purification in the fire of Achala's irreversible eighth bhūmi.

~ 938 ~

A dark dream last night: *I was in an art museum, about to leave. The cashier (for some reason I had to pay on exit) noticed I was wearing a bracelet with gray, rough, cone-shaped, sandstone-like beads. She wanted to charge me based on the value of the bracelet. "The bracelet is very valuable," she said.*

I found myself back in the museum, where a staff person befriended me. She walked toward the backroom, and I followed her. There were many people there, asking me what I was doing there. "I just wandered in," I said. It was very dark, and I got lost amid the boxes and objects d'art trying to find my way out.

Then I found myself in a lit but empty room. The people said, "Lock her inside the room." I pulled on the door from the inside to open it and escape, but felt the people on the other side pulling it shut. I prevailed, and got out. The vision of the bracelet came up again.

From dreammoods.com:

> **Museum** – To dream that you are in a museum represents the things you value in life. Objects in the museum symbolize memories and talents.

> **Bracelet** – To see or wear a bracelet in your dream refers to an expression of deep passion and fire. The dream also highlights your need to reach out to others.

> **Stones** – To see a stone in your dream symbolizes strength, unity, and unyielding beliefs. Look at the shape, texture and color of the stone for additional significance. If the stones

are rough, then it represents your quest in recognizing and developing your self-identity. Part of this quest is to also become aware of your subconscious and suppressed thoughts.

Cone – To see a cone in your dream represents a flow of ideas and feelings.

Gray – Gray indicates fear, fright, depression, ill health, ambivalence and confusion. You may feel emotionally distant, isolated, or detached. Alternatively, the color gray symbolizes your individualism.

Door – To dream that you are entering through a door signifies new opportunities that are presented before you. You are entering into a new stage in your life and moving from one level of consciousness to another. In particular, a door that opens to the outside signifies your need to be more accessible to others, whereas a door that opens into the inside denotes your desire for inner exploration and self-discovery.

To dream that the door is closed or locked signifies opportunities that are denied and not available to you or that you have missed out on. Something or someone is blocking your progress. It also symbolizes the ending of a phase or project. In particular, if you are outside the locked door, then it suggests that you have anti-social tendencies. If you are inside the locked door, then it represents harsh lessons that need to be learned.

Room – To dream that you are in a room represents a particular aspect of yourself or a specific relationship. Dreams about various rooms often relate to hidden areas of the conscious mind and different aspects of your personality. To dream that you are in an empty white room indicates a fresh start. It is like a blank canvas where you want to start life anew.

I was being locked out of the things that I value in life. But those trying to block me did not succeed. I escaped being stuck behind the locked door where harsh lessons need to be learned. (There was another locked door in a past dream that did presage harsh lessons. [~524~]) The empty lit room represents my conscious waking life, and the dark museum beyond the room, my subconscious spirit life. I refuse to be locked inside my physical life and isolated from my guiding spirits in the collective unconscious. (I have been feeling that the confining demands of my worldly life are sidetracking my spiritual development.) The very valuable bracelet is my divine love, solid as a rock and unyielding in the immovable eighth bhūmi, my individual self-identity, flowing to others.

~ 939 ~

Emily texted that we might get together next week ... or maybe the week after, or maybe not until January when she is back from her trip to see Danny. I suggested we go to a movie, but she said no, she had plans to go to the movies with other people. And by the way, she will be off the grid, no phone, while she is away, because a "very special event" is coming up. I asked, "Getting married?" There was no reply.

She dangles the carrot of a meeting in front of my nose and then puts off seeing me, goes out with other people, announces plans to cut me off from communication, and won't tell me what the "special event" is.

She tortures me with surgical precision. She is doing her devilish job – the job God sent her to do – holding up to me the mirror that needs polishing, wringing out of me every last shred of clinging desire, sticking a stiletto precisely into my most vulnerable spot, burning up my illusory landscape of samsara, preparing me for nirvana. Dashing my hope, my last temptation.

And yet ... nothing has changed. Divine love continues without the slightest interruption through it all. I am purified in Achala's fire, but not consumed. I am singed by the flaming swords of the cherubim who guard the Tree of Eternal Life, lighting the passage back into the Garden of Eden at the narrow gate.

~ 940 ~

Why then did you go out? To see a prophet? Yes, I tell you, and more than a prophet. This is he of whom it is written, "Behold, I send my messenger before thy face, who shall prepare thy way before thee." Truly, I say to you, among those born of women there has risen no one greater than John the Baptist; yet he who is least in the kingdom of heaven is greater than he. (Matthew 11:7-11 RSV)

I always wondered how "the least in the kingdom of heaven" could be greater than John the Baptist. Wasn't John, of all men, worthy of the greatest greatness? The clue to the meaning of this passage is in Jesus' reference to those "born of women" – those who identify with their illusory physical bodies, know only the world of duality that they were born into, and are tainted by original sin. Those in the kingdom of heaven, who are "born of the spirit," know the eternal reality behind the illusion of life and have been released from the law and sin, and thus are greater than all those born of women.

Sometimes those in the kingdom of heaven return to the world in human form, as Jesus did, to bring others into the kingdom. They are bodhisattvas. They inhabit earthly bodies, but they identify with the indwelling spirit that imbues the body with eternal life, not with the matter, lower energies, and ego that drive the dualistic world. Those born of women take direction from the lower three chakras; those in the kingdom of heaven direct the power of the lower three chakras to the upper three and make the spiritual connection between heaven and earth via the 4th chakra.

I have no doubt that after his death John the Baptist joined the awakened souls in the kingdom of heaven, transcended duality, and so exceeded even his earthly greatness. As John Wesley says, he rose from being a *servant* of God to being a *son* of God. (~894~)

~ 941 ~

Emily said that my texts and emails are "a bit much" and I should respect her privacy. Meaningful conversation between us ended months ago, and now she wants no conversation at all. Shards of pain are shooting through me.

Just now I drew this angel card: *"Peace"* – *Archangel Chamuel: "Peace comes from remembering that only love is real."*

Anthony de Mello said that all anyone ever needs is to "be love." Emily's cruel rejection brings me St. Francis' perfect joy, destroying the last remnant of ego, polishing the last bit of dust from my mirror, so the love that I am can flow unimpeded, the full moon perfectly reflecting the invisible light of the sun.

Emily told me when The Unnamed One rejected me, "When he rejects you, he rejects himself." When she rejects me, she rejects herself. But I do not reject her. I hold her in endless eternal embrace.

~ 942 ~

Suddenly out of nowhere, a slew of texts, beginning at 3:36 p.m. and ending at 4:27 p.m.:

Can you come take me to dinner? If not see you next year.

The last sentence was a tip-off that she wouldn't take no for an answer, and some kind of manic episode would soon follow. I was already committed for the evening, so I replied, "Cannot tonight, but would love to get together later in the week."

> *Ok, see you next year.*
> *I really felt you ignored my birthday after I celebrated yours.*
> *Not very nice Betty.*
> *You always tell me you love me but is not love but obsession.*

You are not a true friend, just another person who wanted me.
I say goodbye.
You disgust me.
You are a fake.
You use people emotionally.
We are not toys or puppets, we are real.
I hope you get help.
I will pray for you.
You are gay, just admit it.
You are false.
You have used me.
I have lost all respect for you.
Goodbye.
If you really cared you would have made sure you took care of my birthday and
at least tried to be here tonight.
All talk.
OK guess I am done.

She projects onto me her own self-loathing and all of the detestable things she believes about herself. This kind of tirade is typical of her when she is insecure, in a state of uneasy transition.

Even though she tries to pull away from me, there's something in her that snaps back to me like a bungee cord. I feel that some part of her, perhaps the wounded inner child who is angry with me for not paying enough attention to her on her birthday, nevertheless knows that I am the one she can safely cry out to, so she does. She cries out, and lashes out. Deep down, she knows what we are, but her troubled psyche is confused and conflicted. She can't stop being drawn to me, if only to abuse me, no matter how hard she tries to distance herself.

~ 943 ~

The next day, a text:

If you want to bring some really good Chinese soup, a little spicy, that would be
nice, and a little wine.

We ate soup and drank wine and talked for about two hours. We cleared the air, agreed that we are still friends. Yesterday's histrionics burned themselves out.

Like The Unnamed One, Emily cannot conceive of an intimate relationship without sex. She thinks that my descriptions of divine love are me "wanting" her and seeking a sexual relationship, as it has always been with her men. My love is so much more than that.

PART 40

Radha Krishna

December 2015 – January 2016

~ 944 ~

I woke up at 3:00 a.m. thinking about Radha Krishna, a great Hindu love story. I went to the computer and did some research. The relationship of Radha Krishna is described in many beautiful metaphors as one soul in two bodies:

> Radha, daughter of Vrishabhanu, was the mistress of Krishna during that period of his life when he lived among the cowherds of Vrindavan. Since childhood they were close to each other—they played, they danced, they fought, they grew up together and wanted to be together forever, but the world pulled them apart. He departed to safeguard the virtues of truth, and she waited for him. *[like Fatima and the alchemist: ~721~]* He vanquished his enemies, became the king, and came to be worshipped as a lord of the universe. She waited for him. He married Rukmini and Satyabhama, raised a family, fought the great war of Ayodhya, and she still waited. So great was Radha's love for Krishna that even today her name is uttered whenever Krishna is referred to, and Krishna worship is thought to be incomplete without the deification of Radha.[65]

> Krishna quietly digested what had been said and then replied softly but firmly. "Radha lives for me and in me and I live for her and in her." They reached their destination and huddled close together on the mossy grass. They kissed tentatively at first, but the pent-up passions soon engulfed them and they united in body and soul. After a while Radha got up and began to tie her disheveled tresses into a knot. "Will we always be together after we are married?" she inquired uncertainly. Krishna replied that they were inseparable and that they had just gotten married according to the Gandharva tradition.[66] *[compare the Parzival story: ~787~]*

> Krishna is not only the ultimate object of all love, but also is the topmost enjoyer of all loving relationships. To do this, He expands Himself into the dual form of Krishna and Radha, His eternal consort and topmost devotee. In other words, Radha is the feminine aspect of Lord Krishna and is non-different from Krishna, but together (both the masculine and feminine aspects).

Krishna was the eighth incarnation of Vishnu, the Preserver of Universe. He took the human form to redeem mankind from evil forces. *[Jesus]* Radha was a childhood friend and soulmate of Krishna and the two were inseparable as playmates and later as lovers. Theirs was a love hidden from society, given Radha's status of a married woman. *[compare Campbell's courtly love: ~643~]*

Radha's love for Krishna is all consuming and compels her to ignore her family honor and disregard her husband. *[as Jesus' disciples left home and family to follow him]* Radha is the soul; Krishna is the God. Krishna is the *shaktiman*—possessor of energy—and Radha is His *shakti*—energy. She is the female counterpart of the Godhead. She is the personification of the highest love of God, and by her mercy the soul is connected with the service and love of Krishna. *[as the Virgin Mary intercedes for Man to God]*

The relationship between Radha and Krishna is the example of the highest and purest love, an indissoluble union of the highest intermingling and completion; it is also a love expressed through music. Music underlines the illicit relationship; this love shadowed by secrecy, adultery, and scorn, finds its outlet in Krishna's charming and passionate musical talents. *[as Lou, The Unnamed One, and even Emily and I found in music a vehicle for our spiritual connection]*

In this relationship, Love reigns supreme as Krishna surrenders to Radha. Krishna is lovestruck while Radha has taken over control. He has surrendered to the Power of Love. Very few people really understand this relationship and the message it contains. The supreme object of devotion, Krishna, worships the highest devotion, Radha.

Radha Krishna is the original principle of loving relationships (conjugal Love). The sex principle exists in the Absolute in its pure form without any inebriety or impurity, because Krishna is in fact Radha. In other words, the Lord is one, but for His pleasure and enjoyment, He expands himself to enjoy loving relationships. The original expansion is Radha. *[as Eve was created from Adam's rib]* Together, Radha and Krishna enjoy eternal pastimes of transcendental love.[67]

Around this time two years ago I told Emily that we are the same person. At the time I don't think either of us quite knew what I meant by that, but now I do – we are Radha Krishna, one soul in two bodies – separate and apart in the flesh, one in the spirit. We are both Radha and both Krishna: Emily goes off to distant lands, fights wars, and forms relationships, while I am patiently waiting rapt in divine love, playing music, safeguarding truth, and redeeming mankind.

Knowing this story of Radha Krishna makes it so much easier for me to understand and accept the long distances and silences between us in space and time, and the unusual joy that we experience when we finally come together again. Her physical distance and her emotional distance while in relationships with other people are but passing illusions, not at all interrupting our "eternal pastimes of transcendental love." Danny may be the love of Emily's worldly life, but I am the love of her spiritual life.

The concept of Radha Krishna gives great meaning to Jesus' remark to the Sad'ducees: "For in the resurrection they neither marry nor are given in marriage, but are like angels in heaven." (Matthew 22:30) In their separate worldly lives, Radha and Krishna are married to other people, but in their eternal lives, marriage – even the very concept of it – is meaningless. They are Radha Krishna, not separate, but one with each other and with all things, like angels in heaven.

> Out beyond ideas of rightdoing and wrongdoing,
> there is a field. I'll meet you there.
> When the soul lies down in that grass,
> the world is too full to talk about.
> Ideas, language, even the phrase "each other"
> doesn't make any sense.
>
> – Rumi, from "A Great Wagon"

I went back to sleep. When I awoke this morning, I discovered that my surge of vaginal secretions, absent for many months, had returned. My reunion with Emily in the spirit had again become real in the flesh. Radha Krishna reunited. In my relationship with The Unnamed One, our tantric union manifested in the realm of the native love gods; today the Hindu love gods preside.

Before I slept last night, I prayed for a sign to give me direction and reassurance. As if on cue, a sign appeared. I never cease to be amazed at how the myths and metaphors of every place and time come alive in me.

~ 945 ~

The Judeo-Christian world has a parallel to Radha Krishna in the creation of Sophia (Wisdom, "the Word" in the gospel of John[68]) out of the primordial God:

> Does not wisdom call,
>   Does not understanding raise her voice? ...
> The Lord created me at the beginning of his work,
>   the first of his acts of old.
> Ages ago I was set up,

at the first, before the beginning of the earth.
When there were no depths I was brought forth,
    when there were no springs abounding with water.
Before the mountains had been shaped,
    before the hills, I was brought forth;
before he had made the earth with its fields,
    or the first of the dust of the world.
When he established the heavens, I was there,
    when he drew a circle on the face of the deep,
when he made firm the skies above,
    when he established the fountains of the deep,
when he assigned to the sea its limit,
    so that the waters might not transgress his command,
when he marked out the foundations of the earth,
    then I was beside him, like a master workman;
and I was daily his delight,
    rejoicing before him always,
rejoicing in his inhabited world
    and delighting in the sons of men.

    (Proverbs 8:1 ... 22-31 RSV)

The idea of Radha being created out of Krishna – as Eve is created out of Adam, as Shakti emerges out of Shiva, as God creates Sophia out of his eternal singularity to help him finish his creation – has revealed another layer of understanding.

Radha Krishna is like a deck of cards, all the cards making one unified deck. The deck is given life when all the cards are separated out of the unity, spread out like the colors of a rainbow. As life unfolds, the cards are shuffled, dealt, played in games that send the cards into and out of complex relationships, and then gathered up again, returned to the oneness of a single deck.

Radha Krishna is also like a folding fan. When the fan is closed, it is the one singular God. Then the fan opens and reveals the folded panels that are hidden in the unity of the fan. When we use the fan, it comes alive, flutters and processes through space and time. Birth, the creation of the universe, is the opening of the fan. Death, the implosion of the universe, is closing it again, collapsing all the panels back into each other, into the oneness of the folded fan.

This explains why good is not separate from evil. Every deck of cards must have all fifty-two cards (and a couple of jokers) if it is to be able to play all the games invented for it. Removing any of the panels from the folding fan destroys its integrity and its usefulness. All the jewels of Indra's Net, the light and the dark and all the hues in between, are necessary to make a complete whole.

~ 946 ~

Once again I am struck dumb by the revelations that have come to me. My new understanding of Radha Krishna has sent me to a yet higher plateau of awakening. Over the last seven years or so, since the miracles and synchronicities began exploding in my life, I have come to understand the Hebrew and Christian Bible, Buddhist and Hindu scriptures, native mythologies, and all the parallel wisdom of the ages at a depth that leaves me in humble wonder. Thousands of people have spent their entire lives in devoted study of these writings but have barely begun to touch the deep meaning of them. I am grateful for the mystical experiences, the myths and legends coming alive in me, that enable me to understand the wisdom behind mystical words.

I see how my sufferings – the death of Lou, the rejection of The Unnamed One, and my continuing trials with Emily – are all gifts from God, necessary lessons for me on my spiritual journey. I feel the touch of God, his hand taking me by the scruff of the neck, his love coursing through me like a mighty wave, overriding every sensation of the body, mind, and soul.

I surrender. I have no choice. I trudge up the hill of sacrifice willingly, dutifully, as a Lamb of God must.

> He issued the law: Learn through suffering.
> Sorrow enters even sleep, dripping into the heart,
> Sorrow which cannot forget suffering.
> And even those who are unwilling learn to be wise.
>
> – Aeschylus, *Oresteria*

~ 947 ~

In his later years, Joe was fond of recalling how Schopenhauer, in his essay "On the Apparent Intention in the Fate of the Individual," wrote of the curious feeling one can have, of there being an author somewhere writing the novel of our lives, in such a way that through events that seem to us to be chance happenings there is actually a plot unfolding of which we have no knowledge. – Robert Walter, "About Joseph Campbell," Joseph Campbell Foundation

I invited Rita and Martha over for a feast in honor of Joseph Campbell. The menu included rare roast beef and Glenlivet, Campbell's favorites. I warned Rita that parking was tight in my neighborhood, but just as she arrived, a huge parking space opened up on the street in front of my house. As we three talked, more fascinating connections emerged: dancers, musicians, artists, philosophers, healers and mystics we did not realize we all knew.

Serendipities and synchronicities abound, all the threads of Indra's Net coming together. Synchronicity is the name of our mystical game, the sign of our deep spiritual connection. Campbell, Krishna, Kuan Yin, and all our guiding spirits living and dead sip Glenlivet with us. This is really living, a plot unfolding as we act out the novel of our lives.

> All the world's a stage,
> And all the men and women merely players;
> They have their exits and their entrances;
> And one man in his time plays many parts,
> His acts being seven ages.

> – William Shakespeare, *As You Like It*

~ 948 ~

I just spent a lovely five hours with Emily. We ate a little, drank a bottle of wine, played computer games, watched my new TV, exchanged gifts, and had a really peaceful, pleasant time together. A tiny bit of our Radha Krishna connection came through. She can't help loving me, as much as she tries not to.

Soon she will leave for two weeks with Danny. As much fun as we had tonight, I am not fooled. The torments and temptations will continue. I remind myself that there is no hope. Satan and Mara are still in charge of her, and I am still alone.

~ 949 ~

FULL MOON – NEW MOON, Part 8

Christmas falls during the full moon this year, a most auspicious sign. The full moon is the light of the sun fully reflected to earth. It is God with form, the Word made Flesh, the bodhisattva Christ who came into the world to dwell among us.

The Council of Nicaea in A.D. 325 set the date of Easter as the Sunday following the paschal full moon, which is the full moon that falls on or after the vernal equinox. The church fathers were right to use the lunar calendar for this calculation, but they got the timing wrong. Easter should be on the new moon, when the moon is absorbed into the light of the sun at the 7th chakra – resurrection. By this symbology, Christmas should also be a moveable feast, always on the full moon as it is this year.

~ 950 ~

The rose does not preen herself to catch my eye. She blooms because she blooms. A saint is a saint until he knows he is one. – Anthony de Mello, *One Minute Wisdom* [69]

Alas, I am no longer a saint. Now that I know I am not one, does that mean I *am* one?

I know what Tony means. He is warning me about the temptation of self-glorification, of feeling privileged or specially graced, about doing good deeds to curry favor or build merit, about answering the call of ego rather than the call of love. A saint doesn't consciously try to be saintly. Saintliness is spontaneous, unconscious, unintentional, arising when the force behind everything is love. I hear you, Tony.

~ 951 ~

Emily said that she has decided not to get married. She is cutting her visit with Danny short, then going to Argentina, where she is picking up with Arthur, the man she was involved with when she met me, the man she broke up with at this time two years ago because, so she said, I came along.

"Help us to find God."
"No one can help you there."
"Why not?"
"For the same reason that no one can help the fish to find the ocean."
    – Anthony de Mello, *One Minute Wisdom* [70]

Emily looks for happiness everywhere but never finds it. Bliss is right in front of her nose, but she can't see it. She is swimming in the sea of my divine love, but she can't find the ocean. I am content for this condition to persist for now, because until she can see beyond her old ways of limited and conditional loving, she cannot open to the true spiritual love that I already share with her, perfected, in the spirit realm.

~ 952 ~

"After he had dismissed the crowds, he went up on the mountain by himself to pray."

Has it ever occurred to you that you can only love when you are alone? What does it mean to love? It means to see a person, a thing, a situation, as it really is and not as you imagine it to be, and to give it the response it deserves. You cannot love what you do not even see.

And what prevents you from seeing? Your concepts, your categories, your prejudices and projections, your needs and attachments, the labels you have drawn from your conditioning and from your past experiences.

To drop your conditioning in order to see is arduous enough. But seeing calls for something more painful still. The dropping of the control that society exercises over you. You were given a taste for the drug called Approval, Appreciation, Attention, the drug called Success, Prestige, Power. You must tear away from your being the roots of society that have penetrated to the marrow. You must drop out. Externally everything will go on as before, you will continue to be in the world, but no longer of it. And in your heart you will now be free at last and utterly alone. To come to the land of love, you have to pass through the pains of death, for to love persons is to have died to the need for persons and to be utterly alone.

"What will it profit a man, to gain the whole world, if he loses his life?"

Recall the kind of feeling you get when someone praises you, when you are approved, accepted, applauded. And contrast that with the kind of feeling that arises within you when you look at the sunset or the sunrise or Nature in general or read a book or watch a movie you thoroughly enjoy.

Attempt to understand the true nature of worldly feelings, namely, the feelings of self-promotion, self-glorification. They are not natural, they were invented by your society and culture to make you productive and to make you controllable. – Anthony de Mello, "The Way to Love" [71]

"Has it ever occurred to you that you can only love when you are alone?" De Mello perfectly describes the solitude of the bodhisattva of which I have written so often, seeing things as they really are, in a way that is only possible when you are alone in the land of love.

De Mello also explains Emily's weakness for the flattery and attention she receives from her lovers. With their attentions her infatuated boyfriends feed her narcissism; they give her what she wants to get what they want. She thinks she is in control of these relationships, but her acculturated need for approval and glorification makes her productive and controllable. Her men control her, and she produces for them.

She is a victim of her success at luring lovers; she draws them in and holds them to satisfy her desires, but she is gullible and cannot resist their adoration, expensive gifts and shiny baubles, and she is drawn into their web as they are drawn into hers. The predator becomes the prey. Neither Emily nor her lovers are able to see past the illusion of physicality and desire.

Unlike the others, I love her best when I am alone, away from the distractions of physical attraction and repulsion, where I can see her as she really is. That is the place where I make tantric love with her, where we are free of all needs and desires. I can love her so completely because I have "died to the need for persons;" in divine love there is no need for anyone to produce anything, to control or be controlled. To be utterly alone in the land of love is the solitude of the bodhisattva.

Emily's lovers prey upon her societal conditioning; I pray upon her eternal essence.

~ 953 ~

Saw Elaine today, first time in a long time. We were so glad to see each other. She remarked, "You look so pretty today."

I chuckled and said, "Thank you, but I always feel disheveled."

"It's an inner beauty," she replied.

This evening my Kuan Yin picture began to slip out of its frame again. I slid the picture back into its frame, reglued the bottom of the frame, and started to put the picture back up on the wall. But then, one of the nails in the wall holding up the picture frame fell out of its hole in the wall. I fetched it off the floor and put it back in its hole, but as I tried to position the frame on the nails, the nail fell down again. And then the other nail got pushed deeper into the wall. I finally got the picture back up, but it seemed that the Fates were conspiring to keep Kuan Yin from assuming her old position. Is there meaning in this?

From dreammoods.com:

> **Picture** – To see a picture in your dream symbolizes a mental imprint that remains persistent in your mind. Your actions are irreversible. There is no turning back in what you do. To dream that you are hanging a picture represents acceptance of the image that is depicted in the picture.

> **Picture Frame** – To see or place a picture in a picture frame represents a wish to have a current situation or relationship remain the same as it is now. Perhaps you are reminiscing of the past. Consider what is depicted on the picture for additional significance.

For some time now I have accepted my role in the world as that of Kuan Yin, Goddess of Compassion; I give life to the image in the picture. Does Kuan's resistance to being in the frame and being replaced on the wall indicate that she wants "a current situation or relationship" to change?

~ 954 ~

In my continuing research into the teachings of Anthony de Mello, I discovered a document condemning the teachings of de Mello: "Notification Concerning the Writings of Fr. Anthony de Mello, S.J.," written in 1998 by Joseph Ratzinger, Cardinal-Prefect (who later became Pope Benedict XVI). Cardinal Ratzinger's objections to de Mello's writings were:

1) In place of the revelation which has come in the person of Jesus Christ, he substitutes an intuition of God without form or image, to the point of speaking of God as a pure void;

2) For him, to think that the God of one's own religion is the only one is simply fanaticism. "God" is considered as a cosmic reality, vague and omnipresent; the personal nature of God is ignored and in practice denied;

3) Jesus is not recognized as the Son of God, but simply as the one who teaches us that all people are children of God;

4) On various occasions, the question of destiny after death is declared to be irrelevant; only the present life should be of interest;

5) With respect to this life, since evil is simply ignorance, there are no objective rules of morality. Good and evil are simply mental evaluations imposed upon reality.

Consistent with what has been presented, one can understand how, according to the author, any belief or profession of faith whether in God or in Christ cannot but impede one's personal access to truth. The Church, making the word of God in Holy Scripture into an idol, has ended up banishing God from the temple. She has consequently lost the authority to teach in the name of Christ.

With the present Notification, in order to protect the good of the Christian faithful, this Congregation declares that the above-mentioned positions are incompatible with the Catholic faith and can cause grave harm.[72]

Rather than convincing me that de Mello's teachings are blasphemy, this document further cements my awe for de Mello's truth and his courage in speaking it. His teachings may have been "incompatible with the Catholic faith," but they were not incompatible with the teachings of Jesus.

Jesus often invoked the image of the Hebrew anthropomorphic God, a personal God, calling him "Father" and describing God's judgment, vengeance, and anger in Old Testament terms. He did this because he was talking to people who had no concept of God but this one. All of the names given to this Man-God, including Yahweh, Emmanuel, Elohim, and my favorite Adonai, represent worldly aspects of the Godhead, of the ultimate Source, the Way that cannot be named. Jesus had to speak to the masses in terms they could understand, starting their journey to salvation with baby steps.

But in conversation with more elevated individuals, Jesus could take longer strides. Jesus – God with form – made known a new concept of God to those capable of awakening to it. Jesus' description of the ultimate God – de Mello's "God without form or image" – can be found in his conversation with Nicodemus:

> Truly, truly, I say to you, unless one is born of water and the Spirit, he cannot enter the kingdom of God. That which is born of the flesh is flesh, and that which is born of the Spirit is spirit. Do not marvel that I said to you, "You must be born anew." The wind blows where it wills, and you hear the sound of it, but you do not know whence it comes or whither it goes; so it is with everyone who is born of the Spirit. (John 3:5-8 RSV)

Jesus thus described God without form, without beginning or end, and without any of the dualistic attributes that characterize those born of the flesh.

I love the wind metaphor. A footnote to this passage of scripture tells us that the same Greek word means both "wind" and "spirit." The spirit resides in the wind, and in the flame. In these metaphors we learn how God can be experienced in this world, in ways perceptible to the senses: When the wind blows we hear the sound of it (aural), and we feel it against our skin (tactile); in the flame we see that God is light (visual), and we feel its heat (tactile again). I wonder, can we smell God? How does God taste? Perhaps God also resides in the sweet fragrance of a flower and in the stench of rotting garbage. Perhaps God tastes like everything we put into our mouths. It does not take a huge leap of faith to extend this train of thought into infinity, to know that God resides everywhere in everything, in us.

Joseph Campbell, like de Mello, remained true to the essence of his Roman Catholic faith, not to its superficial doctrines, but to the meaning of Jesus' enlightened teaching, although, like de Mello, he was criticized by the Catholic establishment for expanding that teaching to embrace and harmonize concepts from non-Christian philosophies and religions. Campbell commented on the inability of the Catholic hierarchy to understand its own scripture:

You believe that God, the source of energy, is there, and you are here, and He may come into your life or He may not. No, no—that source of eternal energy is here, in you, now. That is the essence of Gnosticism, Buddha consciousness, and so forth. St. Paul got close to the idea when he said, "I live now, not I, but Christ in me." (Galatians 2:20) I once made this observation in a lecture, and a priest in attendance said, "That's blasphemy"—an example of the church not conceding the very sense of the symbol.[73]

Bertrand Russell said, "Every great idea starts out as a blasphemy."

~ 955 ~

HEAD vs. HEART

People mistakenly assume that their thinking is done by their head; it is actually done by the heart which first dictates the conclusion, then commands the head to provide the reasoning that will defend it. – Anthony de Mello, *One Minute Wisdom* [69]

Compare process thought, as expressed by John B. Cobb, Jr.:

The brain is a complex society of events and so is the mind. In fact, the term 'mind' is misleading in that it quickly leads us, as it did Descartes, to attend to thinking. The term 'psyche' is less misleading, in that with psyche we often associate emotion as much as thought. For Whitehead, even in human experience, emotion is much more fundamental than conscious thinking. He also assumes that emotion does not have to be conscious; indeed, even in human beings, most of it is not conscious.[74]

I suspect that Whitehead and Cobb use the word "emotion" in this context to mean not just the sensory feelings and mental formations that erupt from the body-mind, but also the bliss, rapture, joy, and sublime esthetic arrest that spill over into the soul, that connect the sensory lower chakras to the extrasensory upper ones through the heart chakra of divine love.

As one man said, "I got a pretty good education. It took me years to get over it." That's what spirituality is all about, you know: unlearning. Unlearning all the rubbish they taught you. – Anthony de Mello, *Awareness* [69]

Compare Campbell:

The question sometimes arises as to whether the experience of mystery and transcendence is more available to those who have undergone some kind of religious and spiritual training, for whom, as I have said, it has all been named completely. It may be less available to them precisely because they have got it all named in the book. One way to deprive yourself of an experience is indeed to expect it. Another is to have a name for it before you have the experience. Carl Jung said that one of the functions of religion is to protect us against the religious experience.[61]

And Lewis:

Many a man, brought up in the glib profession of some shallow form of Christianity, who comes through reading Astronomy to realise for the first time how majestically indifferent most reality is to man, and who perhaps abandons his religion on that account, may at that moment be having his first genuinely religious experience. C.S. Lewis, *Miracles*[27]

And Goethe:

We know accurately only when we know little; with knowledge doubt increases.

And the Kena Upanishad:

That [which is beyond every name and form] is comprehended only by the one with no comprehension of it: anyone comprehending knows it not. Unknown to the knowing, it is to the unknowing known.

These writers knew what Jesus meant when he said, "Truly, I say to you, whoever does not receive the kingdom of God like a child shall not enter it." (Luke 18:17 RSV) And the Shōrinji school of Zen that tells us to learn as "plain and naïve as an infant." Wisdom comes from knowing the unknowable. When Adam and Eve ate of the Tree of the Knowledge of Good and Evil, their new knowledge, their newfound consciousness of duality, clouded their plain and naïve innate wisdom that transcends knowledge.

I am also reminded of John Wesley's admonition against putting too much faith in scripture. (~894~) Scripture is not itself truth, but it may point the way to truth. Being educated, having acquired knowledge, is not the same as knowing. If we are not careful, knowledge can be a barrier to knowing.

All the great mystical writers were inspired to write by their personal revelatory experience, not by their education or intellect. Even a life-long scholar like Campbell did not arrive at his enlightened understanding as a result of his scholarship; he knew in his heart the truth of which he spoke, and his research was, as de Mello described it, his head commanding him to confirm and defend what his heart already knew.

It is the same with me; all my recent reading and study has given me no new knowledge, but it has validated and deepened what I already know and given me the confidence to go forward bravely in the face of rejection and persecution. I may be utterly alone in this world, but not in the spirit. I am in good company there.

~ 956 ~

Emily asked Danny for thirty days without contact so she can decide what to do about their relationship without pressure from him. She doesn't want to get married, deal with in-laws, or live with him fulltime. But she enjoys his attentions. She is going to visit Arthur next month, but doesn't see a future with him. She took my hands and said that she might end up marrying a woman. Is she beginning to open to our love, or is she just tempting me, saying what she thinks I want to hear to keep me on the string?

Then she did a tracing of our hands, one superimposed on top of the other. In this bit of therapeutic art, she captured not just our hands, but our souls, interlocked and inseparable.

~ 957 ~

HEALTH, Part 8

In an intuitive session tonight, Martha talked about the meaning of healing. Healing is not "fixing" something, she said. It is reconnecting with the eternal perfection, renewing the perfect balance of body, mind, and soul.

She pointed out that Jesus healed not only by the laying on of hands, but also by just being in the presence of the afflicted. His divine energy, alignment with the Source, was so high that he could clearly see the eternal perfection within the physical form of the afflicted. By the power of his eternal vision, the affliction – blindness, lameness, demonic possession, or even death – was removed to conform the external physical form to the perfection of the indwelling spirit that he saw.

Martha explained, "Energetic clarity gets things done. Think it done. Anything on the physical plane can be transmuted. No anger, no resistance, no doubt. Affirm that the body can filter out toxins. Rising above the laws of physics, the spiritual firewalker is not burned. Beekeepers who love bees are not poisoned by bee stings."

I have always wondered about the miraculous healings in the Bible. Did they really happen? Jesus was reported to have healed many people, sometimes without knowing them, seeing them, or even knowing he was doing it.

Although I suppose it is possible that these healings actually happened on the physical plane, it doesn't really matter. There is a metaphysical plane on which these healing stories have meaning. The healings in the Bible are almost always tied to faith, an elevated state of absolute trust and acceptance:

> ... And he said to her, "Daughter, your faith has made you well; go in peace, and be healed of your disease." (Mark 5:34 RSV)

> ... The blind men came to him; and Jesus said to them, "Do you believe that I am able to do this?" They said to him, "Yes, Lord." Then he touched their eyes, saying, "According to your faith be it done to you." And their eyes were opened. (Matthew 9:28-30 RSV)

> ... "Lord, I am not worthy to have you come under my roof; but only say the word, and my servant will be healed. ... When Jesus heard him, he marveled, and said to those who followed him, "Truly, I say to you, not even in Israel have I found such faith." (Matthew 8:8...10 RSV)

> And when they came to the crowd, a man came up to him and kneeling before him said, "Lord, have mercy on my son, for he is an epileptic and he suffers terribly; for often he falls into the fire, and often into the water. And I brought him to your disciples, and they could not heal him." ... Then the disciples came to Jesus privately and said, "Why could we not cast it out?" He said to them, "Because of your little faith." (Matthew 17:14...20 RSV)

Faith healing can be seen as a kind of placebo effect in which faith – absolute trust and surrender – allows one to accept whatever happens in peaceful equanimity, not desperation. A sufferer heals himself by letting go and letting God. Physical healing can indeed be physical, the result of releasing the fear that is the cause of all illness, as Anita Moorjani explained. (~497~) Or it could be a metaphor for spiritual healing, a metaphysical condition expressed in physical terms.

The Dean of Lourdes said at the end of the movie *The Song of Bernadette*, about the miracles at Lourdes, "For those who believe in God, no explanation is necessary; for those who do not believe in God, no explanation is possible."

~ 958 ~

GOOD AND EVIL, Part 5

At Ignacio's theology discussion group we discussed an article on Islam by Jay McDaniel.[75] Near the beginning of the article we learn about signs of Allah:

The happening we know best is the web of life on earth. Its rhythms and sounds, its colors and textures, reveal the Beauty of the divine mystery. Whenever we experience beauty we experience a sign of Allah.... Signs reveal archetypal patterns within the mind of Allah. All finite realities participate in these patterns, and their participation is revealed in their beauty. Allah is the Beauty within the beauty.... Allah is also the Goodness within goodness. Whenever we experience wisdom and mercy, justice and compassion, we are witnessing signs of Allah.

I asked, "What about the other side of the Old Testament God, the dark side, with vengeance, anger, judgment, and punishment?"

Cecilia said, "Hold that question; we'll get to that in the Day of Reckoning." And sure enough, we did:

A Day of Reckoning occurs in moments when the fog of personal misunderstanding is lifted, and we see ourselves clearly. Moments of reckoning have an apocalyptic dimension to them. In moments of reckoning the familiar world falls away and we feel we cannot hang on to the prior objects of attachments. We stand naked in the presence of the Unity. We know ourselves as we are known by the Knowing.... In moments of reckoning we may have a sense of being punished. But the punishment is not an infliction of suffering on the part of Allah. It is an awakening into self-awareness in which we feel remorse, because we see ourselves clearly. We understand the selfishness of our prior intentions; we understand the harm we have caused others; we understand the ways we have abandoned the Unity.

My concern, reflected in my question, was the absence of equal balance in this Islamic portrayal of God in the world. The "rhythms and sounds" and "colors and textures" of life on earth can be discordant as well as harmonious, glaring and rough as well as soft and soothing. It's not all beautiful. And then the key to reconciling beauty and ugliness, good and evil, was introduced with the idea of "Beauty within beauty" and "Goodness within goodness."

At the Day of Reckoning we face our dark side, the other side of the dualistic coin, experience the punishing side of God, and then recognize the God that rises above and lifts us out of duality; we come to know the difference between Beauty and beauty, Goodness and goodness. When we "stand naked in the presence of the Unity," "know ourselves as we are known by the Knowing," and experience the most elevated signs of Allah – "wisdom and mercy, justice and compassion" – we are experiencing not goodness, but Goodness.

The Abrahamic religions have often placed God in the world as the "good" side of the coin and Satan (Iblis in Islam) as the opposing "bad" side. Indeed, the anthropomorphic gods of the Bible, given names like Yahweh and Emmanuel, fill that role, but the ultimate God, the Source, the Unity, the Way that cannot be named, contains the good and the bad, Yahweh and Satan, and harmonizes all into the emptiness, the Great Void, where all and nothing are found, where there is no beginning and no end, no good and no evil.

C.S. Lewis wrote this in *Mere Christianity*, which seems to conflict in a way with the above understanding:

> Confronted with a cancer or a slum the Pantheist can say, "If you could only see it from the divine point of view, you would realise that this also is God." The Christian replies, "Don't talk damned nonsense." It thinks God made the world—that space and time, heat and cold, and all the colours and tastes, and all the animals and vegetables, are things that God "made up out of His head" as a man makes up a story. But it also thinks that a great many things have gone wrong with the world that God made and that God insists, and insists very loudly, on our putting them right again.[76]

Lewis confuses the dual aspects of God portrayed in the Bible with the one unified eternal Godhead that Jesus represented on earth in human form. The perfect world that God – the Godhead, the "Knowing" of Islam – "made up out of His head" includes cancer and slums. It also includes animals who eat their young, bacteria that infect and kill other living things, and wildfires that lay waste to forests and all who live in them. These are not things that have gone wrong with the world contrary to God's will, but simply the natural balance necessary in God's dualistic creation.

The faith healing that Martha described (~957~) is the "putting right" that Lewis says God wants, but it is not fixing things that have gone wrong, not removing pain and suffering, but rather moving our spiritual alignment and life energy to a higher hermetic level, rising above the tugs and pulls of duality toward the perfect Beauty and Goodness of the Unity that is Allah.

Lest one think that suffering could be eliminated from this world, or that it would be desirable to do so, consider this, from *An Introduction to Existentialism* by Robert G. Olson:

> Since compassion is by definition a form of love or sympathy for those who suffer, compassion would be logically impossible in a world without suffering. One cannot, therefore, attempt to eliminate suffering without at the same time attempting to eliminate compassion. Most people would probably say that a world with no suffering and no compassion is better than a world with suffering and compassion, since the disvalue of suffering is greater than the value of compassion.[9]

There must be suffering in the world in order for compassion to arise, as opposites naturally arise together by mutual consent in the field of duality – interdependent co-arising. This is the world, such as it is, that God made. It is a world of suffering and compassion, samsara. But God also made a world with no suffering and thus no need for compassion. You can go there anytime you want. It is, by definition, nirvana.

~ 959 ~

The minister today made a very apt analogy comparing baptism to a gym membership. Some people get a gym membership but never actually go to the gym, so they never receive the benefits that gym membership makes available to them. Baptism does not in itself provide salvation; it is just an invitation to take the first steps toward salvation, to begin the journey that is the Way and the Truth and the Life. Many are baptized, but few enter through the narrow gate.

~ 960 ~

GOOD AND EVIL, Part 6

Cecilia wrote:

> *Thanks for your spiritual musings on Islam. (~958~) I get the yin/yang thing about balance, but does that mean that humankind can never cease the suffering we inflict on each other? If that is a necessary part of the balance, then why do we even bother with prayer, hoping for peace? Let's just accept it and lob another explosive projectile?*

I responded:

The answer lies in the existential quote by Olson (~958~) about suffering and compassion. In the field of duality, we can't totally eradicate suffering, but we can bring it down in amplitude, along with its companion, compassion. The goal is to narrow the arc of the pendulum swings between the dualistic extremes, coming closer and closer to a stop in the middle, to the Middle Way.

Suffering could be reduced to just an occasional argument over squeezing the toothpaste tube at the end or the middle, and compassion could be reduced to kissing a child's sore finger to make it better. No more would suffering mean genocide, and no more would compassion require sacrifice. Evil would not demand killing, and Jesus, al-Hallaj, Joan of Arc, Gandhi, Martin Luther King, and Bonhoeffer would not have to give their lives in compassionate counterpoint to the extreme evil around them.

The other way to reduce suffering is to be lifted out of duality, to rise above the fray even while in it, to awaken to the eternal emptiness where, as the *Heart Sutra* describes, there is neither suffering nor no suffering, where form and emptiness flow endlessly in and out of each other. The *Heart Sutra* ends with this mantra: "gate gate pāragate pārasamgate bodhi svāhā," meaning "gone, gone, everyone gone all the way to the other shore, awakening. Amen." This is where the Godhead, the Source, the Force, is.

Every year at Christmastime we pray for peace on earth, goodwill toward men. Yet even after thousands of years of uttering this prayer, every new generation brings yet another round of war and atrocity, a renewed upwelling of greed and fear. Jesus said the poor are always with us, and they are, no matter what we do. Jesus also said, "Do not resist one who is evil. But if any one strikes you on the right cheek, turn to him the other also; and if any one would sue you and take your coat, let him have your cloak as well; and if any one forces you to go one mile, go with him two miles." (Matthew 5:39-41 RSV)

This is the hardest instruction to follow. Give up everything you have without reservation, retaliation, or reward. Remain vulnerable, even unto death. At the height of *agape*, that vulnerability opens one to ridicule, rejection, and self-sacrifice – as on a cross. Not a shred of self or ego is left. This is what it is to be enlightened, or "born again."

At this highest level of awareness, there are no righteous wars, not even in defense. The only way to win against evil, to have peace on earth, is to find peace in the presence of evil, as did Victor Frankl and Maximillian Kolbe in Nazi concentration camps, as did Dietrich Bonhoeffer in a Nazi prison, as did Jesus on the cross.

The distinction between a bodhisattva and a buddha is that a bodhisattva remains in the fray, in the field of duality knowing both suffering and compassion, hearing the world's cries, suffering with the people and bringing compassion to help them; while a buddha lives in eternity, in pure spiritual contemplation and meditation. Trungpa said, "A buddha begins to realize that he has no role to play anymore, but to be."

Please continue to pray – couldn't hurt!

The End of Volume Three

to be continued ...

First in the Series:

Volume One
The First Awakenings

Volume Two
Soul of Darkness

Next in the Series:

Volume Four
The Mystic Milieu

Volume Five
Plumbing the Depths Above the Clouds

Cast of Characters

Each of the five volumes of *Love and Loss* can stand alone, but for those who read later volumes without having read the earlier volumes, it may be helpful to know the roles played by the recurring characters introduced early on:

Lou – my husband and first karmic love

The Unnamed One – my second karmic love

Emily – my third karmic love

Jean & Joan – the twins who reawakened my ability to love

Archie – a brief but meaningful love object

James – my rude office colleague who taught me to see through bad behavior

Ignacio & Cecilia – my Christian angels

Kathy – my niece who hears me in her dreams but is afraid to listen

John – Lou's favorite brother

Elaine – John's wife and my Buddhist angel

Natalie – John's and Elaine's daughter

Joe – a business associate and my atheist angel

June & Marilyn – a lovely gay couple who understood my pain

Vincent, Arthur, & Danny – Emily's on-again, off-again lovers

Martha & Rita – my intuitive angels

Hugh & Josie – my shamanic angels

Patrick – my best friend in the band

Acknowledgments

One of the great virtues I have discovered in my life's journey is gratitude. I am grateful for all the joy and all the sorrow, and especially for all those who helped me learn and grow through the joys and sorrows. There are so many over the decades who gave me encouragement, comfort, understanding, and support, whose tender care kept me from falling off a cliff of despair. Some of these people go back thousands of years, others are alive and with me now. I cannot thank my contemporaries by name or the anonymity of this book would be destroyed. But you know who you are! Thank you all so much. A few of these angels are characters in the book; you do not know their true names, but you know their true souls.

Of course, at the top of the gratitude list are the heroes of this book, my karmic loves, to whom I literally owe my life in the spirit. Fanning out from them, I also thank their families, ancestors, and descendants to and from whom our eternal love will always flow. Speaking of ancestors and descendants, I humbly thank my parents, who raised me well, kept every door of opportunity open, and prepared my heart and mind to welcome the wisdom of every place and every age. And I thank my siblings and their children, who had the temerity to challenge my beliefs and make me think about the difference between what is true and what I *think* is true, testing the mettle of my ideas in the fire of their skepticism.

This story includes many different religious and philosophical perspectives. I pay homage to the many branches of the Judeo-Christian tradition, as well as the Eastern traditions of Buddhism, Hinduism, and Daoism; the Greco-Roman gods and goddesses; several ancient indigenous religions; and various world philosophies with little or no religious basis. My spiritual growth would not have been possible without major input from luminaries in all the arts and sciences. I am therefore especially indebted to the writers of the Bible, the Hindu, Daoist, and Buddhist scriptures, and the work of, among many others: William Shakespeare, Albert Einstein, Dave Brubeck, Pang-yun, John Wesley, Deepak Chopra, Joseph Campbell, John Milton, Jacobo Timerman, Felix Mendelssohn, Robert Olson, Martin Luther King, Jr., Carol Burnett (and her fabulous comedic cast), Kahlil Gibran, Anthony de Mello, Plato, Henrietta Lacks, St. Francis of Assisi, Sandi Patti, Martin Heidegger, Dietrich Bonhoeffer, Marianne Williamson, T. S. Eliot, Lao-tzu, David Oistrakh, C. S. Lewis, Socrates, Wayne Dyer, Thomas Hardy, the Dalai Lama, Jorge Luis Borges, Brené Brown, Vince Gill, Carl Jung, St. Augustine, Thich Nhat Hanh, Alan Watts, J. S. Bach, Doreen Virtue, Alexander Pope ...

and on and on and on ... and the myriad artists, scientists, authors, philosophers, and other great souls of every age who influenced them.

I must give a special nod to the filmmakers. Like most people of my generation, I came of age watching movies, and I marched faithfully in step with my contemporaries as the movies moved from theaters to television to videocassette to DVD to the Internet. A great film is a work of art, like great literature, stage plays, and opera, with which they often share common themes and subject matter. I owe the screenwriters, actors, directors, producers, designers, cinematographers, composers, musicians, and all the creative people who make movies a debt of gratitude for putting deep spiritual messages into sounds and pictures – dramas, musicals, and documentaries – that can reach into the hearts of the masses. I will name the movies that I can remember contributing to my spiritual growth, but I know there are many more that escape my recollection: *Song of Bernadette, Star Wars (all episodes), It's A Wonderful Life, Gandhi, Guess Who's Coming To Dinner, Flight, The Buddha, Sophie's Choice, The Last Samurai, Mary and Tim, Einstein's Universe, The Heart Is A Lonely Hunter, Judgment At Nuremberg, Avatar, Romeo and Juliet, West Side Story (R&J modernized and musicalized), Invasion of the Body Snatchers, Julia, The Shawshank Redemption, Titanic, WarGames, Inherit The Wind,* and the Jesus flicks: *Greatest Story Ever Told, Jesus of Nazareth, Jesus Christ Superstar, King of Kings, Ben-Hur.*

Everyone who has passed through my life, in person or through writings, art, music, or historic legacy, has added a piece to my spiritual puzzle. Some pieces are larger than others, but each piece is essential to completing the puzzle. The final piece I must add myself.

Virtually all of my thoughts and opinions in this book were developed with inspiration from the great work of others, as reflected in the references below. I do not claim to be a Bible scholar, Zen master, psychologist, or an expert in history, literature, art, science, or humanities. I am a layperson relating what inspiring works of art, science, religion and philosophy say to me, amplified by my own experience and revelation. No religious or scholarly authority has formally endorsed my interpretations. However, like the infinitely connected jewels in Indra's Net, all ideas are connected to all others. I claim no originality in any of the thoughts herein; as Goethe said, "Everything has been thought of before; the task is to think of it again."

As is the case with most diaries, in this journal I am talking to myself. In that private environment of my own heart and mind, there were no holds barred, no subjects off limits, no level of intimacy too deep. Under normal circumstances the deeply personal thoughts, feelings, ideas, analyses, and speculations herein would only be shared with the most intimate confidants, if at all. I am sharing this journal now because the miraculously abnormal circumstances of my life demand it. So my final acknowledgment goes to the Source, however you know it, and to you, the readers of this book, who have all become my most intimate confidants and who are yourselves miraculous manifestations of the Source.

A Word About Sex

I thought long and hard about how much sexually explicit material to include in this book. I knew I had to include some; the evolution of my sexuality, as concerns the crossing from spirit to flesh and back again, is central to my story. In such stories, the sexual questions are the ones usually left unanswered, in deference to modesty, privacy, and propriety, yet are the ones on everyone's mind:

What is the role of sex in divine love? When does "having sex" become "making love"? How does a widow for whom joy in sex has ended find satisfaction with a man whom she has never even seen naked? And with a woman thousands of miles away? How does the eternal creative union of Shiva and Shakti play out in real life – and in real-life body chemistry? How do the urges of the body, the thoughts of the mind, and the wisdom of the spirit each play a role in the act of sex, and in the larger sense, of creation? What is tantric love? How does love in the spirit feel in the body?

I knew I had to answer these questions, so I left most of the sexy stuff in, taking a chance that more readers would be grateful and enlightened than offended or titillated.

A Word About Money

The proceeds I receive from the sale of this book after the cost of its production will be donated to nonprofit organizations doing work that is consonant with my spiritual direction. I offer my personal life experiences seeking to enrich the lives of others, not to enrich my own. I have enough money.

Betty Hibod
2020

References & Citations

1. Paulo Coelho, *Manuscript Found in Accra*, trans. Margaret Jull Costa. (Vintage Books/Random House, New York 2013).

2. Joseph Campbell, *Transformations of Myth Through Time.* (Harper & Row, New York 1990).

3. C.S. Lewis, *A Grief Observed.* © 1961 by C.S. Lewis Pte. Ltd. (Bantam/Seabury Press, New York 1963).

4. St. Augustine, *Confessions*, trans. R.S. Pine-Coffin. (Penguin Books, Harmondsworth, England 1961).

5. Jacobo Timerman, *Prisoner without a Name, Cell without a Number*, trans. Toby Talbot. (University of Wisconsin Press, Madison 1930).

6. Joseph Campbell, *The Power of Myth,* transcript of the PBS documentary hosted by Bill Moyers. (Apostrophe S Productions, Inc., New York 1988). Used by permission.

7. Alan Watts, *The Way Of Zen.* Excerpt(s) from WAY OF ZEN by Alan Watts, copyright © 1957 by Penguin Random House LLC, copyright renewed 1985 by Mary Jane Watts. Used by permission of Pantheon Books, an imprint of the Knopf Doubleday Publishing Group, a division of Penguin Random House LLC. All rights reserved.

8. *www.dreammoods.com.* © 2000-2014 Dream Moods, Inc. All rights reserved.

9. Robert Olson, *An Introduction To Existentialism.* (Dover Publications, Inc., New York 1962).

10. Kahlil Gibran, *The Prophet.* (Alfred A Knopf, New York 1923).

11. *wikipedia.com.* Descriptions of the ten bhūmi used in this book are from the Avatamsaka Sutra, as illuminated in commentaries at wikipedia.org: http://en.wikipedia.org/wiki/Ten_bhūmis.

12. Abhaya, http://www.freebuddhistaudio.com/search.php?q=kshanti&r=10&o=ya&b=p&l= en&at= audio&lang=en.

13. C.S. Lewis, *On Stories: And Other Essays on Literature.* © 1982, 1966 by C.S. Lewis Pte. Ltd. All rights reserved.

14. Anita Moorjani, *Dying To Be Me.* (Hay House, Carlsbad CA 2012).

15. C.S. Lewis, *God in the Dock.* © 1970 by C.S. Lewis Pte. Ltd. All rights reserved.

16. Paraphrased from *Traveling the Path of Compassion: A Commentary on the Thirty-Seven Practices of a Bodhisattva* by His Holiness the Seventeenth Karmapa (KTD 2009), translated by Ringu Tulku Rinpoche and Michele Martin. (*from the January 2010 issue of Shambhala Sun*).

17. The Enneagram Institute, www.enneagraminstitute.com. Copyright 2014, The Enneagram Institute. All Rights Reserved. Used with permission.

18. Martin Heidegger, *An Introduction to Metaphysics*, trans. Ralph Manheim. (Yale University Press, New Haven 1959).

19. Cyndi Dale, *The Complete Book of Chakra Healing.* (Llewellyn Publications, Woodbury MN 1996, 2009).

20. Rebecca Skloot, *The Immortal Life of Henrietta Lacks.* (Crown Books 2010).

21. Hsuan Hua, *The Chan Handbook.* (http://psychology.wikia.com/wiki/Dhy%C4%81na_in_Buddhism)

22. http://www.africa.upenn.edu/Articles_Gen/Letter_Birmingham.html.

23. Neale Donald Walsch, *The Complete Conversations with God.* (Putnam/Penguin Group, New York 2005).

24. Viktor Frankl, *Man's Search for Meaning*, Part One, "Experiences in a Concentration Camp." (Pocket Books, pp. 56–57. via *Wikipedia*).

25. Thich Nhat Hanh, *The Thich Nhat Hanh Collection* ("Peace Is Every Step," "Teachings On Love," "The Stone Boy" and other stories), trans. Mobi Warren and Annabel Laity. (One Spirit, New York 2004).

26. Deepak Chopra, *How To Know God.* (Harmony Books/Random House, New York 2000).

27. C.S. Lewis, *Miracles: A Preliminary Study.* © 1947, 1960, 1996 by C.S. Lewis Pte. Ltd. All rights reserved.

28. Joseph Campbell, *The Inner Reaches of Outer Space*. (Novato, CA; New World Library 2002, pp. 39,41,43,86-87, 92, 93-94, 101-102, 103). Quotations from *The Inner Reaches of Outer Space* by Joseph Campbell, copyright © 2002; reprinted by permission of Joseph Campbell Foundation (www.jcf.org).

29. Abbot George Burke, *Dharma for Awakening* (http://www.ocoy.org/dharma-for-christians). Used by permission.

30. https://en.wikipedia.org/wiki/Jiddu_Krishnamurti.

31. Marianne Williamson, *Enchanted Love*. (Touchstone/Simon & Schuster, New York 1999).

32. Tim Flannery, "Only Human: The Evolution of a flawed species." (*Harper's Magazine*, December 2014).

33. Thich Nhat Hanh, *Living Buddha, Living Christ*. (Riverhead Books, New York 1995).

34. Doreen Virtue, *Angel Numbers 101*. (Hay House, Carlsbad CA 2008).

35. Doreen Virtue, "Hermetic Philosophy and the Seven Hermetic Principles." (https://www.youtube.com/watch?v=8t3AkVvFuqk); and *The Kybalion*. (The Yogi Publication Society, Chicago 1912, 1940).

36. Chögyam Trungpa, *Transcending Madness*. (Shambhala Publications, Boston 1992).

37. Marsha Linehan, http://www.nytimes.com/2011/06/23/health/23lives.html?sq=linehan&st=cse&scp=1&pagewanted=all.

38. Cognitive Behavior Therapy: http://psychology.about.com/od/psychotherapy/a/cbt.htm.

39. C.S. Lewis, *Christian Reflections*. © 1967, 1980 by C.S. Lewis Pte. Ltd. All rights reserved.

40. Joseph Campbell, *A Hero's Journey: Joseph Campbell on His Life and Work*. (New World Library, Novato CA 1990, pp. 101, 107-108). Quotation from *The Hero's Journey* by Joseph Campbell, © 2003, reprinted by permission of the Joseph Campbell Foundation (www.jcf.org).

41. Marianne Williamson, https://www.youtube.com/watch?v=4-ZLkxlV1O8.

42. Thich Nhat Hanh, *Going Home: Jesus And Buddha As Brothers*. (Riverhead Books, New York 1999).

43. https://en.wikipedia.org/wiki/Tantra; and http://www.scribd.com/doc/166511911/The-Songs-of-Radha-from-the-Gita-Govinda-erotic-poetry#scribd.

44. Anthony de Mello, *Awareness*. (Center for Spiritual Exchange, New York 1990).

45. https://myfattyjourney.wordpress.com/2010/08/18/paulo-coelho/.

46. Paulo Coelho, *The Alchemist*, trans. Alan R. Clarke. (HarperCollins, New York 1993).

47. Richard Bach, *Illusions: The Adventures of a Reluctant Messiah*. (Dell/Random House, Inc., New York 1977).

48. Julien Green, *God's Fool: The Life and Times of Francis of Assisi*, trans. Peter Heinegg. (HarperCollins, New York 1985).

49. Shari Y. Manning PhD, *Loving Someone with Borderline Personality Disorder*. (The Guilford Press, New York 2011).

50. Doreen Virtue, from the Angel Intuitive Workshop, September 26-28, 2014.

51. Dietrich Bonhoeffer, *The Cost of Discipleship*, p. 84, 86 (1949), trans. Barbara Green and Reihhard Krauss. (2001).

52. https://en.wikipedia.org/wiki/Metatron.

53. Dietrich Bonhoeffer, *Letters & Papers From Prison*. (Touchstone/Simon & Schuster, New York [1953, 1967, 1971] 1997).

54. F.C. Happold, *Mysticism*. (Penguin Books, Harmondsworth, England 1963, 1970).

55. Marianne Williamson, "Reparations for Slavery: The Role of Repentance in Politics," an address at Harvard Divinity School, February 19, 2019.

56. C.S. Lewis, *The Problem of Pain*. © 1940, 1996 by C.S. Lewis Pte. Ltd. All rights reserved.

57. Dr. Henry Cloud and Dr. John Townsend, *Beyond Boundaries*. © 2014 Zondervan; all rights reserved. via Bible Gateway, https://www.biblegateway.com.

58. Anthony de Mello, "A Rediscovery of Life." (https://www.youtube.com/watch?v=8b8TLQh4Q84, https://vimeo.com/9718009).

59. Miguel Serrano, *C.G. Jung & Hermann Hesse: A Record of Two Friendships*, trans. Frank MacShane. (Shocken Books, New York 1966).

60. David Ray Griffin, ed., *Deep Religious Pluralism.* (Westminster John Knox Press, Louisville, KY 2005).

61. Joseph Campbell, *Thou Art That.* (New World Library, Novato CA 2001, pg. 13, 29-30, 82, 99) © Joseph Campbell Foundation (jcf.org) 2001. Used with permission.

62. John Wesley Sermons, "On Divine Providence." (http://www.umcmission.org/Find-Resources/ John-Wesley-Sermons/Sermon-67-On-Divine-Providence#sthash.xGIJNxd5.dpuf). "On Faith." (http://www.umcmission.org/Find-Resources/John-Wesley-Sermons/Sermon-106-On-Faith#sthash. ffTUN2RE.dpuf).

63. A. H. Maslow, "A Theory of Human Motivation." (1943) Originally Published in *Psychological Review*, 50, 370-396 (http://psychclassics.yorku.ca/Maslow/motivation.htm).

64. McLeod, S. A. (2014) "Maslow's Hierarchy of Needs." (www.simplypsychology.org/maslow.html).

65. http://hinduism.about.com/od/scripturesepics/a/lovelgends_4.htm.

66. http://mohitinhere.blogspot.com/2005/08/mysterious-radha-and-her-last-meeting.html.

67. Madhuri Guin, http://www.dollsofindia.com/library/radhakrishna/.

68. Marcus J. Borg, *Meeting Jesus Again for the First Time.* (HarperOne/HarperCollins, New York 1995).

69. Anthony de Mello, https://www.goodreads.com/author/quotes/54195.Anthony_de_Mello

70. Anthony de Mello, http://lazarus.trinityjanesville.org/demello.htm.

71. Anthony de Mello, http://www.demellospirituality.com/the-way-to-love-excerpts/.

72. Congregation for the Doctrine of the Faith, Joseph Card. Ratzinger, Prefect, "Notification Concerning the Writings of Fr. Anthony de Mello, SJ." (http://www.ewtn.com/library/CURIA/ CDFDEMEL.HTM).

73. Diane K. Osbon, *A Joseph Campbell Companion.* (HarperCollins, New York 1991). *Reflections on the Art of Living, A Joseph Campbell Companion.* © Joseph Campbell Foundation (jcf.org) 1991. Used with permission.

74. John B. Cobb, Jr., "Whitehead and Mind-brain Relations: How Psychology and Physiology are Connected." (http://www.jesusjazzbuddhism.org/whitehead-and-mind-brain-relations.html).

75. Jay McDaniel, "A Process Appreciation of Islam: Interpreting Some Key Ideas in the Islamic Tradition in a Process-Relational Way with help from Yusuf Islam." (http://www.jesusjazzbuddhism. org/beautiful-islam.html).

76. C.S. Lewis, *Mere Christianity.* © 1942,1943, 1944, 1952, 1980 by C.S. Lewis Pte. Ltd. All rights reserved.

77. C. G. Jung, *Dreams*, trans. R. F. C. Hull. (Princeton University Press, Princeton NJ 1974).

78. Tenzin Gyatso, His Holiness the XIV Dalai Lama, *Commentary on the Thirty Seven Practices of a Bodhisattva*, trans. Acharya Nyima Tsering. (Library of Tibetan Works and Archives, Dharamsala 1995).